Contents

Contents	4
Introduction	10
Abbreviations Used	13
Alaska	15
Arizona	18
California	20
Colorado	40
Idaho	47
Kansas	53
Montana	79
Nebraska	84
New Mexico	95
North Dakota	101
Oklahoma	110
Oregon	156
South Dakota	181
Texas	196
Washington	239
Appendix A - Alphabetical List of Lakes	252
Appendix B - Districts of the Corps of Engineers	257
Appendix C - Internet Resources	260
Appendix D - Camping and Day-Use Fees	262
Appendix E - National Recreation Reservation Service	265
Appendix F - Golden Age and Golden Access Passport	266
Appendix G - Brief History of the U.S. Army Corps of Engineers	267
Index	270

Contents

Short Contents 3
Introduction 10
Abbreviations Used 13

Alaska

Alaska Resources 15
Chena River Lakes 16

Arizona

Arizona Resources 18
Alamo Lake 19

California

California Resources 20
Black Butte Lake 21
Eastman Lake 22
Englebright Lake 23
Hensley Lake 25
Lake Kaweah 26
Lake Mendocino 28
Lake Sonoma 29
Martis Creek Lake 31
New Hogan Lake 32
Pine Flat Lake 34
Santa Margarita Lake 35
Stanislaus River Parks 36
Success Lake 38

Colorado

Colorado Resources 40
Bear Creek Lake 41
Chatfield Lake 42
Cherry Creek Lake 43
John Martin Reservoir 44

Trinidad Lake 45

Idaho

Idaho Resources 47
Albeni Falls Dam / Lake Pend Oreille 48
Dworshak Reservoir 49
Lucky Peak Lake 51

Kansas

Kansas Resources 53
Big Hill Lake 54
Clinton Lake 55
Council Grove Lake 56
El Dorado Lake 58
Elk City Lake 59
Fall River Lake 61
Hillsdale Lake 62
John Redmond Reservoir 63
Kanopolis Lake 64
Marion Reservoir 66
Melvern Lake 67
Milford Lake 69
Perry Lake 71
Pomona Lake 72
Toronto Lake 74
Tuttle Creek Lake 75
Wilson Lake 77

Montana

Montana Resources 79
Fort Peck Lake 80
Lake Koocanusa 82

Nebraska

Nebraska Resources 84
Harlan County Lake 85
Papio Creek Watershed Projects 86
Glenn Cunningham Lake 86

Standing Bear Lake	87
Wehrspann Lake	88
Zorinsky Lake	88
Salt Valley Lakes	89
Bluestem SRA	90
Branched Oak SRA	90
Conestoga SRA	91
Olive Creek SRA	92
Pawnee SRA	92
Stagecoach SRA	93
Twin Lakes WMA	93
Wagon Train SRA	93
Yankee Hill WMA	94

New Mexico

New Mexico Resources	95
Abiquiu Reservoir	96
Cochiti Lake	97
Conchas Lake	98
Santa Rosa Lake	99

North Dakota

North Dakota Resources	101
Lake Ashtabula	102
Bowman-Haley Lake	103
Homme Lake	104
Pipestem Lake	105
Lake Sakakawea	106

Oklahoma

Oklahoma Resources	110
Arcadia Lake	111
Birch Lake	112
Broken Bow Lake	113
Canton Lake	114
Chouteau Lock and Dam	115
Copan Lake	117
Eufaula Lake	118

Fort Gibson Lake 120
Fort Supply Lake 122
Great Salt Plains Lake 124
Heyburn Lake 125
Hugo Lake 126
Hulah Lake 127
J.W. Trimble Lock and Dam 129
Kaw Lake 130
Keystone Lake 131
Newt Graham Lock and Dam 134
Oologah Lake 135
Optima Lake 137
Pine Creek Lake 138
Robert S. Kerr Reservoir 139
Sardis Lake 141
Skiatook Lake 142
Tenkiller Ferry Lake 144
Lake Texoma 146
W.D. Mayo Lock and Dam 149
Waurika Lake 150
Webbers Falls Lock and Dam 151
Wister Lake 153

Oregon

Oregon Resources 156
Applegate Lake 157
Blue River Lake 158
Lake Bonneville 159
Lake Celilo 161
Cottage Grove Lake 163
Cougar Lake 164
Detroit Lake 165
Dorena Lake 167
Fall Creek Lake 168
Fern Ridge Lake 169
Foster & Green Peter Lakes 170
Hills Creek Lake 172
Lookout Point & Dexter Lakes 173

Lost Creek Lake 175
Lake Umatilla 176
Lake Wallula 178

South Dakota

South Dakota Resources 181
Cold Brook Lake 182
Cottonwood Springs Lake 183
Lake Francis Case 184
Lewis and Clark Lake 186
Lake Oahe 189
Lake Sharpe 193

Texas

Texas Resources 196
Aquilla Lake 197
Bardwell Lake 198
Belton Lake 199
Benbrook Lake 201
Canyon Lake 202
Lake Georgetown 204
Granger Lake 205
Grapevine Lake 207
Hords Creek Lake 209
Jim Chapman Lake 210
Joe Pool Lake 212
Lake O' The Pines 213
Lavon Lake 215
Lewisville Lake 217
Navarro Mills Lake 219
O.C. Fisher Lake 220
Pat Mayse Lake 222
Proctor Lake 223
Ray Roberts Lake 224
Sam Rayburn Reservoir 226
Somerville Lake 228
Steinhagen Lake 230
Stillhouse Hollow Lake 231

Waco Lake 233
Whitney Lake 234
Wright Patman Lake 236

Washington

Washington Resources 239
Lake Bryan 240
Lake Herbert G. West 241
Lower Granite Lake 243
Mill Creek & Bennington Lake 245
Rufus Woods Lake 246
Lake Sacajawea 248
Wynoochee Lake 249

Appendix A

Alphabetical List of Lakes 252

Appendix B

Districts of the Corps of Engineers 257

Appendix C

Internet Resources 260

Appendix D

Camping and Day-Use Fees 262

Appendix E

National Recreation Reservation Service 265

Appendix F

Golden Age and Golden Access Passport 266

Appendix G

Brief History of the U.S. Army Corps of Engineers 267

Index 270

Introduction

About the Corps of Engineers

The US Army Corps of Engineers is the largest engineering organization in the world. It traces is origins to the American Revolution when the Continental Congress established the Army. Since 1775, the Corps has had an ever-changing role. Today they are one of the Nation's largest providers of outdoor recreation. Next to the Department of the Interior, the agency that operates our national park system, the Corps of Engineers manages more recreation areas than any other federal or state agency. There are more than 450 projects nationwide with over 4,300 parks and recreation areas.

About Lakeside Recreation

This book is a compilation of the Corps of Engineers projects constructed in the western United States. The book details nearly 150 lakes and reservoirs and the recreation areas surrounding each lake. In the pages that follow, you'll find information on more than 1,200 lakeside parks, including over 800 campgrounds offering more than 35,000 campsites. *Lakeside Recreation* is the most complete and up-to-date book available on the Corps lakes.

Facilities Chart

Shown below is a sample of the chart that is used to summarize the recreation areas that surround each lake. The chart lists the name of the recreation area and bullets (•) indicate the facilities found in the park. A number preceding the park name corresponds to the number block on the map of each lake.

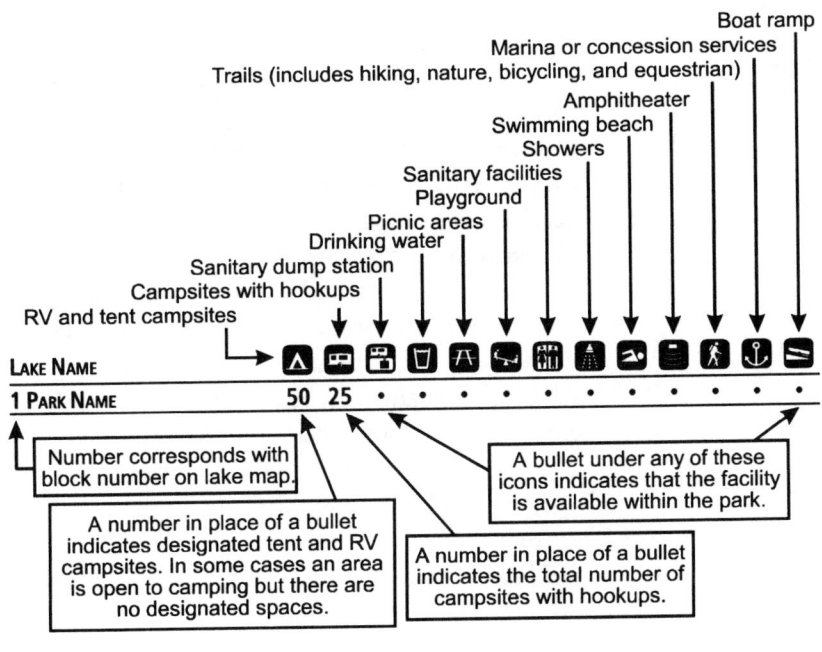

At A Glance Chart

At A Glance chart provides a summary of the facilities and activities available at each lake. Listed below is a description of what each category represents.

AT A GLANCE
✓ AUTO TOURING
✓ BIKING
✓ BOATING
✓ CLIMBING
✓ CULTURAL OR HISTORIC SITES
✓ CAMPING
✓ EDUCATIONAL PROGRAMS
✓ FISHING
✓ GROCERIES / SUPPLIES
✓ HIKING
✓ HORSEBACK RIDING
✓ HUNTING
✓ LODGING
✓ OFF HIGHWAY VEHICLES
✓ VISITOR CENTER

- ***Auto Touring*** indicates that a scenic drive is nearby with interesting sights and scenic vistas along the route. Maps, brochures, and cassette tapes detailing the drive may be available.
- ***Biking*** includes mountain biking, road biking, and bicycle tours. It can also indicate that bicycle rentals are available.

- *Boating* includes sailing, motor boating, canoeing, and kayaking.
- *Camping* indicates that tent and recreational vehicle camping is offered. Campgrounds can range from primitive to highly developed.
- *Climbing* indicates that rock climbing is available nearby or within the project.
- *Cultural or Historic Sites* includes significant and informative cultural and historical landmarks.
- *Educational Programs* includes campfire talks, guided hikes, museums, and exhibits are offered.
- *Fishing* indicates that fishing is permitted. Species of fish are mentioned in the description.
- *Groceries/Supplies* indicates that groceries, snacks, camping, and fishing supplies are available nearby or from concession operations.
- *Hiking* indicates that trails exist within or near the project. This category includes backpacking and nature trails.
- *Horseback Riding* indicates that trail riding or off-trail riding is available within the project. It can also indicate that horse rentals are available.
- *Hunting* indicates that hunting is permitted within the project. Restrictions will apply and permits are required. Check with the project office for more information on regulations.
- *Lodging* indicates that hotels, motels, and cabins are available. Facilities can range from rustic cabins to five-star resort hotels.
- *Off Highway Vehicles* indicates that areas for four-wheel drive, all-terrain vehicles, or motorcycles are within the project or nearby.
- *Visitor Center* indicates that recreation information is available. Visitor centers are staffed with personnel that can answer questions and provide brochures and information about the project. Visitor centers may also include interpretive displays and exhibits.

Abbreviations Used

ATV	All-Terrain Vehicle
BIA	Bureau of Indian Affairs
BLM	Bureau of Land Management
COE	Corps of Engineers
CR	County Road
DOT	Department of Transportation
FSR	Forest Service Road
HMU	Habitat Management Unit
I	Interstate
NF	National Forest
NHS	National Historic Site
NHT	National Historic Trail
NM	National Monument
NP	National Park
NRA	National Recreation Area
NRT	National Recreation Trail
ORV	Off-Road Vehicle
SH	State Highway
SP	State Park
SRA	State Recreation Area
US	U.S. Highway

ALASKA

1 Chena River Lakes

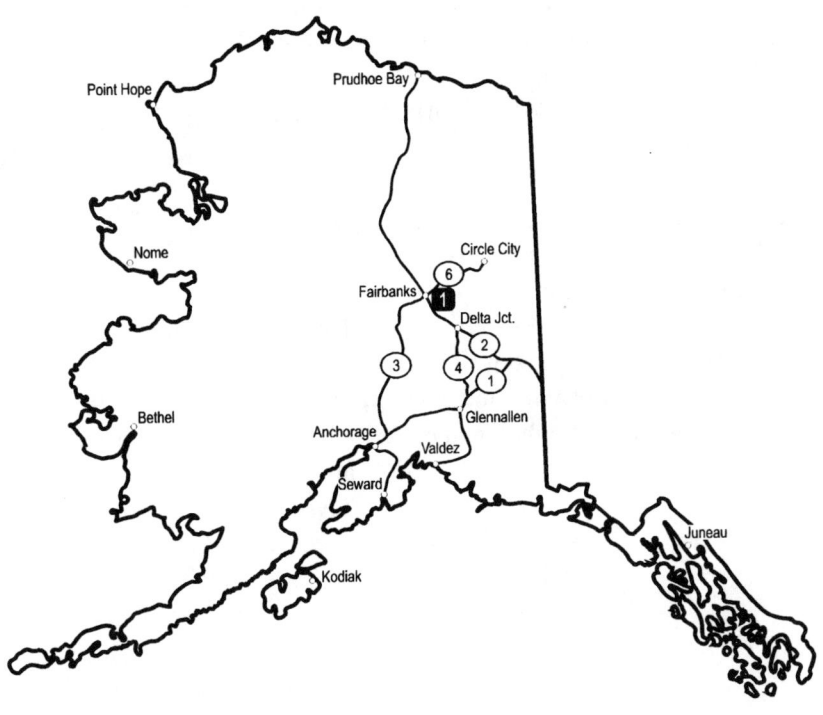

Alaska Resources

- *Alaska Division of Tourism* - P.O. Box 110801, Juneau AK 99811 / (907) 465-2010
- *Alaska Dept. of Fish and Game* - (907) 344-0541
- *Alaska Marine Highway System* - (800) 642-0066 (U.S./Canada)
- *Road Condition Hotline* - (907) 456-7623 (recorded message)
- *Road Construction Hotline* - (907) 273-6037, press 3

Chena River Lakes

Located in Alaska's Interior, approximately 100 miles south of the Arctic Circle and 17 miles east of Fairbanks. The project is reached from Richardson Highway by following Laurance Road north out of North Pole. Tours of the Moose Creek Dam can be scheduled with the Corps office. Additional visitor information is available from the Corps project office and the Fairbanks North Star Borough office, both are located at the entrance of the project.

At A Glance
Auto Touring
✓ Biking
✓ Boating
Climbing
Cultural or Historic Sites
✓ Camping
✓ Educational Programs
✓ Fishing
✓ Groceries / Supplies
✓ Hiking
✓ Horseback Riding
Hunting
Lodging
✓ Off Highway Vehicles
✓ Visitor Center

The 2,000-acre Chena Flood Control Project and Chena Lakes Recreation Area consists of a 260-acre lake and four miles of the Chena River. Gently rolling slopes characterize the landscape of this area dotted with ponds, peat bogs, oxbow lakes and meandering streams. Throughout the area visitors will find walking and bicycle trails, horseshoe pits, picnic areas, volleyball and basketball courts. All recreation areas are managed by the Fairbanks North Star Borough. The *Lake Park Island* recreation area is only accessible by boat. Warm up/change houses for wintertime activities are located in both *Lake Park* and *River Park* recreation areas. Canoe, sail and paddle boats are available for rent at *Lake Park*. A 5-mile bicycle path runs from Laurence and Nelson roads to the project's information kiosk. The kiosk is located near the Chena River in the *River Park* recreation area. The kiosk has information on wildlife viewing opportunities and

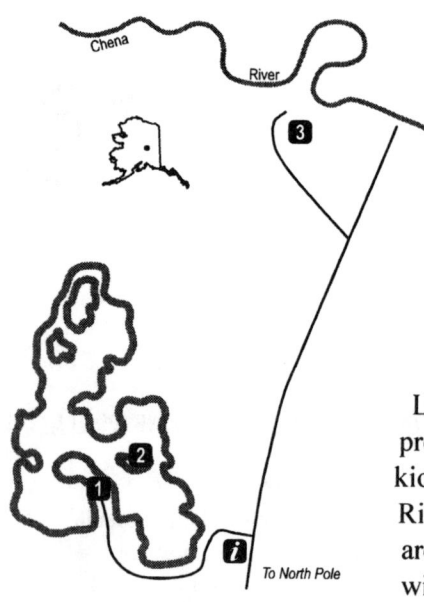

mountain bike tours. A sanitary dump station is located at the entrance of the project.

The clear water of the rivers, ponds and lakes provide excellent fish habitat. The lake is stocked with thousands of game fish every year where anglers will find lake trout and silver salmon. The Chena River offers grayling, northern pike, whitefish, burbot, and is home to a king salmon run every July. During the winter months, ice fishing houses are available for rent.

Information: U.S. Army Corps of Engineers, Chena Project Office, P.O. Box 55270, North Pole AK 99705-5270 / 907-488-2748. Fairbanks North Star Borough, Chena Lakes Recreation Area, P.O. Box 71267, Fairbanks AK 99707 / 907-488-1655.

CHENA RIVER LAKES												
1 LAKE PARK	•			•	•	•	•		•		•	•	•
2 LAKE PARK ISLAND	•				•								
3 RIVER PARK	•			•	•		•				•		•

ARIZONA

1 Alamo Lake

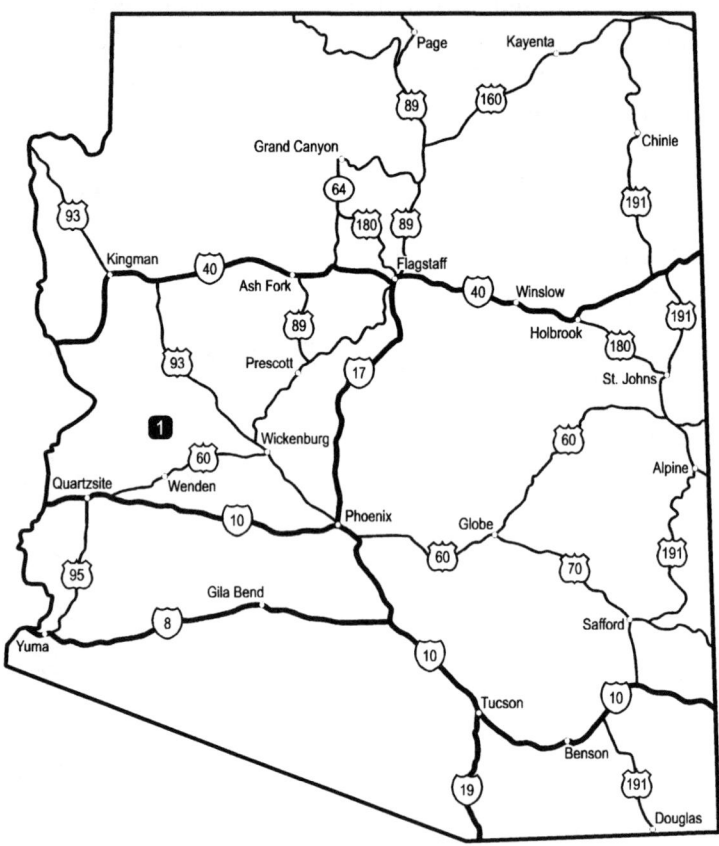

Arizona Resources

- *Arizona Office of Tourism* - 2702 N. 3rd St. Suite 4015, Phoenix AZ 85004 / (800) 842-8257 or (602) 230-7733
- *Arizona Game & Fish Department* - (602) 942-3000
- *Road Condition Hotline* - (602) 861-9400 ext. 7623 (recording)
- *Road Construction Hotlines* - (602) 255-6588 weekdays and (602) 779-2711 (Northern Arizona; recording)

Alamo Lake

Alamo Lake, on the Bill Williams River, is in west-central Arizona about 135 miles northwest of Phoenix. From Wenden travel 38 miles north on Alamo Dam Road off US 60.

Alamo Lake is set in the wide-open spaces of Arizona against a backdrop of the picturesque Rawhide and Buckskin mountains. The 8,400-acre area has one developed recreation area, open year-round, administered by Arizona State Parks. The Bureau of Land Management manages the nearby Rawhide Mountain Wilderness. This area lies southwest of the lake and provides excellent opportunities for open hiking and horseback riding.

At A Glance
Auto Touring
Biking
✓ Boating
Climbing
Cultural or Historic Sites
✓ Camping
Educational Programs
✓ Fishing
✓ Groceries / Supplies
✓ Hiking
✓ Horseback Riding
Hunting
Lodging
Off Highway Vehicles
✓ Visitor Center

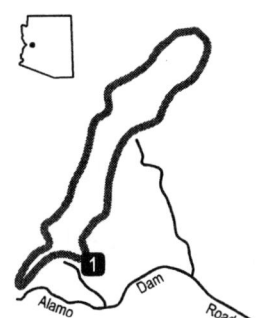

Alamo Lake is one of the best warm water fisheries in the Southwest and one of the best bass lakes in Arizona. The lake teems with largemouth bass, bluegill and catfish. For a fishing report call 520-949-7904. The park store is well stocked with fishing tackle, bait and groceries. The store also rents a good variety of boats—for information call 520-945-7741.

Information: Alamo Lake State Park, P.O. Box 38, Wenden AZ 85357 / 520-669-2088. Arizona State Parks, 1300 W. Washington, Phoenix AZ 85007 / 602-542-4174.

Alamo Lake													
1 Alamo Lake State Park	250	60	•	•	•	•	•	•			•	•	•

CALIFORNIA

1. Black Butte Lake
2. Eastman Lake
3. Englebright Lake
4. Hensley Lake
5. Lake Kaweah
6. Lake Mendocino
7. Lake Sonoma
8. Martis Creek Lake
9. New Hogan Lake
10. Pine Flat Lake
11. Santa Margarita Lake
12. Stanislaus River Parks
13. Success Lake

California Resources

- ***California Division of Tourism*** - P.O. Box 1499 Dept. 200, Sacramento CA 95812-1499 / (800) 862-2543, ext. 200 or (916) 322-2881
- ***California Fish and Game*** - (916) 227-2244
- ***Road Condition Hotline*** - (916) 445-7623 or (916) 445-1534 or (800) 427-ROAD (24-hour information)

Black Butte Lake

Black Butte Lake is situated on Stony Creek eight miles west of Orland off I-5 in north-central California. From Orland travel west on Newville Road (County Road 200). The park office is located southeast of the dam. Group dam tours and ranger programs can be scheduled with the Corps.

At A Glance
Auto Touring
✓ Biking
✓ Boating
Climbing
Cultural or Historic Sites
✓ Camping
✓ Educational Programs
✓ Fishing
✓ Groceries / Supplies
✓ Hiking
✓ Horseback Riding
✓ Hunting
Lodging
✓ Off Highway Vehicles
✓ Visitor Center

This quiet lake, surrounded by beautiful, dark volcanic buttes, is well known for outstanding fishing and sailing. On the south end of the dam is *Observation Point* which has picnic facilities overlooking the dam and lake. A 75-acre ATV area on the north side of the lake near *Buckhorn* offers a variety of hills and trails and is open June through February. There are three self-guided nature trails within the project that offer quiet, pleasurable hikes through the rolling oak foothills. A centrally located amphitheater offers summer campfire programs.

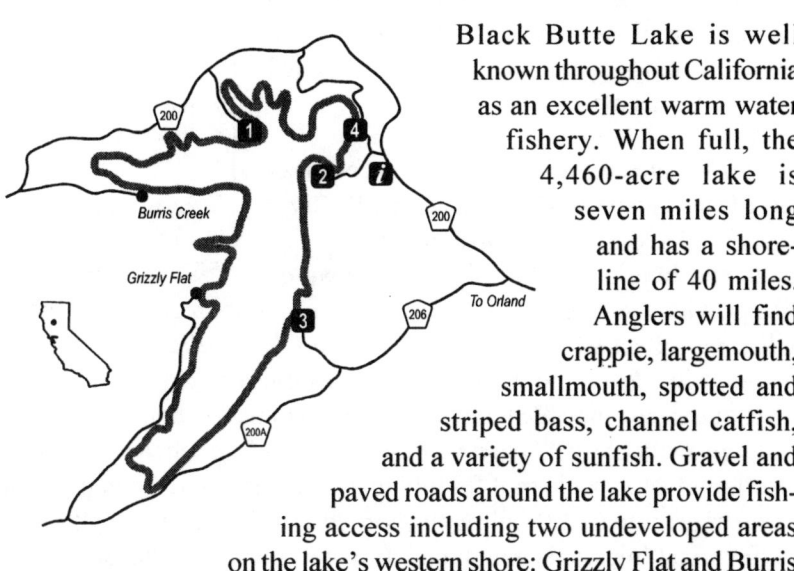

Black Butte Lake is well known throughout California as an excellent warm water fishery. When full, the 4,460-acre lake is seven miles long and has a shoreline of 40 miles. Anglers will find crappie, largemouth, smallmouth, spotted and striped bass, channel catfish, and a variety of sunfish. Gravel and paved roads around the lake provide fishing access including two undeveloped areas on the lake's western shore: Grizzly Flat and Burris Creek. The best angling is usually during the spring and early summer. Fishing supplies are available at the marina in *Buckhorn*.

Hunting is permitted in designated areas using only shotguns or bows and arrows. Wildlife inhabiting the region includes deer, rabbit, and waterfowl.

Information: U.S. Army Corps of Engineers, Black Butte Lake, 19225 Newville Rd., Orland CA 95963-8901 / 530-865-4781.

Black Butte Lake	△	⌂	🚻	🚽	⛱	🚣	🏕	🛏	🌊	🍴	🚶	⚓	〰
1 Buckhorn	85	•	•	•	•	•	•		•	•	•	•	
2 Eagle Pass				•	•							•	
3 Orland Buttes	35	•	•		•	•			•	•			
4 Observation Point				•	•								

Eastman Lake

Located in the Sierra Nevada foothills about 48 miles north of Fresno in central California. From Chowchilla, follow Avenue 26 east to Road 29; turn left and follow Road 29 north to the project. An audiovisual program, displays, and brochures are available at the visitor center located near the south end of the dam. Group tours and ranger programs can be scheduled with the Corps office.

The 1,780-acre lake was created when construction of Buchanan Dam on the Chowchilla River was completed in 1976. Surrounded by grasslands and blue oaks, the rolling oak-covered hills provide a scenic and restful setting for outdoor recreation. Guests will find volleyball and horseshoe pits in *Chowchilla* and a softball diamond in *Monument Ridge*. Both parks close at dark. About four miles of easy to moderate hiking, mountain biking, and horseback riding trails are available in *Monument Ridge*. The *Codorniz* area offers horse corrals and a four mile trail for hiking, biking, and equestrian use. The trail is moderate to difficult with short steep hills and a rocky terrain. Of historical interest is a monument to the town of Buchanan located along the entrance road. This once thriving copper town now exists only in legend and a few old photos.

At A Glance
Auto Touring
✓ Biking
✓ Boating
Climbing
Cultural or Historic Sites
✓ Camping
✓ Educational Programs
✓ Fishing
Groceries / Supplies
✓ Hiking
✓ Horseback Riding
✓ Hunting
Lodging
Off Highway Vehicles
✓ Visitor Center

Eastman Lake has been designated California's first Trophy Bass Fishery by the California Department of Fish and Game. Anglers will find several types of game fish such as rainbow trout, which are planted during the winter months, largemouth bass, bluegill, redear sunfish, crappie, brown bullhead, channel and white catfish. Trout fishing peaks in the fall and winter. In the warmer months, catfish, crappie and bluegill fishing is usually at its best. For bass anglers, fishing is generally good throughout the year.

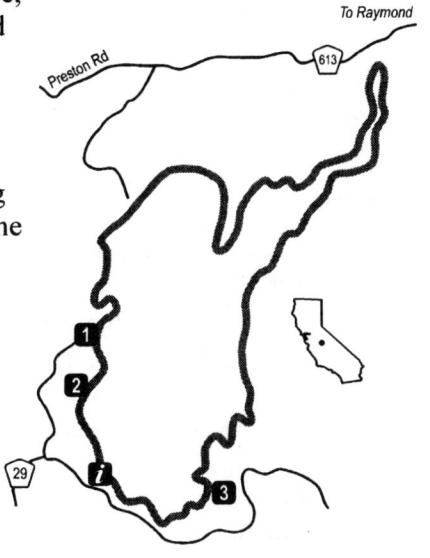

Hunting is permitted on the northern portion of the project's land. Shotgun hunting for dove, quail, waterfowl, squirrel, and rabbit is popular in season. Archery hunters can also hunt for deer with a special park permit.

Information: U.S. Army Corps of Engineers, Eastman Lake Project, 32175 Road 29, P.O. Box 67, Raymond CA 93653 / 209-689-3255.

Eastman Lake	🛆	🚐	🚻	🚽	⛲	🛶	🏚	🚿	🏊	🎣	🚶	⚓	⚡
1 Monument Ridge			•		•					•			
2 Chowchilla					•	•	•	•	•		•		•
3 Codorniz	65	12	•	•		•	•	•		•	•		•

Englebright Lake

Harry L. Englebright Lake is nestled in the scenic Sierra Nevada foothills east of Marysville in north-central California. From Marysville, travel east on SH 20 for 21 miles; watch for roadside signs. Turn left (north) on Mooney Flat Road and travel 2½ miles to the park entrance. The project's visitor center is located in the *Narrows* recreation area just east of the dam. Group tours and ranger programs can be scheduled through the project office.

At A Glance

- Auto Touring
- Biking
- ✓ Boating
- Climbing
- Cultural or Historic Sites
- ✓ Camping
- ✓ Educational Programs
- ✓ Fishing
- ✓ Groceries / Supplies
- ✓ Hiking
- Horseback Riding
- Hunting
- Lodging
- Off Highway Vehicles
- ✓ Visitor Center

Constructed for the storage of hydraulic gold mining debris, Englebright Dam is in the steep Yuba River gorge known as the Narrows, and behind it, a nine-mile long lake with a surface area of 815 acres. Camping at Englebright Lake is unique in that all campsites are accessible only by boat. All of the campgrounds are situated along the lake's 24 miles of shoreline.

The lake's clear, cool water provides the angler with a variety of species. Game fish include rainbow and brown trout, largemouth and smallmouth bass, bluegill, green and redear sunfish, white crappie, channel catfish, brown bullhead, kokanee salmon, and carp. Fish may be taken from the shore or boat by bottom fishing or trolling with bright, flashy lures. Boat rentals, mooring, gas, bait and tackle, sewage pumping, and store facilities are available at the Skippers Cove Marina, phone 530-639-2272, located in the *Joe Miller Ravine* recreation area.

Due to narrow canyons and sharp bends, the upper four miles of the lake are not suitable for water-skiing and/or towing any type of inflatable device. These activities are therefore restricted to the lower five miles of the lake. A counter-clockwise direction of travel is strictly enforced for the safety of park visitors.

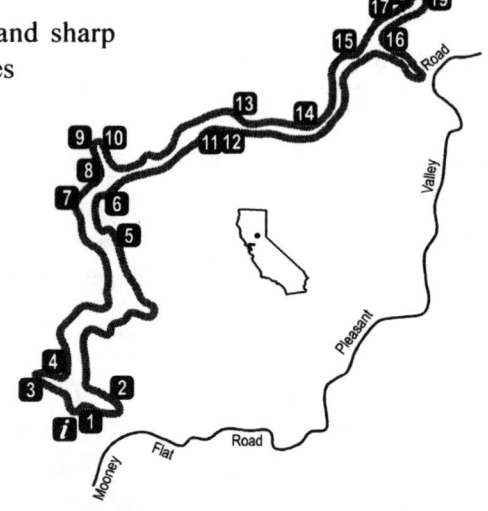

Information: U.S. Army Corps of Engineers, Englebright Lake Project, P.O. Box 6, Smartville CA 95977 / 530-639-2342.

Englebright Lake	⛺	🚐	🚻	🍴	🥾	🏊	🚿	🎣	🚶	⚓	🐟	〰️
1 Narrows				•	•		•			•		•
2 Joe Miller Ravine			•			•				•	•	•
3 Hogback Ravine	8					•						
4 Bonanza Point	3					•						
5 Long's Cove	8					•						
6 Long's Point	5					•						
7 Rocky Bluff	4					•						
8 Singles Point	3					•						
9 Shadyside	4					•						
10 Black's Ravine	1					•						
11 Boston Bar	12					•			•			
12 Upper Boston Bar	6					•						
13 Cherokee	3					•						
14 Buck's Beach	5					•						
15 Dixon Hill	2					•						
16 Point Defiance	8					•						
17 Lower Missouri Bar	4					•						
18 Missouri Bar	15					•						
19 Sunnyside	2					•						
20 Rice's Crossing						•						

Hensley Lake

Hensley Lake is located in central California 37 miles north of Fresno and 17 miles northeast of Madera. To reach the dam from Madera, travel northeast on CR 400. A small visitor center is located at the park office near the west end of the dam. Tours and ranger programs can be scheduled through the office.

Hensley Lake, constructed on the Fresno River, is surrounded by the oak woodlands of the Sierra Nevada foothills. A 500-acre wildlife area is on the north end of the lake. Here you can enjoy hiking, bird watching, hunting, mountain biking, horseback riding, or take in the variety of abundant wildflowers. An equestrian trail and hitching posts can be found in the *Hidden*

At A Glance

Auto Touring
✓ Biking
✓ Boating
Climbing
✓ Cultural or Historic Sites
✓ Camping
✓ Educational Programs
✓ Fishing
Groceries / Supplies
✓ Hiking
✓ Horseback Riding
✓ Hunting
Lodging
Off Highway Vehicles
✓ Visitor Center

View recreation area. Of historical interest is a monument in the *Buck Ridge* recreation area that was erected to the memory of Major James D. Savage. He is credited with the discovery of Yosemite Valley on March 25, 1851 during the Mariposa Indian War. As a trader, Savage established a store on the Fresno River where he made a small fortune trading goods for gold with the local miners.

Numerous game fish abound in the 1,500-acre lake. Anglers will find largemouth black bass, crappie, bluegill, and catfish. Rainbow trout are planted during the winter months. Some of the best fishing is found in the many coves around the lake. Anglers can keep two bass over 15 inches in length.

Information: U.S. Army Corps of Engineers, Hensley Lake Project, P.O. Box 85, Raymond CA 93653 / 559-673-5151.

Hensley Lake													
1 Hidden View	52	10	•	•		•	•	•	•	•	•		•
2 Wakalumi	10						•						
3 Vista Point									•				
4 Buck Ridge				•	•	•	•			•	•	•	

Lake Kaweah

Located on the main southern route into Sequoia-Kings Canyon National Park in central California, 60 miles southeast of Fresno. To reach Lake Kaweah from Visalia follow SH 198 east 20 miles to the park entrance. The project office is north of SH 198 near the west end of the dam; group hikes and ranger programs are scheduled here.

High mountains provide a scenic backdrop for this lake situated on the Kaweah River in the rugged foothills of the southern Sierra Nevada

Mountains. In 1856, cattleman Hale Tharp settled in the area and constructed a ranch at the confluence of the Kaweah River and Horse Creek. He lived in the area until his death in 1912. Numerous landmarks bear his name.

Between *Slick Rock* and *Cobble Knoll* recreation areas is a one-mile hiking trail where visitors enjoy bird-watching, wildflowers, or the simple pleasure of a quiet walk. An amphitheater in *Horse Creek* is the site each Saturday night from Memorial Day weekend through Labor Day weekend for campfire programs. A snack bar is located in the marina at *Lemon Hill* recreation area.

At A Glance
Auto Touring
Biking
✓ Boating
Climbing
Cultural or Historic Sites
✓ Camping
✓ Educational Programs
✓ Fishing
✓ Groceries / Supplies
✓ Hiking
Horseback Riding
Hunting
Lodging
Off Highway Vehicles
Visitor Center

Lake Kaweah offers both lake and stream fishing for rainbow trout, largemouth bass, bluegill, catfish, and crappie. Bass must be a minimum of 12 inches long before they can be kept by the angler. Trout are especially abundant during the winter because of regular stocking by the California Department of Fish and Game. The marina at *Lemon Hill* offers boating and camping supplies, fishing tackle, boat rentals and fuel. Fishing licenses can also be purchased at the marina. For information about boating registration and operating regulations, contact the Tulare County Boat Patrol Office at 209-597-2437.

Information: U.S. Army Corps of Engineers, Lake Kaweah Project, P.O. Box 44270, Lemon Cove CA 93244 / 209-597-2301.

Lake Kaweah	⛺	🚐	🚻	🗑	🪑	🧺	👥	🪜	🍽	🥾	⚓	🌊
1 Lemon Hill							•				•	•
2 Kaweah			•	•			•	•				•
3 Horse Creek	80		•	•	•	•	•			•	•	
4 Slick Rock							•					
5 Cobble Knoll											•	

Lake Mendocino

Lake Mendocino is situated on the East Fork of the Russian River in northwestern California. The lake is 64 miles northwest of Santa Rosa just north of Ukiah. From Ukiah travel three miles north on US 101, then east on Lake Mendocino Drive. A visitor center is found on the north end of the lake in the *Pomo* recreation area.

A hiking and horseback riding trail can be accessed in the *Kaweyo* and *Mesa* recreation areas. This trail follows the eastern shore of the lake and through the wildlife area. A hiking and bicycling trail is accessed in the *Overlook* and *Pomo* recreation areas. This trail follows the western shore of the lake. Primitive boat-in camping is available at designated sites on the east shore. Camping is permitted in the *Kaweyo* area by permit only.

At A Glance
Auto Touring
✓ Biking
✓ Boating
Climbing
Cultural or Historic Sites
✓ Camping
Educational Programs
✓ Fishing
✓ Groceries / Supplies
✓ Hiking
✓ Horseback Riding
✓ Hunting
Lodging
Off Highway Vehicles
✓ Visitor Center

The 1,822-acre lake provides a challenging and rewarding fishing experience for the avid angler and novice alike. Anglers will find large and smallmouth bass, striped bass, crappie, bluegill, and catfish. The marina on the northern end of the lake has complete fishing, camping, and boating supplies and services.

The 689-acre wildlife area on the lake's eastern shore provides a natural habitat for black-tailed deer, wild turkey, gray fox, red-tailed hawk, osprey, and valley quail. Hunting for waterfowl and upland game is permitted in much of this area.

Information: U.S. Army Corps of Engineers, Lake Mendocino Project, 1160 Lake Mendocino Dr., Ukiah CA 95482 / 707-462-7581.

LAKE MENDOCINO													
1 JOE RILEY		•	•	•	•						•		
2 CHE-KA-KA	21		•		•	•					•		•
3 OVERLOOK			•	•	•	•					•		
4 POMO			•	•	•	•	•	•	•	•	•		
5 KY-EN	103	•	•				•	•		•			
6 BU-SHAY	164	•	•		•	•	•			•	•		
7 MESA				•	•	•	•				•		
8 OAK GROVE				•	•		•						
9 MITI	17						•		•		•		
10 KAWEYO		•			•		•						
11 MARINA			•	•		•						•	•

Lake Sonoma

Lake Sonoma lies west of US 101 in the coastal foothills of northern California, 26 miles northwest of Santa Rosa. From Healdsburg, travel 10 miles northwest on Dry Creek Road. A visitor center and fish hatchery is located near the dam.

Warm Springs Dam, which formed the 2,700-acre lake, was completed in 1983. The lake extends westward for nine miles on Dry Creek and four miles on Warm Springs Creek. Forty miles of trails surround the lake for use by hikers and horseback riders. A detailed brochure on the trail system is available at the visitor center. *Liberty Glen* is the only campground within the park that is accessible by road. There are 15 primitive, boat-in campgrounds surround-

AT A GLANCE
AUTO TOURING
✓ BIKING
✓ BOATING
CLIMBING
CULTURAL OR HISTORIC SITES
✓ CAMPING
EDUCATIONAL PROGRAMS
✓ FISHING
✓ GROCERIES / SUPPLIES
✓ HIKING
✓ HORSEBACK RIDING
HUNTING
LODGING
OFF HIGHWAY VEHICLES
✓ VISITOR CENTER

ing the lake. Nine of these can also be reached from hiking and equestrian trails. Backcountry camp permits are required and may be obtained free of charge at the visitor center.

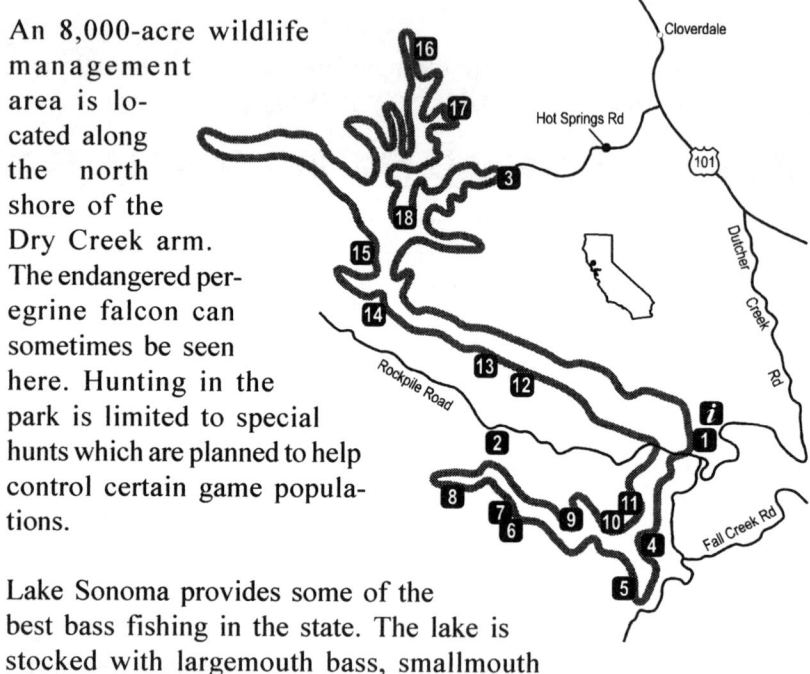

An 8,000-acre wildlife management area is located along the north shore of the Dry Creek arm. The endangered peregrine falcon can sometimes be seen here. Hunting in the park is limited to special hunts which are planned to help control certain game populations.

Lake Sonoma provides some of the best bass fishing in the state. The lake is stocked with largemouth bass, smallmouth bass, channel catfish, and various sunfish. Rainbow trout can also be found in the lake. The Warm Springs Creek arm is subject to closure to boating due to fluctuating water levels. The marina, located off Stewart Point Road, offers complete boating and fishing supplies and services as well as boat rentals. Information regarding the marina may be obtained by phoning Lake Sonoma Resort at 707-433-2200.

Information: U.S. Army Corps of Engineers, Lake Sonoma Project, 3333 Skaggs Springs Rd., Geyserville CA 95441 / 707-433-9483.

Lake Sonoma													
1 Warm Springs Dam				•	•	•	•				•	•	•
2 Liberty Glen	113	•	•				•	•		•	•		
3 Yorty Creek					•		•		•				•
4 Quicksilver		•				•			•				

continued next page

Lake Sonoma (continued)	⛺	🚐	🚻	🚰	🛣	🛶	🏘	🏊	⛵	🗑	🚶	⚓	≋
5 Island View	•						•			•			
6 Black Mountain	•						•			•			
7 Buck Pasture	•						•			•			
8 Old Sawmill Camp	•						•			•			
9 Madrone Point	•						•			•			
10 Lone Pine	•						•			•			
11 Bummer Peak	•						•			•			
12 Broken Bridge	•						•						
13 Falcons Nest	•						•						
14 Homestead	•						•						
15 Loggers Camp	•						•						
16 Skunk Creek	•						•						
17 Thumb Camp	•						•						
18 Rustler	•						•						

Martis Creek Lake

Martis Creek Lake is set among the Sierra Nevada Mountains near Lake Tahoe in northeastern California. From I-80 at Truckee, take the Central Truckee exit and turn south onto SH 267. Travel southeast six miles and turn left at the entrance sign. Group tours and ranger programs can be scheduled with the Corps.

> **At A Glance**
> Auto Touring
> ✓ Biking
> Boating
> Climbing
> Cultural or Historic Sites
> ✓ Camping
> ✓ Educational Programs
> ✓ Fishing
> Groceries / Supplies
> ✓ Hiking
> Horseback Riding
> Hunting
> Lodging
> Off Highway Vehicles
> Visitor Center

When full, Martis Creek Lake has a surface area of 770 acres. Hiking trails are nearby throughout the 1,050-acre Wildlife Management Area. The area provides unique opportunities to spot wildlife on a recurring basis. An amphitheater is located in *Alpine Meadows* where campfire programs are offered to visitors on weekend evenings. Park facilities are closed during the winter months but cross-country skiing is permitted.

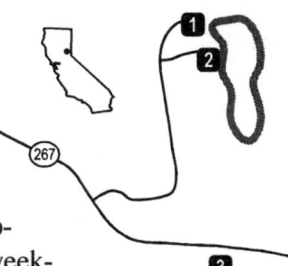

Anglers will find a variety of trout in the lake including rainbow, brown, and Lahontan cutthroat. A "catch and release" program is in effect at the lake. Anglers must use barbless hooks and artificial lures only and all trout caught must be released back into the lake. Due to the small size of the lake, no motor-powered boats (gas or electric) are permitted.

Information: U.S. Army Corps of Engineers, Martis Creek Lake Project, P.O. Box 6, Smartville CA 95977 / 530-639-2342.

Martis Creek Lake	⛺	🚐	🚻	🚰	⛽	💧	🚹	🪜	🎣	🗑	🚶	⚓	〰
1 Alpine Meadows	25			•		•			•				
2 Sierra View						•	•						
3 Wildlife Area						•	•					•	

New Hogan Lake

Located about an hour east of Stockton in central California near historic gold rush towns of the California Mother Lode. From Valley Springs, take SH 26 one-half mile south to Hogan Dam Road. Turn left (east) onto Hogan Dam Road and travel about one mile to the main entrance. The project office is found north of the dam. Group dam tours and ranger programs can be scheduled with the Corps office.

At A Glance
- Auto Touring
- ✓ Biking
- ✓ Boating
- Climbing
- Cultural or Historic Sites
- ✓ Camping
- Educational Programs
- ✓ Fishing
- ✓ Groceries / Supplies
- ✓ Hiking
- ✓ Horseback Riding
- ✓ Hunting
- Lodging
- Off Highway Vehicles
- ✓ Visitor Center

New Hogan Lake is set against the oak and brush-covered foothills of the Sierra Nevada Mountains on the Calaveras River. The 4,400-acre lake, when full, has 50 miles of shoreline and extends nearly eight miles upstream.

Visitors to the project will find numerous trails surrounding the lake. The "River of Skulls" hiking trail is located below the dam at the *Monte Vista* recreation area. This area is also a staging area for an eight mile equestrian trail on a scenic loop that winds along the lake and through the foothill chaparral. A nearly two-mile bicycle trail connects park headquarters to *Wrinkle Cove*.

California

Camping facilities are available in five recreation areas. The *Deer Flat* area is a boat-in campground generally open from May through September. An amphitheater in *Acorn East* campground of- fers weekend campfire programs.

New Hogan Lake provides year-round fishing for striped bass, largemouth and smallmouth bass, bluegill and other sunfish, crappie, and catfish. Some of the best fishing is found in protected coves around the lake. Trout fishing is available downstream of the dam in the Calaveras River. New Hogan Marina offers boating and fishing supplies, slip and boat rentals, and boat storage. For additional information on the marina call 209-772-1462.

A variety of wildlife inhabits the area including black-tailed deer, fox, coyote, skunk, wild turkey, and bobcat. New Hogan Lake is also a winter home for the bald eagle. Limited hunting is available on the south shore of the lake. Contact the project office for more information.

Information: U.S. Army Corps of Engineers, New Hogan Lake Project, 2713 Hogan Dam Rd., Valley Springs CA 95252 / 209-772-1343.

New Hogan Lake	▲	⌂	🚻	🚰	⛽	🍴	🏕	🚿	🎣	🗑	🚶	⚓	〰
1 Oak Knoll	50	•	•			•				•			
2 Coyote Point	•		•			•							
3 Acorn West	58	•	•			•	•		•				
4 Acorn East	69	•	•			•	•			•	•		•

continued next page

New Hogan Lake (continued)	▲	🚐	🚻	🚰	🎿	🍴	🏚	🎣	🥫	🚶	⚓	〰️
5 Fiddleneck		•	•		•					•	•	•
6 Wrinkle Cove		•	•		•			•	•			
7 Observation Point		•	•		•							
8 Monte Vista					•				•			
9 Whiskey Creek					•							
10 Bear Creek					•							
11 Deer Flat	30				•							

Pine Flat Lake

Pine Flat Lake is located in central California north of SH 180 within the Sierra and Sequoia National Forests. From Fresno, follow Belmont Avenue east to the town of Piedra. To visit the dam and park office, turn right on Pine Flat Road. To visit the recreation areas, follow Trimmer Springs Road north. Group dam tours and ranger programs are available and can be scheduled with the Corps at the project office.

Pine Flat Dam is an impressive structure that impounds the waters of the Kings River. Sightseers can enjoy scenic views of the lake from Trimmer Springs Road and the *Observation Area* at the dam. Below the dam, the shady banks of the Kings River offer picnic sites and streamside walking trails. The Blue Oak Nature Trail, located at *Island Park*, is a pleasant and informative walk. *Kirch Flat* is a no-fee campground administered by the Forest Service. There are six areas along the lake where overnight mooring is permitted, inquire with the Corps.

At A Glance
Auto Touring
Biking
✓ Boating
Climbing
Cultural or Historic Sites
✓ Camping
✓ Educational Programs
✓ Fishing
✓ Groceries / Supplies
✓ Hiking
Horseback Riding
✓ Hunting
Lodging
Off Highway Vehicles
Visitor Center

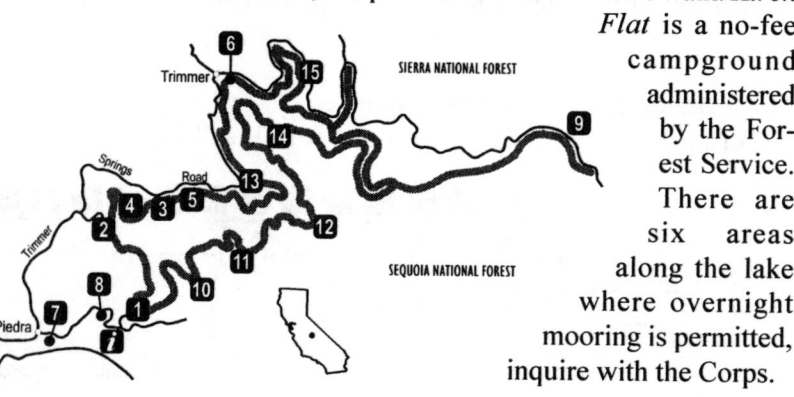

California

Anglers will find the lake filled with rainbow and brown trout, large and smallmouth bass, bluegill, catfish, and crappie. The two marinas offer boat and slip rentals, fuel, fishing tackle and camping supplies. Provisions are also available at the numerous stores near the lake. Boaters are reminded that there is a counter-clockwise direction of travel on the lake and that water surface levels fluctuate daily.

Information: U.S. Army Corps of Engineers, Pine Flat Lake Project, P.O. Box 117, Piedra CA 93649 / 559-787-2589.

Pine Flat Lake	🛆	🚐	🏠	🚽	🎣	🚣	🍴	🚿	⛽	🥫	🚶	⚓	〰️
1 Observation Area				•	•		•						
2 Deer Creek							•					•	•
3 Island Park	52	•	•				•	•			•	•	•
4 Deer Creek Point	•			•			•						
5 Lakeview							•						•
6 Trimmer	•			•	•		•	•				•	•
7 Choinumni	•		•	•	•		•						
8 Pine Flat	•		•	•	•		•						
9 Kirch Flat	19					•	•						
10 Zebe Creek							•						
11 Lawless Cove							•						
12 Flume Cove							•						
13 Edison Point													
14 Big Creek							•						
15 Horse Collar							•						

Santa Margarita Lake

Located about 225 miles north of Los Angeles, Santa Margarita Lake lies between US 101 and I-5 about 45 miles east of San Luis Obispo, off SH 58. From Santa Margarita follow SH 58 east two miles to Pozo Road and then south about seven miles to the project entrance.

Santa Margarita Lake is nestled among the rolling oak and pine covered hills of southwest California. Though noted for its excellent fishing, the park also provides a wide range of hiking and riding trails that offer breathtaking views of the lake and surrounding mountains. The county of San Luis Obispo manages the lake and its only developed recreation area. Beyond the developed area is several thousand acres of open space officially designated the Santa Margarita Lake Natural Area. This area is accessible to hikers, bicyclists and equestrians.

The seven-mile long lake, with 1,100 surface acres and 22 miles of shoreline, offers great year-round fishing. Anglers will find largemouth bass, smallmouth bass, striped bass, channel catfish, crappie, bluegill, rainbow trout, treadfin shad and pumpkinseed. The biggest fish are taken in March and April, during the spring spawn. Largemouth bass average two to three pounds. Rainbow trout are planted November through April. The full service Anglers Outpost Marina is open seven days a week, phone: 805-438-4682.

At A Glance
Auto Touring
✓ Biking
✓ Boating
Climbing
Cultural or Historic Sites
✓ Camping
Educational Programs
✓ Fishing
✓ Groceries / Supplies
✓ Hiking
✓ Horseback Riding
Hunting
Lodging
Off Highway Vehicles
✓ Visitor Center

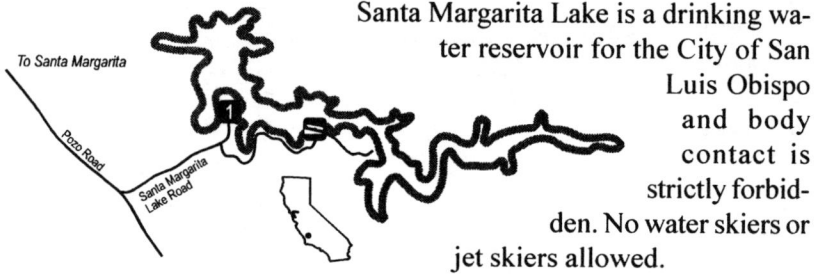

Santa Margarita Lake is a drinking water reservoir for the City of San Luis Obispo and body contact is strictly forbidden. No water skiers or jet skiers allowed.

Information: U.S. Army Corps of Engineers, Santa Margarita Lake Project, P.O. Box 532711, Los Angeles CA 90053 / 213-452-3391. Santa Margarita Lake, County Government Center Room 460, San Luis Obispo CA 93408 / 805-781-5930. Lake office phone: 805-438-5485.

Santa Margarita Lake												
1 Santa Margarita Park	20	•	•	•	•	•	•	•	•	•	•	•

Stanislaus River Parks

This Corps of Engineers project encompasses nearly 60 miles of the Stanislaus River in central California. Nearby communities include Modesto, Salida, Ripon, Riverbank, Oakdale, and Knights Ferry. From Modesto travel 22 miles east on SH 108; from Oakdale, 12 miles east on SH 108/120 to Kennedy Road. Follow the signs to the park headquarters. The information center in Knights Ferry has detailed information about recreation on the river.

Ten recreation areas are scattered along the river as it stretches from Goodwin Dam to its confluence with the San Joaquin River. *Caswell Memorial State Park* is operated by the California Department of Parks and Recreation, the other nine areas are managed by the Corps. Four miles of rapids above Knights Ferry draw those interested in kayaking or whitewater rafting. The Corps requires canoeists stick to the portion of the river below Knights Ferry. Hiking trails in *Goodwin Canyon, Knights Ferry, Valley Oak* and *McHenry Avenue* offer short tours of lush river woodlands. Three environmental camping areas (access by boat, foot, or bicycle only) are available along the river for those wishing to take an extended river trip. Reservations are recommended. Advanced reservations may be made at the information center in Knights Ferry. An attraction at Stanislaus River Parks is a 330-foot long historic covered bridge built in 1863.

At A Glance
Auto Touring
Biking
✓ Boating
Climbing
✓ Cultural or Historic Sites
✓ Camping
✓ Educational Programs
✓ Fishing
Groceries / Supplies
✓ Hiking
Horseback Riding
Hunting
Lodging
Off Highway Vehicles
✓ Visitor Center

The information center in Knights Ferry offers displays on the history of the area as well as the covered bridge and a century-old flour mill.

From Goodwin Dam to Orange Blossom Bridge, the river is characterized by rapids and deep pools of cold water. Anglers in search of rainbow trout should try their luck along this portion of the river. Below the Orange Blossom bridge, the river slows and the water warms, slightly. Here anglers can fish for smallmouth bass, striped bass, carp, channel catfish, white catfish, and black crappie. Boat put-ins and take-outs are located at various spots along the river. The use of motorized boats is limited. Please note that from mid-October to the end of December the river is closed to all fishing in order to protect chinook salmon during the spawning season.

Information: U.S. Army Corps of Engineers, Stanislaus River Parks, P.O. Box 1229, Oakdale CA 95361 / 209-881-3517. Caswell Memorial State Park, California Dept. of Parks and Recreation, P.O. Box 942896, Sacramento CA 94296 / 916-653-6995 or 800-444-7275.

Stanislaus River Parks											
1 Goodwin Dam								•		•	
2 Two-Mile Bar								•		•	
3 Knights Ferry				•	•			•		•	
4 Horseshoe Road	11				•	•		•			
5 Honolulu Bar					•	•		•			
6 Orange Blossom				•	•	•		•			
7 Valley Oak	13			•	•			•			
8 Oakdale								•		•	
9 McHenry Avenue	16			•	•			•			
10 Caswell Memorial State Park	65			•	•			•	•		•

Success Lake

Success Lake is nestled among the Sierra Nevada foothills eight miles east of Porterville and 70 miles southeast of Fresno in south-central California. From Porterville, follow SH 190 east to the park entrance. Group hikes and ranger programs can be arranged with the Corps at the project office.

Success Lake was formed with the completion of the dam constructed on the Tule River in 1961. The 2,450-acre lake is 3½ miles long with 30 miles of shoreline when full. There is only one developed recreation area on the lake that has camping facilities. More than 100 camp-

At A Glance
Auto Touring
Biking
✓ Boating
Climbing
Cultural or Historic Sites
✓ Camping
✓ Educational Programs
✓ Fishing
✓ Groceries / Supplies
Hiking
✓ Horseback Riding
✓ Hunting
Lodging
Off Highway Vehicles
Visitor Center

sites are available to tent campers and RVers. Campfire programs are presented at the amphitheater here each Saturday night from Memorial Day weekend through Labor Day. Downstream of the dam is *Bartlett Park* which is operated by Tulare County. There are some large fishing ponds here for youngsters to try out their fishing skills. A nature trail is also found here.

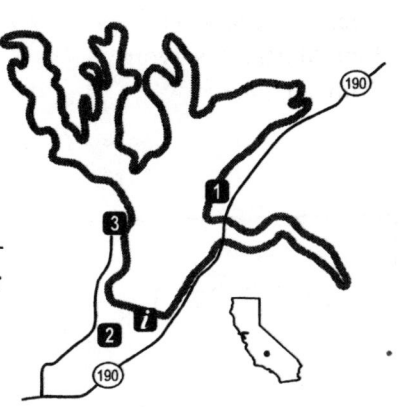

Success Lake provides good habitat for black bass, white crappie, bluegill, and channel catfish. In the spring and summer months, high water covers shoreline vegetation creating superb shoreline angling. Fish attracters have been placed in the area of the north *Tule* boat ramp and in *Kincade Cove*. Each fall and winter, the California Department of Fish and Game stocks the lake with several thousand rainbow trout. Success Marina in the *Tule* recreation area offers complete fishing and boating supplies, boat rentals and fuel.

Hunting is permitted in the 1,400-acre wildlife management area located on the north end of the lake. The most popular game includes pheasant and dove. Game may be taken with shotguns only.

Information: U.S. Army Corps of Engineers, Success Lake Project, P.O. Box 1072, Porterville CA 93258 / 209-784-0215. A 24-hour information line is available by calling 209-783-9200.

Success Lake	▲	🚐	🚻	🚽	⛽	🍴	🏚	🎣	🛟	🚶	⚓	〰
1 Tule	104	•		•	•	•	•		•		•	•
2 Bartlett			•	•	•				•			
3 Rocky Hill				•	•							•

Colorado

1 Bear Creek Lake
2 Chatfield Lake
3 Cherry Creek Lake
4 John Martin Reservoir
5 Trinidad Lake

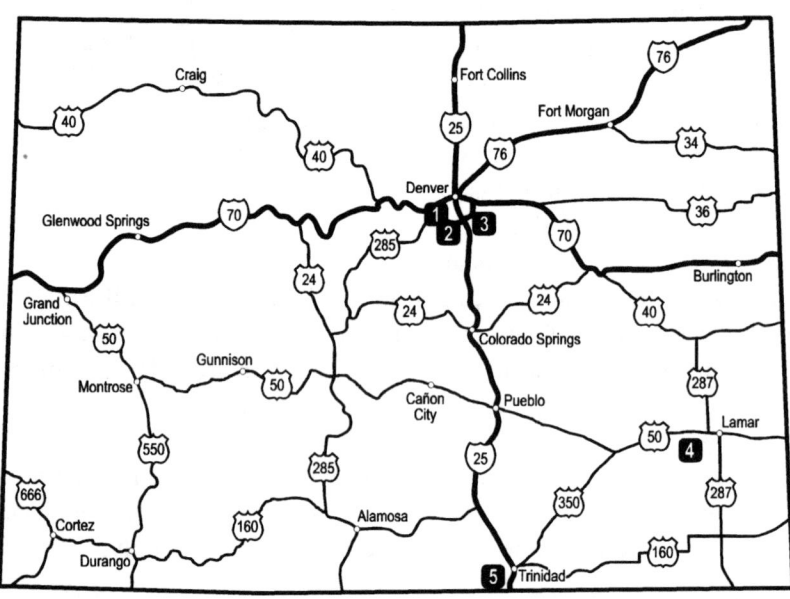

Colorado Resources

- ***Colorado Travel & Tourism Authority*** - P.O. Box 22005, Denver CO 80222 / (800) 265-6723
- ***Colorado Division of Wildlife*** - (303) 297-1192
- ***Road Condition Hotlines*** - (303) 639-1234 (recording) or (303) 639-1111 (within 2 hours of Denver)
- ***Road Construction Hotline*** - (303) 757-9228 (weekdays)

Bear Creek Lake

Located at the base of the Rocky Mountain foothills southwest of downtown Denver. Bear Creek Lake is one of three in the surrounding Denver area as part of the Omaha District's Tri-Lakes Project. Take the Morrison Road exit east off C-470 and follow the signs.

Bear Creek is owned by the Corps and leased to the City of Lakewood. Also considered a part of this project are the nearby Soda Lakes that are owned and operated by Lakewood. In addition to camping and fishing, visitors will find an archery range and golf course. Winter activities include ice fishing and cross-country skiing. The area provides over 20 miles of biking, hiking, and equestrian trails. Also found within the project is a nature study area and a water ski school that is located on Little Soda Lake. A series of campfire programs are offered Memorial Day through Labor Day. Individual environmental education programs are also available upon request.

At A Glance
Auto Touring
✓ Biking
✓ Boating
Climbing
Cultural or Historic Sites
✓ Camping
✓ Educational Programs
✓ Fishing
Groceries / Supplies
✓ Hiking
✓ Horseback Riding
Hunting
Lodging
Off Highway Vehicles
✓ Visitor Center

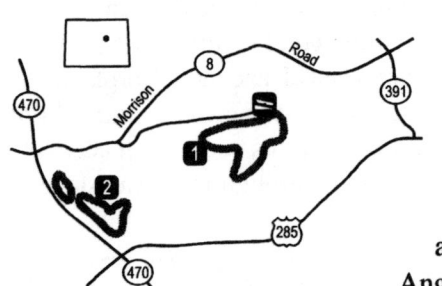

The 110-acre Bear Creek Lake is less than one mile long and reaches a depth of 48 feet. Anglers will find the waters stocked with smallmouth bass, rainbow trout and tiger muskie. Boat rentals are available at the marina on Big Soda Lake.

Information: U.S. Army Corps of Engineers, Tri-Lakes Project Office, 9307 SH 121, Littleton CO 80128 / 303-979-4120. Bear Creek Lake Park, 15600 West Morrison Rd., Morrison CO 80465 / 303-697-6159. For camping reservations call 800-678-2267 or 303-470-1144 in the Denver and Aurora area.

Bear Creek Lake	🔺	🚐	🚻	🚰	⛱	🎣	🏕	🚿	⛵	🥾	🚶	⚓	〰
1 Bear Creek Park	40	16	•	•		•				•	•		•
2 Soda Lakes			•	•	•	•		•			•	•	

Chatfield Lake

Chatfield Lake is situated in the lower foothills of the Front Range on the southwestern edge of Denver. The lake is one of three that comprise the Tri-Lakes Project. The lake can be accessed from either the Santa Fe Drive or Wadsworth Boulevard exits off C-470, then following the signs. The South Platte Visitor Center is located at the northwestern end of the project.

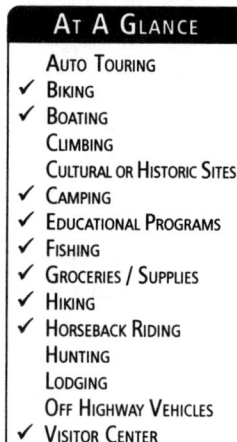

AT A GLANCE
- Auto Touring
- ✓ Biking
- ✓ Boating
- Climbing
- Cultural or Historic Sites
- ✓ Camping
- ✓ Educational Programs
- ✓ Fishing
- ✓ Groceries / Supplies
- ✓ Hiking
- ✓ Horseback Riding
- Hunting
- Lodging
- Off Highway Vehicles
- ✓ Visitor Center

Formed behind the dam on the South Platte River, Chatfield Lake is two miles long and reaches a depth of 47-feet. The area is owned by the Corps and leased to Colorado State Parks and the City of Denver. A heron and marsh bird observatory is located on the project, as is a fish holding facility and sailboat harbor. Also open to visitors is the Botanic Gardens' arboretum for environmental studies. The park also offers a balloon launch and model airplane area.

Winter activities include ice fishing, skating, and cross-country skiing. The barrier-free design of the facilities provides convenient access for the handicapped. A series of trails winds through the area; maps are available at the park's main entrance.

Anglers fish the 1,500-acre Chatfield Lake for largemouth bass, smallmouth bass, crappie, walleye, channel catfish, and sunfish. Brown trout, rainbow trout, and sometimes cutthroat trout occupy the cold waters of the South Platte River. The lake is periodically stocked with

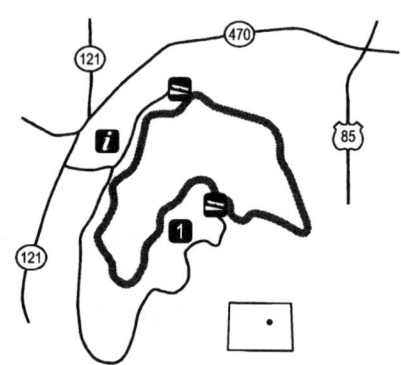

rainbow trout and other fish by the Colorado Division of Wildlife. Ice fishing in the winter produces trout, perch and crappie. For ice and snow conditions call: 303-791-7275. Fishing tackle and supplies are available in the Chatfield Marina, phone 303-791-7547.

Information: U.S. Army Corps of Engineers, Tri-Lakes Project Office, 9307 SH 121, Littleton CO 80128 / 303-979-4120. Chatfield Lake State Park, 11500 N. Roxborough Park Rd., Littleton CO 80125 / 303-791-7275. For camping reservations call 800-678-2267 or 303-470-1144 in the Denver and Aurora area.

Chatfield Lake													
1 Chatfield Lake State Park	153	51	•	•	•	•	•	•	•		•	•	•

Cherry Creek Lake

Cherry Creek Lake is one of three lakes in the surrounding Denver area as a part of the Corps' Tri-Lakes Project. This lake is located southeast of downtown Denver in the suburb of Aurora. Take either the Parker Road or Yosemite Street exits south off I-225 and follow the signs.

At A Glance
Auto Touring
✓ Biking
✓ Boating
Climbing
Cultural or Historic Sites
✓ Camping
✓ Educational Programs
✓ Fishing
✓ Groceries / Supplies
✓ Hiking
✓ Horseback Riding
Hunting
Lodging
Off Highway Vehicles
✓ Visitor Center

The State of Colorado manages and maintains the recreational facilities at Cherry Creek. The extensive trail system and bike lanes are a popular destination year-round. Horse rental and boarding are available from the stables near the east gate entrance. Miles of trails offer the equestrian a real treat. For information on the stables phone 303-690-8235. Other recreational facilities include a nature study area, model airplane field, archery and rifle range. Food concessions, bathhouse and first-aid station are located at the beach area. Fixed targets for rifles and pistols and a trap area for shotguns can be found in the southwestern area of the park, for details call: 303-693-1765. Hunting is not allowed.

Anglers are attracted to the 880-acre Cherry Creek Lake for the warmwater fishing opportunities. Some of the 26 species includes walleye,

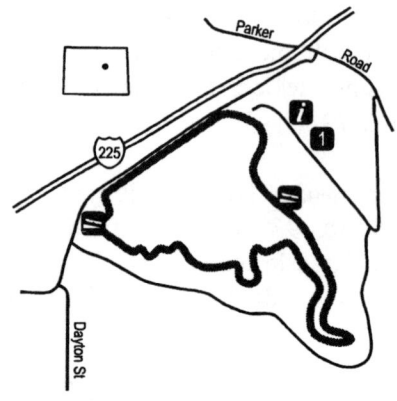

tiger muskie, northern pike, largemouth bass, bluegill, carp, flathead and channel catfish. The Tower Loop area near the dam is a popular spot as well as the quiet of the south end of the reservoir. Fishing supplies, slip rental and fuel is available at the A & H Marina, phone 303-779-6144. They also offer lessons for the beginner sailor, windsurfer or water-skier.

Information: U.S. Army Corps of Engineers, Tri-Lakes Project Office, 9307 SH 121, Littleton CO 80128 / 303-979-4120. Cherry Creek State Park, 4201 S. Parker Rd., Aurora CO 80014 / 303-699-3860. For camping reservations call 800-678-2267 or 303-470-1144 in the Denver and Aurora area.

Cherry Creek Lake														
1 Cherry Creek State Park	102	40	•	•	•	•	•	•	•			•	•	•

John Martin Reservoir

John Martin Reservoir, on the Arkansas River, lies two miles south of US 50 in southeastern Colorado near Hasty. From Las Animas, travel 15 miles east on US 50 to Hasty, then 2 miles south on CR 24. The project visitor center is located inside the project office near the south end of the dam.

The project's only camping area is situated adjacent to the small 72-acre Lake Hasty located below the dam. This area also has 3 enclosed group picnic shelters that are available for rent and a 4½ mile interpretive trail with waterfowl viewing area. Interpretive films are shown every weekend during the peak season in the amphitheater.

At A Glance
Auto Touring
Biking
✓ Boating
Climbing
Cultural or Historic Sites
✓ Camping
Educational Programs
✓ Fishing
Groceries / Supplies
✓ Hiking
Horseback Riding
✓ Hunting
Lodging
Off Highway Vehicles
✓ Visitor Center

John Martin Reservoir offers excellent duck and goose hunting opportunities during the waterfowl season. Hunting is permitted west of the dam only; check with a Corps of Engineers ranger for more information.

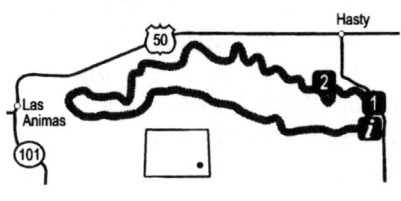

Fishing in Lake Hasty is good to excellent with a variety of species caught. A 1,600-acre pool is maintained in the reservoir for boating, water-skiing and fishing. Anglers will find carp, western white sucker, bullhead, largemouth bass, and bluegill in both the reservoir and Lake Hasty. Rainbow trout, walleye, and channel catfish are stocked annually.

Information: U.S. Army Corps of Engineers, John Martin Reservoir, 29955 CR 25¾, Hasty CO 81044 / 719-336-3476.

John Martin Reservoir	△	▭	🚻	🚰	🔥	⛴	🏕	⛺	🐾	■	🚶	⚓	〜
1 Lake Hasty	64	29	•	•	•	•	•	•	•	•	•		•
2 Overlook						•	•						

Trinidad Lake

Trinidad Lake is situated on the Purgatoire River in southern Colorado 87 miles south of Pueblo. The lake is south of SH 12 three miles west of Trinidad. Information about the lake is available at the project office located nearly one mile west of the dam just off SH 12 and the State Park Visitor Center in the *Trinidad Recreation Area*.

Trinidad Lake is nestled in the foothills of the Culebra Range of the Sangre de Cristo Mountains. All of the recreation areas within the project are operated and maintained by the Colorado Division of Parks and Outdoor Recreation. There are five separate recreation areas that comprise Trinidad Lake State Park. Situated along the northern shore

At A Glance
✓ Auto Touring
✓ Biking
✓ Boating
Climbing
Cultural or Historic Sites
✓ Camping
Educational Programs
✓ Fishing
Groceries / Supplies
✓ Hiking
✓ Horseback Riding
✓ Hunting
Lodging
Off Highway Vehicles
✓ Visitor Center

of the lake is the 143-acre *Carpios Ridge Campground*. More than 60 campsites, most with electric hookups, are available. The 102-acre *Trinidad Recreation Area*, located on the north end of the dam, has a three-lane boat ramp, picnic sites and an overlook. The 318-acre *Southside Recreation Area* provides hiking and equestrian trail access, shore fishing, and six covered picnic sites. The *Long Canyon Wildlife Area* is a 250-acre area that includes a 90-acre lake, wildlife viewing blind, and various trails. The *Levsa Canyon Recreation Area* is a 157-acre area designated for primitive camping and is accessible only by boat and/or foot. There are no developed facilities located here. From Memorial Day through Labor Day the state park staff presents campfire programs on weekends and holidays. Please note that swimming is prohibited in the lake.

Trinidad Lake averages 750 surface acres and provides excellent fishing opportunities. The lake is stocked with trout, largemouth bass, channel catfish, crappie, wipers, bluegill and walleye. Anglers may fish at any point along the shore or lake except at boat docks and ramps.

Small game hunting is permitted in designated areas using only shotguns or bows and arrows. Information on boundaries, seasons, and regulations is available from the visitor center or project office.

Information: U.S. Army Corps of Engineers, Trinidad Lake, P.O. Box 771, Trinidad CO 81082 / 719-846-7990. Trinidad Lake State Park, 32610 Highway 12, Trinidad CO 81082 / 719-846-6951.

Trinidad Lake	▲	⌂	🚻	🥤	🛣	🍴	🏕	🎣	🏊	🚶	⚓	〰
1 Carpios Ridge Campground	62	49	•	•	•	•	•	•		•	•	
2 Trinidad Recreation Area					•							•
3 Southside Recreation Area					•		•			•		
4 Long Canyon Wildlife Area											•	
5 Levsa Canyon Recreation Area	•											

IDAHO

1. Albeni Falls Dam / Lake Pend Oreille
2. Dworshak Reservoir
3. Lucky Peak Lake

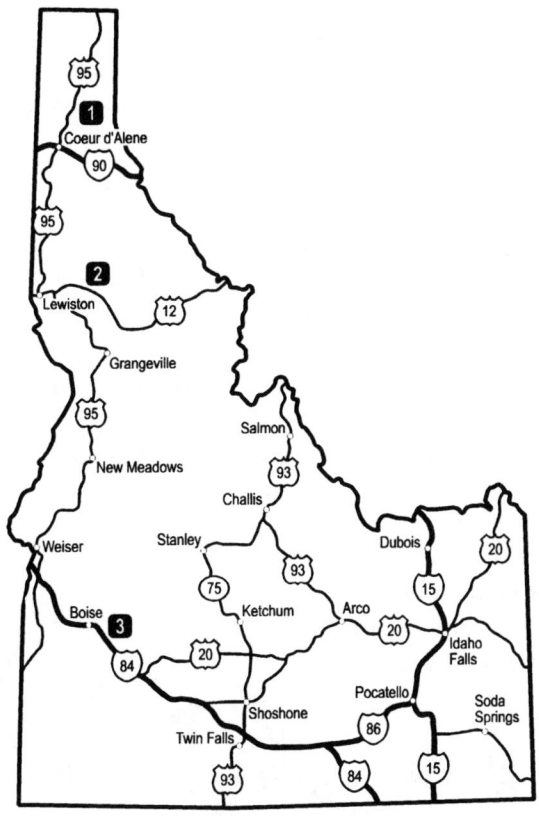

Idaho Resources

- *Idaho Division of Tourism Development* - P.O. Box 83720, Boise ID 83720-0093 / (800) VISIT-ID, (800) 847-4843 or (208) 334-2470
- *Idaho Department of Fish & Game* - (208) 334-3700
- *Road Condition Hotline* - (208) 336-6600 (recording, during winter months)
- *Road Construction Hotline* - (208) 334-8888 (recording)

Albeni Falls Dam / Lake Pend Oreille

Albeni (pronounced Albany) Falls Dam / Lake Pend Oreille (pronounced Pond O'Ray) is in northern Idaho 45 miles north of Coeur d'Alene and 50 miles northeast of Spokane, Washington. The dam is accessed off US 2, just west of Priest River, Idaho. One-hour long tours of the dam are given daily from Memorial Day through Labor Day. The tour begins at the visitor center. A short hike on a paved trail from the visitor center offers a view of the dam's spillway and powerhouse.

At A Glance
- ✓ Auto Touring
- ✓ Biking
- ✓ Boating
- Climbing
- ✓ Cultural or Historic Sites
- ✓ Camping
- ✓ Educational Programs
- ✓ Fishing
- ✓ Groceries / Supplies
- ✓ Hiking
- Horseback Riding
- ✓ Hunting
- Lodging
- Off Highway Vehicles
- ✓ Visitor Center

Forests and mountains, clear water, sandy beaches and excellent trout fishing are a few of the many attractions found here. Albeni Falls Dam sits on the Pend Oreille River about 90 miles upstream from where it enters the Columbia River. Behind the dam, the waters stretch 65 miles through a glacially carved, U-shaped valley that separates three lofty mountain ranges. During the winter, the bald eagle is a common site along the Pend Oreille River as it perches atop the ponderosa pines. *Trestle Creek* recreation area and the powerhouse are popular eagle observation areas. Visitors to the *Farragut State Park* will find a radio-controlled model airplane and glider flying field and shooting ranges. For winter activities the park offers cross-country ski trails, snowmobile area and sledding hill.

Idaho

With nearly 95,000-acres, Lake Pend Oreille is one of the largest and deepest natural lakes in the western United States with some areas reaching a depth of 1,152 feet. Some of the challenges awaiting the angler include kokanee salmon, rainbow trout, whitefish, and kamloops in the river and lake.

Information: U.S. Army Corps of Engineers, Albeni Falls Dam Project, 2376 E Hwy 2, Oldtown ID 83822 / 208-437-3133. Farragut State Park, 13400 E Ranger Rd., Athol ID 83801 / 208-683-2425. Round Lake State Park, P.O. Box 170, Sagle ID 83860 / 208-263-3489.

Lake Pend Oreille		Camping	Picnic	Restrooms	Water	Fee	Boat Ramp	Showers	Swimming	Fishing	Hiking	Anchor	Lake
1	Visitor Center			•	•		•				•		
2	Albeni Cove	14		•	•		•		•				•
3	Priest River	20	•	•	•	•	•		•	•	•		•
4	Riley Creek	67	•	•	•	•	•		•	•	•		•
5	Morton Slough	5			•		•						•
6	Springy Point	40	•	•			•		•				•
7	Trestle Creek			•			•		•				•
8	Johnson Creek	•			•		•						•
9	Samowen	80	•	•			•	•	•		•		•
10	Garfield Bay	27		•			•	•	•		•		•
11	Farragut State Park	137 45	•	•	•		•	•	•	•	•	•	•
12	Round Lake State Park	53	•	•	•		•	•	•	•	•		•

Dworshak Reservoir

The Dworshak Dam & Reservoir is in northwestern Idaho nearly 45 miles east of Lewiston. The lake is accessed from US 12, four miles north of Orofino. The project's visitor center is located on the north end of the dam. Tours are given daily throughout the summer and begin in the main lobby of the visitor center.

This 54 mile long lake provides the visitor a variety of recreational opportunities. Scattered along the 184 miles of shoreline are more than 130 boat accessible mini-camps at 80 locations along both sides of the lake. A map is available

At A Glance
Auto Touring
Biking
✓ Boating
Climbing
Cultural or Historic Sites
✓ Camping
Educational Programs
✓ Fishing
Groceries / Supplies
✓ Hiking
Horseback Riding
✓ Hunting
✓ Lodging
Off Highway Vehicles
✓ Visitor Center

from the Corps of Engineers showing the location of these primitive camps. In addition, the Three Meadows Group Camp in *Dworshak State Park* offers eight tent-only sites, six RV-only sites (35-foot maximum length), cabins, lodge with two cabins, and group grill area. The cabins provide overnight facilities for up to 100 people. The access road to Three Meadows is steep, narrow, and one lane with no turnouts. The area is generally open April through December. Contact the state park for additional information and reservations.

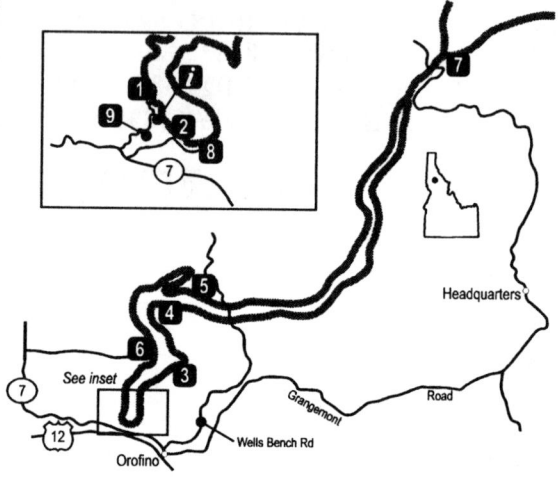

Construction of the dam on the North Fork of the Clearwater River created this 19,824-acre lake. Anglers will find kokanee salmon, rainbow trout, and smallmouth bass in the reservoir and river. The Dworshak National Fish Hatchery, located downstream from the dam, is the largest steelhead trout hatchery in the world. Every spring they release steelhead trout into the river.

Information: U.S. Army Corps of Engineers, Dworshak Dam & Reservoir, 100 Fair Street, Clarkston WA 99403 / 509-751-0240. U.S. Army Corps of Engineers, Dworshak Project Manager, P.O. Box 48, Ahsahka ID 83520 / 208-476-3294. Dworshak State Park, P.O. Box 2028, Orofino ID 83544 / 208-476-5994. Recorded reservoir information can be obtained by calling 800-321-3198.

Dworshak Reservoir	▲	🚻	🚽	🚰	♨	🍽	🏕	🛏	🏊	🍴	🚶	⚓	≋
1 Big Eddy						•	•		•		•	•	•
2 Bruces Eddy				•	•		•				•		•
3 Canyon Creek	12					•	•				•		•
4 Cold Springs Group Camp	•					•	•		•				

continued next page

Idaho

Dworshak Reservoir (cont.)	⛺	🚐	🚻	🚽	🪑	💧	⛲	🎣	🏊	🥾	🚶	⚓	〰️
5 Dent Acres	50	50	•	•	•	•	•	•	•		•		•
6 Dworshak State Park	105	46	•	•	•	•	•	•	•		•		•
7 Grandad	6				•		•						•
8 Merrys Bay					•		•				•		
9 Picnic Glen					•						•	•	

Lucky Peak Lake

Lucky Peak Lake is located in the mountains of southwest Idaho just ten miles southeast of Boise, off SH 21. Tours of the dam and information about the project is available at the visitor center located immediately below the dam.

Lucky Peak Lake provides only day-use areas within the project; there are no developed, overnight camping facilities. Many of the areas are accessible only by boat. The Idaho Department of Parks and Recreation operates three areas as units of Lucky Peak Lake State Park. These units are: *Discovery*, *Sandy Point*, and *Spring Shores*. All three state park units and *Barclay Bay*, *Foote Park / Lydle Gulch*, *Lucky Peak Viewpoint*, *Macks Creek*, *Mores Creek Park*, *Robie Creek*, and *Turner Gulch* are accessible by road. Bicycle paths can be found in the *Discovery* and *Sandy Point* recreation areas.

At A Glance
- ✓ Auto Touring
- ✓ Biking
- ✓ Boating
- Climbing
- ✓ Cultural or Historic Sites
- Camping
- Educational Programs
- ✓ Fishing
- ✓ Groceries / Supplies
- ✓ Hiking
- Horseback Riding
- ✓ Hunting
- Lodging
- Off Highway Vehicles
- ✓ Visitor Center

Those interested in exploring the area will want to follow the Ponderosa Pine Scenic Byway, a nationally designated scenic drive. This route follows SH 21 between Boise and Stanley, passing through the Boise National Forest. Travelers of the byway are treated to spectacular views of the rugged Sawtooth Mountains, much of which are protected from development by the 217,000-acre Sawtooth Wilderness. The U.S. Forest Service has constructed many camping areas directly along the byway and throughout the national forest.

Lucky Peak Dam was constructed on the Boise River and completed in 1955. When the lake behind the dam is full, it stretches for 12 miles and has 42 miles of shoreline. Anglers come to the 2,800-acre lake year-round in search of rainbow trout and kokanee salmon. A full service marina can be found in the *Spring Shores* unit of the state park.

Information: U.S. Army Corps of Engineers, Lucky Peak Lake Project, 9723 E Hwy 21, Boise ID 83716 / 208-343-0671. Lucky Peak State Park, HC 33 Box 1027, Boise ID 83706 / 208-334-2679.

LUCKY PEAK LAKE	🏕	🍴	🚻	🚰	⛺	⛱	🏨	🛣	🚤	🏊	🥾	⚓	〰
1 BARCLAY BAY	•	•		•					•			•	•
2 BIRCH CREEK				•					•				
3 BROWNS GULCH				•									
4 CHARCOAL CREEK				•	•				•				
5 CHIMNEY ROCK				•	•				•				
6 DEAD DOG CREEK				•					•				
7 DEER FLAT				•	•				•				
8 FOOTE PARK / LYDLE GULCH				•					•				
9 GOOSE NECK BAY				•					•				
10 LUCKY PEAK VIEWPOINT				•	•								
11 MACKS CREEK	•	•		•							•		•
12 MORES CREEK PARK				•	•								
13 PIPELINE GULCH				•					•				
14 PLACER POINT				•	•				•				
15 ROBIE CREEK	•	•	•	•			•		•				•
16 ROBIE CREEK SOUTH				•					•				
17 SHEEP CREEK				•					•				
18 TURNER GULCH	•			•	•				•			•	•
19 TURNAROUND POINT				•					•				
20 SANDY POINT (STATE PARK)	•	•		•	•	•	•	•					
21 SPRING SHORES (STATE PARK)	•	•		•		•		•			•	•	•
22 DISCOVERY (STATE PARK)	•	•		•		•	•	•					

Kansas

1 Big Hill Lake
2 Clinton Lake
3 Council Grove Lake
4 El Dorado Lake
5 Elk City Lake
6 Fall River Lake
7 Hillsdale Lake
8 John Redmond Reservoir
9 Kanopolis Lake
10 Marion Reservoir
11 Melvern Lake
12 Milford Lake
13 Perry Lake
14 Pomona Lake
15 Toronto Lake
16 Tuttle Creek Lake
17 Wilson Lake

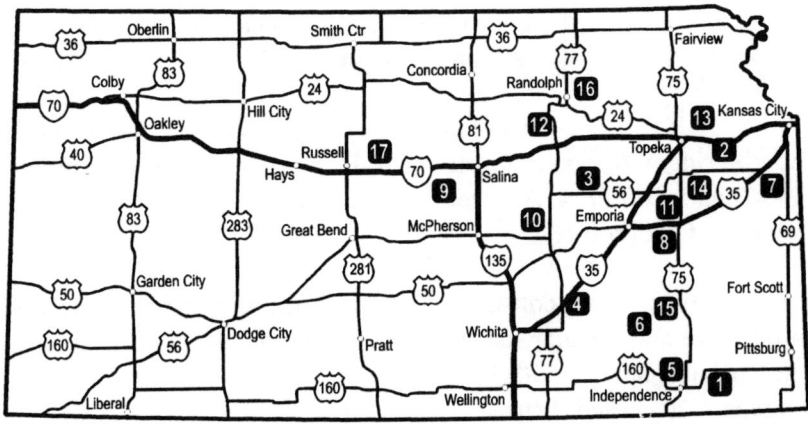

Kansas Resources

- *Kansas Travel and Tourism Development Division* - 700 S.W. Harrison Street Suite 1300, Topeka KS 66603 / (800) 2-KANSAS, (800) 252-6727 (lower 48 states) or (785) 296-2009
- *Kansas Dept. of Wildlife & Parks* - (785) 296-2281
- *Road Condition Hotlines* - (785) 291-3000 (recording) or (800) 585-7623 (KS only)

Big Hill Lake

Big Hill Lake is in southeast Kansas 11 miles southwest of Parsons and four miles east of Cherryvale. Information about the project is available from the office located near the dam.

At A Glance
Auto Touring
Biking
✓ Boating
Climbing
Cultural or Historic Sites
✓ Camping
Educational Programs
✓ Fishing
Groceries / Supplies
✓ Hiking
✓ Horseback Riding
✓ Hunting
Lodging
Off Highway Vehicles
Visitor Center

The area surrounding Big Hill Lake has long been noted for its rolling prairies and tree-dotted valleys. Wildflowers are abundant in the area during the spring and fall.

Opportunities for hiking and horseback riding exist around the lake. The Ruth Nixon Memorial Hiking Trail is a one-mile trail along the lake's western shoreline extending from the *Overlook* area to *Cherryvale Park*. The Big Hill Lake Horse Trail surrounds three-fourths of the lake and is about 17 miles long. The trail offers tethering areas and three large turfed parking areas that may be used for overnight camping by trail riders. Access points to the trail are found in *Cherryvale Park* and *Timber Hill Park*. Another access point is on US 160 at the northern end of the project

This 1,240-acre lake, constructed on Big Hill Creek, is one of the most productive and popular fisheries in the area. Anglers will find largemouth bass, smallmouth bass, crappie, channel and flathead catfish, walleye, bluegill, and other sunfish native to the area. Fishing docks are located in *Cherryvale* and *Overlook* recreation areas.

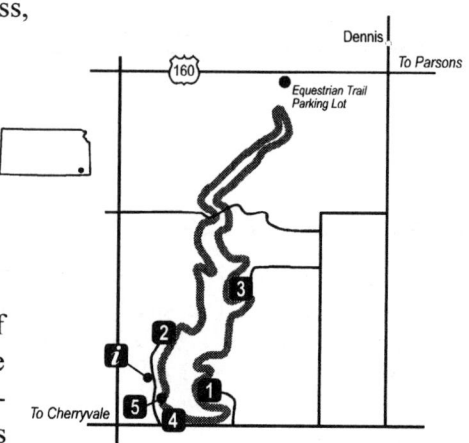

Those interested in hunting will find hundreds of acres of land within the project that are open to the public. About one-half mile east of the lake is

1,350 acres of land managed by the Kansas Department of Wildlife and Parks also open to the public for hunting. Game species vary and include bobwhite quail, rabbit, wild turkey, and white-tailed deer.

Information: U.S. Army Corps of Engineers, Big Hill Lake Project Office, P.O. Box 426, Cherryvale KS 67335 / 316-336-2741.

Big Hill Lake														
1 Mound Valley	90	74	•	•	•		•	•	•		•		•	
2 Cherryvale Park	30	30	•	•		•	•	•			•			
3 Timber Hill Park	20		•	•			•				•		•	
4 Downstream Point	9			•	•		•							
5 Overlook			•	•			•				•			

Clinton Lake

Located in eastern Kansas among the rolling woodlands about 45 miles west of Kansas City near Lawrence. To reach the dam from Lawrence travel west on Clinton Parkway. Information is available from the project office near the north end of the dam.

Clinton Lake, with its high bluffs, wooded shoreline, and clear water is unequaled among Kansas lakes for the beauty of its setting. Five developed recreation areas around the lake provide the visitor with plenty of camping and picnicking opportunities. The *Woodridge* area, on

At A Glance
Auto Touring
✓ Biking
✓ Boating
Climbing
Cultural or Historic Sites
✓ Camping
Educational Programs
✓ Fishing
✓ Groceries / Supplies
✓ Hiking
✓ Horseback Riding
✓ Hunting
Lodging
Off Highway Vehicles
✓ Visitor Center

the lake's western end, is undeveloped and highly recommended for the backpacker or nature lover. For the hiker and equestrian, *Rockhaven* offers access to more than 30 miles of bridle and hiking trails. Cross-country snow skiers find *Clinton State Park* an ideal spot for winter recreation. The City of Lawrence operates the *Outlet* park, a day use area below the dam, that offers two picnic shelters, a playground and softball field. The city also operates the Eagle Bend Golf Course, an 18-hole course, below the dam.

The 7,000-acre Clinton Lake, on the Wakarusa River, stretches eight miles up the Wakarusa Valley and offers the angler 85 miles of shoreline. Species of fish include largemouth and smallmouth bass, channel catfish, crappie, white bass, walleye, bluegill, and various other species of sunfish. A marina in the state park provides boating equipment and services as well as fishing supplies.

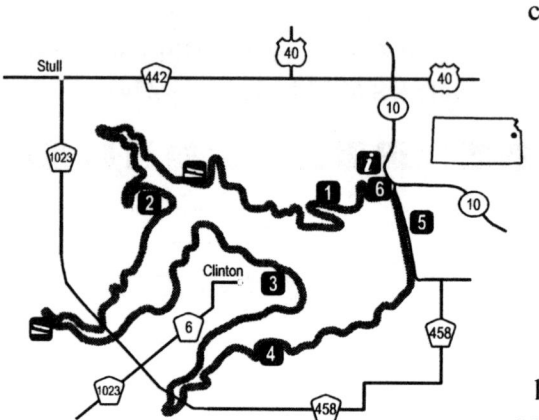

Over 9,000 acres of land within the project is open to the public for hunting. Wildlife found around Clinton Lake includes mourning dove, quail, squirrel, rabbit, deer, raccoon, and opossum. Waterfowl are usually numerous on the lake late in the year.

Information: U.S. Army Corps of Engineers, Clinton Lake Project Office, 872 N 1402 Rd., Lawrence KS 66049 / 785-843-7665. Clinton State Park, 798 N 1415 Rd., Lawrence KS 66049 / 785-842-8562. City of Lawrence Parks and Recreation Department, 785-832-7900.

CLINTON LAKE														
1 CLINTON STATE PARK	464 240	•	•	•	•	•	•	•	•		•	•	•	
2 WOODRIDGE		•			•			•				•		
3 BLOOMINGTON	382 220	•	•	•	•	•	•	•	•	•				•
4 ROCKHAVEN	50		•		•			•				•		
5 OUTLET				•	•	•	•							
6 OVERLOOK				•	•	•	•					•		

Council Grove Lake

Council Grove Lake is nestled in the northern quarter of the Flint Hills in east-central Kansas about 60 miles southwest of Topeka. The dam is two miles northwest of Council Grove off US 56. Information about the lake is available at the lake office on the west end of the dam.

Council Grove Lake is one of the top outdoor recreation sites in Kansas. The lake is in a beautiful setting with rolling bluestem hills highlighted with hickory, oak, walnut, and elm along the streams. Nine developed recreation areas surround the lake and all offer camping. Nature trails near the lake office and in *Richey Cove* provide visitors the opportunity for walks among the trees. An all-terrain vehicle area is found below the dam in Outlet Channel East park.

At A Glance
Auto Touring
Biking
✓ Boating
Climbing
Cultural or Historic Sites
✓ Camping
Educational Programs
✓ Fishing
✓ Groceries / Supplies
✓ Hiking
Horseback Riding
✓ Hunting
✓ Lodging
✓ Off Highway Vehicles
✓ Visitor Center

Council Grove Lake was constructed on the Neosho River and provides 3,310 acres for boating and fishing. With 40 miles of shoreline, anglers are afforded numerous spots from which to fish. Species include white crappie, walleye, channel catfish, flathead catfish, white bass, largemouth bass, and a variety of sunfish. Council Grove is best known for its crappie fishing but the cat fishermen have always done well also. Concession services are available at the marina, west of the dam.

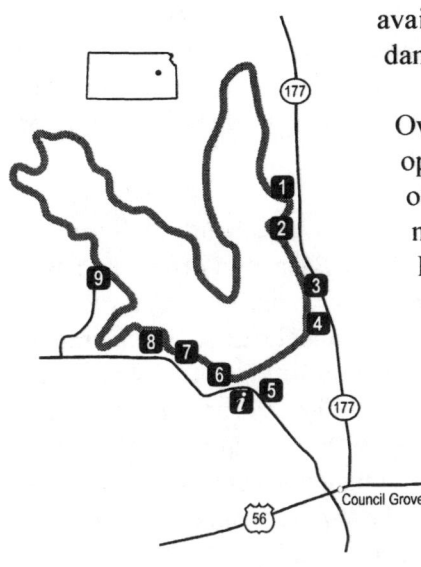

Over 2,600 acres of project land is operated by the Kansas Department of Wildlife and Parks for wildlife management and public hunting. Hunters find plentiful populations of quail, pheasant, prairie chicken, wild turkey and deer.

Information: U.S. Army Corps of Engineers, Council Grove Lake Office, 945 Lake Road, Council Grove KS 66846 / 316-767-5195.

Council Grove Lake	⛺	🚐	🚻	🍽	🏕	🚿	🏛	🏊	🗑	🥾	⚓	🚤
1 Custer Park	10		•	•		•						•
2 Richey Cove	50	48	•	•	•	•	•	•	•	•	•	•
3 Kit Carson Cove	14	12		•	•		•					•
4 Kansa View	5			•	•							
5 Outlet Channel	4			•	•		•					
6 Neosho Park	8	8		•	•		•					•
7 Marina Cove	4	3		•	•		•		•		•	•
8 Santa Fe Trail	39	33		•	•	•	•					•
9 Canning Creek Cove	45	38	•	•	•	•	•	•	•	•		•

El Dorado Lake

El Dorado Lake is in an area of rolling terrain in southeast Kansas about 25 miles northeast of Wichita. Information is available from the project office east of the dam. To reach the office from El Dorado, follow US 54 east for about four miles to Bluestem Road and then north for two miles.

At A Glance
- Auto Touring
- ✓ Biking
- ✓ Boating
- Climbing
- Cultural or Historic Sites
- ✓ Camping
- Educational Programs
- ✓ Fishing
- ✓ Groceries / Supplies
- ✓ Hiking
- ✓ Horseback Riding
- ✓ Hunting
- ✓ Lodging
- Off Highway Vehicles
- ✓ Visitor Center

Four recreation areas surround the lake and all are leased, operated, and maintained by the Kansas Department of Wildlife and Parks as units of the El Dorado State Park. The four areas combined offer more than 1,000 campsites for tent campers and RVers. Five camping cabins are also available in the *Bluestem Point* campground.

El Dorado Lake covers about 8,000 acres of the Walnut River Basin and offers the angler nearly 100 miles of shoreline. The reservoir is inhabited by a variety of sport fish including bluegill, walleye, channel catfish, black crappie, largemouth and smallmouth bass. Anglers will also find white crappie, flathead catfish, white bass, black bullhead, drum and carp. Rainbow trout are stocked seasonally below the dam in the *Walnut River* campground. A public fishing area is maintained below the dam at the reservoir outlet. Boating, fishing, and camping supplies may be found at the marina within *Shady Creek* campground.

The Flint Hills area surrounding the reservoir provides good opportunities for hunting quail, prairie chicken, dove, wild turkey, and deer. The primary area that is open to the public for hunting is along the northern Walnut River arm of the lake.

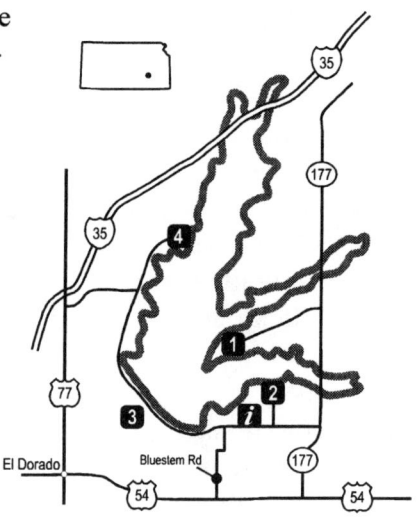

Information: U.S. Army Corps of Engineers, El Dorado Lake, 2710 NE Shady Lake Rd., El Dorado KS 67042 / 316-321-9974. El Dorado State Park, 618 NE Bluestem Rd., El Dorado KS 67042 / 316-321-7180.

El Dorado Lake														
1 Bluestem Point	552	•	•	•	•	•	•	•	•		•		•	
2 Shady Creek	238	•	•	•	•	•	•					•	•	
3 Walnut River	155	•	•	•	•	•	•	•	•	•	•			
4 Boulder Bluff	155		•	•	•	•	•				•	•	•	

Elk City Lake

Elk City Lake is situated on the Elk River in southeastern Kansas. The dam is about seven miles east of Elk City and 11 miles northwest of Independence. To reach the dam from Independence, follow US 75 north for five miles to 5400 Road; travel west four miles and then south for two. Maps and information is available from the Fish & Wildlife Office located near the west end of the dam.

Elk City Lake is set among the rolling pastures and sheer bluffs of southeast Kansas. In autumn,

At A Glance

Auto Touring
✓ Biking
✓ Boating
Climbing
Cultural or Historic Sites
✓ Camping
Educational Programs
✓ Fishing
Groceries / Supplies
✓ Hiking
Horseback Riding
✓ Hunting
Lodging
Off Highway Vehicles
Visitor Center

the native hardwoods bring an abundance of color to the area. The lake is well known for its six scenic trails, three of which are National Recreation Trails. These trails meander through the colorful oak and hickory woods surrounding the lake and take the hiker through some of the most interesting rock formations in Kansas. The trails range from a 15-mile scenic trek to a one-mile all-weather and handicap accessible trail.

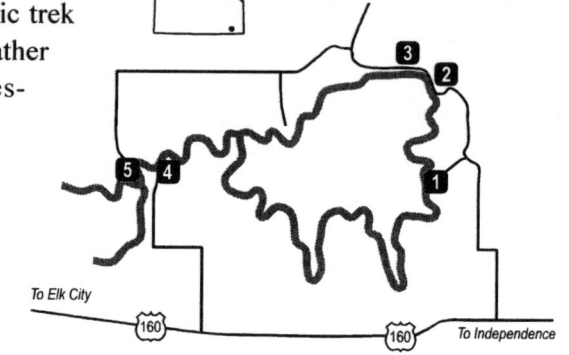

The 4,460-acre lake offers excellent opportunities for fishing. The lake is stocked with a variety of sunfish, largemouth bass, white crappie, wipers, saugeye, white bass, channel catfish, and flathead. Although there are no marinas in any of the recreation areas, supplies can be found in Independence.

The Kansas Department of Wildlife and Parks, Fish & Wildlife Division manages more than 12,000 acres of land for wildlife management and public hunting. Wildlife common to the area includes bobwhite quail, cottontail rabbit, mourning dove, fox, squirrel, white-tailed deer, wild turkey, and a variety of ducks and geese.

Information: U.S. Army Corps of Engineers, Elk City Project Office, P.O. Box 426, Cherryvale KS 67335 / 316-336-2741. Elk City State Park Office, P.O. Box 945, Independence KS 67301 / 316-331-6295.

Elk City Lake														
1 Elk City State Park	165	95	•	•	•	•	•	•	•	•	•	•		•
2 Memorial Overlook				•	•		•				•			
3 Outlet Channel	15		•	•	•		•							
4 Card Creek	16	16	•	•	•		•				•			•
5 Oak Ridge	11					•	•				•			•

Fall River Lake

Fall River Lake is in southeast Kansas about 75 miles east of Wichita and 17 miles southeast of Eureka. The dam forming the lake was constructed on Fall River, a tributary of the Verdigris River. It is four miles northwest of the town of Fall River, north of US 400. Information about the lake and its recreation areas is available at the project office near the western end of the dam.

Positioned between the cross-timbered Chautauqua Hills to the east and the grasslands of the Flint Hills to the west, Fall River Lake provides a remarkable variety of landscape and wildlife for the outdoor enthusiast. The lake is about a mile wide at the damsite and stretches 15 miles up Fall River. Canoeists are afforded many access points along the river. Canoe rentals are available in nearby Eureka.

Anglers will find the 2,450-acre Fall River Lake stocked with largemouth bass, white bass, crappie, flathead and channel catfish, and a variety of sunfish. In the spring, white bass runs can be excellent, especially in both Otter Creek and Fall River above the reservoir.

Kansas Department of Wildlife and Parks manages over 8,000 acres of land within the project for wildlife management and public hunting. Wildlife species common to the area includes white-tailed deer, squirrel, cottontail rabbit, greater prairie chicken, mourning dove, turkey, duck, goose, and bobwhite quail.

At A Glance

- Auto Touring
- Biking
- ✓ Boating
- Climbing
- Cultural or Historic Sites
- ✓ Camping
- ✓ Educational Programs
- ✓ Fishing
- ✓ Groceries / Supplies
- ✓ Hiking
- Horseback Riding
- ✓ Hunting
- Lodging
- Off Highway Vehicles
- ✓ Visitor Center

Information: U.S. Army Corps of Engineers, Fall River Project Manager, P.O. Box 37, Fall River KS 67047 / 316-658-4445. Fall River State Park, RR 1 Box 44, Toronto KS 66777 / 316-637-2213.

Fall River Lake													
1 Overlook				•		•							
2 Damsite	33	21	•	•	•	•	•	•					
3 Quarry Bay (State Park)	25			•	•		•	•	•		•		•
4 Whitehall Bay	25	24	•	•	•		•	•	•				•
5 Browns Cove	N	O		F	A	C	I	L	I	T	I	E	S
6 Fredonia Bay (State Park)	105	45	•	•	•		•	•		•			•
7 Rock Ridge Cove North	44	25	•	•	•		•				•		•
8 Rock Ridge Cove South (SP)	30				•		•						•

Hillsdale Lake

Hillsdale Lake is in east-central Kansas 30 miles southwest of Kansas City and nine miles north of Paola. To reach the dam from Paola, follow US 169 north to the Hillsdale exit and then west on 255th Street for two miles. A Corps of Engineers visitor center and state park office are located on the east end of the dam.

At A Glance
- Auto Touring
- ✓ Biking
- ✓ Boating
- Climbing
- Cultural or Historic Sites
- ✓ Camping
- ✓ Educational Programs
- ✓ Fishing
- ✓ Groceries / Supplies
- ✓ Hiking
- ✓ Horseback Riding
- ✓ Hunting
- Lodging
- Off Highway Vehicles
- ✓ Visitor Center

The Kansas Department of Wildlife and Parks manages all of the project's 8,000 acres of land including the only developed recreation area on the lake, *Russell L. Crites*. Visitors will find 200 campsites here with most having electric hookups. On the lake's east shore is the Marysville equestrian area which has about 30 miles of marked and unmarked trails for the horseback rider. Those interested in model airplane flying will find an area south of the dam for enjoying their craft.

With the construction of the dam on Big Bull Creek, Hillsdale Lake covered 4,580 acres of surrounding land. Over 70 percent of the standing timber was left in the lake basin to enhance fish habitat. The lake, with 51 miles of shoreline, is stocked with largemouth bass, crappie, catfish, walleye, and a variety of sunfish.

Kansas

Wildlife is abundant in the hardwood forests surrounding the project. Approximately 7,000 acres of land within the project is open to the public for hunting. White-tailed deer, raccoons, beavers, squirrels, rabbits, coyotes, and bobcats are among the wildlife inhabiting the area. A large variety of birds make this area home year-round with guests of migrating waterfowl and shorebirds using the lake as a rest stop.

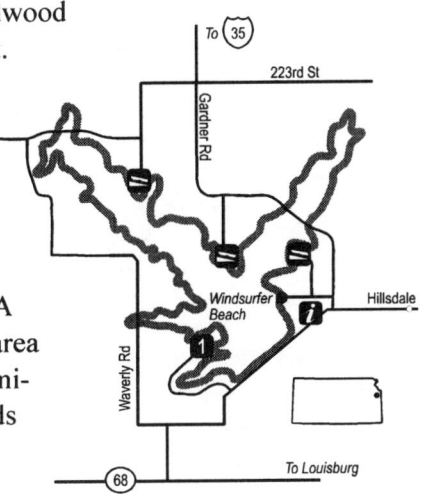

Information: U.S. Army Corps of Engineers, Hillsdale Lake Office, 26000 W 255th St., Paola KS 66071 / 913-783-4366. Hillsdale State Park, 26001 W 255th St., Paola KS 66071 / 913-783-4507.

Hillsdale Lake	▲	▭	▤	▯	⛽	⛵	🍴	▦	▨	▣	🚶	⚓	▬
1 Russell L. Crites	200	120	•	•			•	•	•		•		•

John Redmond Reservoir

John Redmond Reservoir is in east-central Kansas 55 miles south of Topeka. The dam, constructed on the Neosho River, is accessed three miles north and one mile west of Burlington, just off US 75. The Corps' project office is located on the north end of the dam.

John Redmond Reservoir is surrounded by rolling grassland and wooded areas of elm, black walnut and hickory. Visitors to this project will find five developed recreation areas that have camping facilities for tents and recreational vehicles.

At A Glance
Auto Touring
Biking
✓ Boating
Climbing
Cultural or Historic Sites
✓ Camping
Educational Programs
✓ Fishing
Groceries / Supplies
✓ Hiking
✓ Horseback Riding
✓ Hunting
Lodging
✓ Off Highway Vehicles
Visitor Center

The 9,400-acre lake, with nearly 60 miles of shoreline, offers excellent fishing opportunities. Anglers will find the lake filled with largemouth bass, white crappie, channel and flathead catfish, and various species of sunfish. Anglers will find access to good fishing on the Neosho River in the *Hartford* recreation area.

More than 18,000 acres of land surrounding the project is managed by the U.S. Fish and Wildlife Service as the Flint Hills National Wildlife Refuge. This area is open to the public for hunting during the appropriate season. The area north of Neosho River is closed during migratory waterfowl season. Wildlife common to the area includes white-tailed deer, squirrel, cottontail rabbit, bobwhite quail, mourning dove, and greater prairie chicken.

Information: U.S. Army Corps of Engineers, John Redmond Project Office, 1565 Embankment Rd. SW, Burlington KS 66839 / 316-364-8613.

John Redmond Reservoir	▲	⛴	🍴	🚻	♿	☕	🏠	🚿	🏊	🥫	🚶	⚓	〰
1 Damsite	25	21	•	•	•	•	•	•	•		•		•
2 Hartford	9			•	•		•						•
3 Riverside East	53	53	•	•		•					•		
4 Riverside West	43	37	•	•	•	•	•	•			•		•

Kanopolis Lake

Kanopolis Lake, constructed on the Smoky Hill River, is in central Kansas about 33 miles southwest of Salina. To reach the dam from Salina, travel 26 miles southwest on SH 140 and then south on SH 141 for seven.

Kansas

Visitors to Kanopolis Lake will find four developed recreation areas on the lake. Two of these areas, *Langley Point*, located on the south end of the dam and *Horsethief*, located on the north side of the lake, are managed by the Kansas Department of Wildlife and Parks. The *Riverside* area, located below the dam, and *Venango*, located on the north end of the dam, are managed by the Corps of Engineers. All parks offer a full range of recreational opportunities including camping, fishing and picnicking.

At A Glance
✓ Auto Touring
✓ Biking
✓ Boating
Climbing
✓ Cultural or Historic Sites
✓ Camping
✓ Educational Programs
✓ Fishing
✓ Groceries / Supplies
✓ Hiking
✓ Horseback Riding
✓ Hunting
Lodging
✓ Off Highway Vehicles
✓ Visitor Center

Nestled along the Smoky Hill River toward the northwest portion of the project is Faris Caves, which were carved by early pioneers and served as milk house, school house, and living quarters. Horsethief Canyon on the north end of the lake offers 26 miles of trails for hikers, horseback riders, and bicyclists.

The 3,800-acre lake with 41 miles of shoreline is well known for its excellent white bass and walleye fishing, but catches of crappie and channel cat can be equally good. March and April bring the best walleye fishing as they spawn along the face of the dam. March to May is the best time for crappie, however, they can be caught year-round. Gravel and dirt roads lead to Yankee Run Point and Boldt Bluff Public Use Areas on the western shore of the lake. Anglers will find some good fishing spots in these areas but no boat access to the lake. A marina in *Langley Point State Park* offers a general store and snack bar.

Nearly 13,000 acres of land surrounding the lake is open to the public for hunting. Most of this land is in the northwest portion of the project along the Smoky Hill River. Pheasant, quail, prairie chicken, rabbit, white-tailed deer, and mule deer are most common in this area. A variety of ducks and geese inhabit the area during spring and fall migrations. Other wildlife inhabiting the region includes coyote, fox, squirrel, beaver, raccoon, and opossum.

Information: U.S. Army Corps of Engineers, Kanopolis Lake Information Center, 105 Riverside Dr., Marquette KS 67464 / 785-546-2294. Kanopolis State Park, 200 Horsethief Rd., Marquette KS 67464 / 785-546-2565.

Kanopolis Lake													
1 Riverside (Outlet Area)	40	9	•	•	•	•	•	•					
2 Venango	219	66	•	•	•	•	•	•	•		•		•
3 East Shore (State Park)	143	30	•	•	•	•	•	•	•	•	•		•
4 Langley Point (State Park)	200	88	•	•	•	•	•	•	•	•	•		•

Marion Reservoir

Marion Reservoir is located just north of US 56 in central Kansas between Marion and Hillsboro. Marion is nearly 60 miles northeast of Wichita. The dam forming the lake was constructed on the Cottonwood River and completed in 1968. Information about the lake and recreation areas is available from gate attendants, park rangers, or at the project office near the northeast end of the dam.

> **At A Glance**
> Auto Touring
> Biking
> ✓ Boating
> Climbing
> ✓ Cultural or Historic Sites
> ✓ Camping
> Educational Programs
> ✓ Fishing
> Groceries / Supplies
> ✓ Hiking
> Horseback Riding
> ✓ Hunting
> Lodging
> Off Highway Vehicles
> Visitor Center

Marion Reservoir is surrounded by seven recreation areas with four having facilities for tent campers and RVers. The largest of these, *Cottonwood Point*, has nearly 100 campsites and all have electric hookups. Wildlife observers will enjoy the Willow Walk Nature Trail found in this park.

Marion Reservoir encompasses 6,200 acres and 60 miles of shoreline. Anglers will find largemouth bass, crappie, white bass, channel catfish, and flathead catfish. The lake is also stocked with walleye and wiper, a striped bass and white bass hybrid. A fisherman's parking area with fish attractors and feeders is in *Cottonwood Cove*. Boat ramps are in all but two of the recreation areas.

Approximately 4,100 acres of land within the project is managed by the Kansas Dept. of Wildlife and Parks for public hunting and wildlife management. Most of this land is located in the upper reaches of the lake. Wildlife inhabiting the area includes bobwhite quail, mourning dove, cottontail rabbit, pheasant, squirrel, deer, and wild turkey. A map showing the location of land open to the public for hunting is available from the project office.

Information: U.S. Army Corps of Engineers, Marion Reservoir, Route 1 Box 102, Marion KS 66861 / 316-382-2101.

Marion Reservoir	△	▭	▯	▯	⛽	🌊	🏠	🛣	⛰	🚶	⚓	〰
1 Durham Cove												•
2 French Creek Cove	20			•	•		•					•
3 Hillsboro Cove	51	51	•	•	•	•	•	•		•		•
4 Spillway Area							•					
5 Marion Cove	6			•	•		•					•
6 Cottonwood Point	92	92	•	•	•	•	•		•	•	•	•
7 Overlook				•	•	•		•				

Melvern Lake

Melvern Lake lies on the eastern edge of the scenic Flint Hills region in east-central Kansas. The lake is 40 miles south of Topeka just west of US 75 and north of I-35. The dam forming the lake was constructed on the Marais des Cygnes River. Information about the lake and surrounding recreation areas is available from the project office near the south end of the dam.

> **At A Glance**
> ✓ Auto Touring
> ✓ Biking
> ✓ Boating
>   Climbing
> ✓ Cultural or Historic Sites
> ✓ Camping
> ✓ Educational Programs
> ✓ Fishing
> ✓ Groceries / Supplies
> ✓ Hiking
> ✓ Horseback Riding
> ✓ Hunting
>   Lodging
>   Off Highway Vehicles
> ✓ Visitor Center

The Flint Hills are characterized by gently rolling hills covered with tall native grasses. Native woodlands occur in the bottomlands along tributaries of the Marais des Cygnes. Recreational opportunities are abundant at this Corps' project. *Eisenhower State Park*, operated by the Kansas Department of Wildlife and Parks, is the largest recreation area and is located on the north shore near the eastern end of the lake. There are 300 campsites in this park suitable for tents and recreational vehicles. If you're interested in a primitive setting for camping, *Sun Dance* offers 30 sites.

Those interested in hiking or horseback riding will find six trails within the project. A 22-mile equestrian trail follows the southern shore of the lake between *Sun Dance* and *Arrowrock*. Nature trails can be found in the *Outlet* and *Coeur D'Alene* recreation areas as well as the state park.

Melvern Lake is stocked with largemouth bass, white bass, walleye, sauger, channel catfish, crappie, and a variety of sunfish. The lake has a surface area of 6,930 acres and 101 miles of shoreline. A marina is in the *Coeur D'Alene* park and provides complete boating, fishing, and camping supplies. Boat ramps are located in all of the parks.

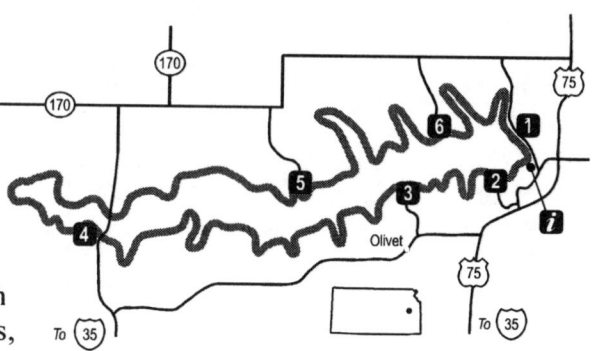

Wildlife species found around the lake include bobwhite quail, prairie chicken, mourning dove, cottontail rabbit, white-tailed deer, and squirrel. Thousands of geese and ducks rest here during fall and spring migrations. Hunting is permitted in season on all public land surrounding the project except for developed recreation areas and land near the dam. A wildlife refuge on the lake's western end is closed to hunting from mid-October through mid-January.

Information: U.S. Army Corps of Engineers, Melvern Lake Project Office, 31051 Melvern Lake Pkwy., Melvern KS 66510 / 785-549-3318. Eisenhower State Park, 29810 S Fairlawn Rd., Osage City KS 66523 / 785-528-4102.

Melvern Lake														
1 Outlet	150	150	•		•	•	•	•	•	•	•			•
2 Coeur D'Alene	60	34	•		•	•	•	•	•			•	•	•
3 Arrowrock	45	19	•		•	•	•	•				•		•
4 Sun Dance	30				•	•		•				•		•
5 Turkey Point	50	36	•		•	•	•	•						•
6 Eisenhower State Park	300	195	•		•	•	•	•	•	•	•	•		•

Milford Lake

Milford Lake is situated on the Republican River in northeast Kansas four miles north of Junction City and 60 miles west of Topeka. Either side of the dam is accessed from SH 57 off US 77. Additional information about the project is available from the information center on the south end of the dam.

Visitors to this project will find 11 public use areas surrounding the lake with camping available in eight. The *Milford State Park*, just north of the dam, is the largest park with over 200 campsites available. Adjacent to the *Outlet Park* is the Milford Education Center and Fish Hatchery. There is an off-road vehicle area along the lake's western shore, just north of the *School Creek* campground. This area is reached

At A Glance
- Auto Touring
- ✓ Biking
- ✓ Boating
- Climbing
- Cultural or Historic Sites
- ✓ Camping
- ✓ Educational Programs
- ✓ Fishing
- ✓ Groceries / Supplies
- ✓ Hiking
- ✓ Horseback Riding
- ✓ Hunting
- ✓ Lodging
- ✓ Off Highway Vehicles
- ✓ Visitor Center

from the dam by following SH 244 west and then CR 837 north. East of the dam off US 77 is a golf course for those interested in enjoying an afternoon playing golf.

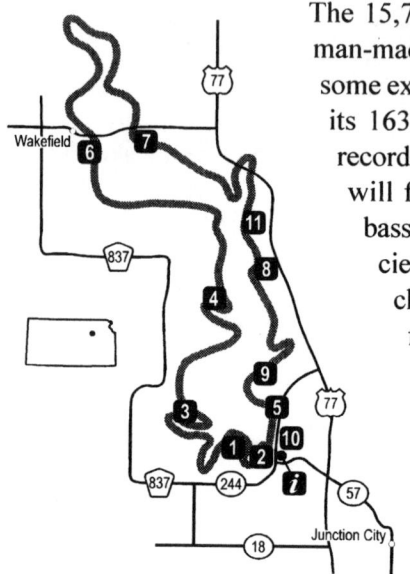

The 15,700-acre Milford Lake, the largest man-made lake in Kansas, offers the angler some excellent fishing opportunities along its 163 miles of shoreline. Several state records have come from this lake. Anglers will find largemouth bass, smallmouth bass, white bass, and wipers. Other species of fish include walleye, crappie, channel catfish, and a variety of sunfish. Complete fishing and boating supplies are available in two marinas, one in *West Rolling Hills* and the other in *Milford State Park*.

More than 23,000 acres of land within the project is open to the public for hunting. Wildlife inhabiting the area includes quail, pheasant, prairie chicken, duck, goose, rabbit, squirrel, deer, and turkey.

Information: U.S. Army Corps of Engineers, Milford Lake Information Center, 4020 W K-57 Highway, Junction City KS 66441 / 785-238-5714. Milford State Park, 8811 State Park Rd., Milford KS 66514 / 785-238-3014.

Milford Lake	△	⌂	🚻	🚰	🏕	🛋	🍴	🚿	🏊	🎣	🚶	⚓	🚤
1 West Rolling Hills	62	40	•	•			•	•	•			•	•
2 East Rolling Hills					•	•	•		•				•
3 Curtis Creek	81	67	•	•			•	•	•				•
4 School Creek	44				•	•		•			•		•
5 North Overlook						•	•	•					
6 Clay County Park	•	•	•	•	•	•	•	•	•				•
7 South Timber Creek	34				•	•	•	•					•

continued next page

Kansas

Milford Lake (continued)

	△	🚐	🚻	🚰	⛱	👥	🚿	🏊	🛢	🚶	⚓	📞
8 Farnum Creek	76	46	•		•	•						•
9 Milford State Park	222	123	•	•	•	•	•	•		•	•	•
10 Outlet Park				•	•	•	•		•			•
11 Milford City Park	•	•	•	•	•	•	•	•	•			•

Perry Lake

Perry Lake lies to the north of US 24 in northeast Kansas about 17 miles east of Topeka. The dam forming the lake was constructed on the Delaware River and completed in 1969. The dam can be reached from the town of Perry on US 24 by following Ferguson Road north for three miles. The project office is located near the east end of the dam; more information about the lake and its recreation areas is available here.

At A Glance
Auto Touring
✓ Biking
✓ Boating
Climbing
Cultural or Historic Sites
✓ Camping
Educational Programs
✓ Fishing
✓ Groceries / Supplies
✓ Hiking
✓ Horseback Riding
✓ Hunting
✓ Lodging
✓ Off Highway Vehicles
✓ Visitor Center

There are eight recreation areas surrounding the lake including *Perry State Park,* which is operated by the Kansas Department of Wildlife and Parks. The state park is the largest recreation area and has 400 campsites for tents and RVs. Horseback riders will be interested in the trail running through the state park and *Rock Creek.* For the hiker, there's a 30-mile long trail that follows the eastern shore and Slough Creek arm of the lake. The trail can be accessed from *Slough Creek* and *Longview* recreation areas. A mountain bike trail can also be found in the state park. A motorcycle and ATV trail is south of the dam, adjacent to the *Outlet* park.

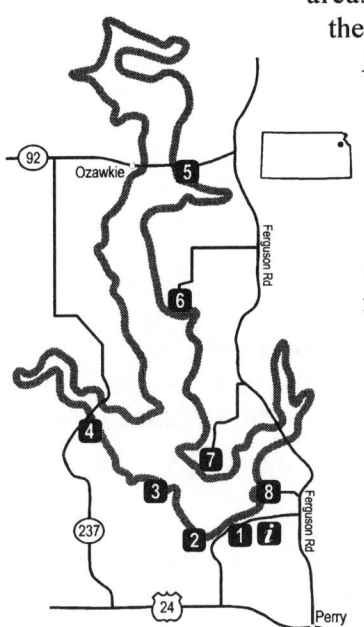

The 11,150-acre Perry Lake, surrounded by rolling hills and forested areas of hardwood trees, provides many good fishing spots along its 160 miles of shoreline. The lake supports a variety of species of fish including largemouth bass, crappie, sauger, walleye, catfish, bluegill and other sunfish. The reservoir is known for its excellent crappie and channel cat fishing. Fishing and boating supplies are available from the marina.

Wildlife found in the area includes quail, wild turkey, pheasant, duck, goose, rabbit, squirrel, and deer. Much of the project land is open to the public for hunting during the appropriate season. Wildlife refuges on the northern end of the project are closed to the public from October through mid-January.

Information: U.S. Army Corps of Engineers, Perry Lake Project Office, 10419 Perry Park Dr., Perry KS 66073 / 785-597-5144. Perry State Park, 5441 West Lake Rd., Ozawkie KS 66070 / 785-246-3449.

Perry Lake														
1 Outlet		•			•		•			•				
2 Thompsonville					•	•								
3 Rock Creek	106 53	•	•	•	•	•	•							•
4 Perry State Park	370 124	•	•	•	•	•	•	•	•			•		•
5 Old Town	104 33	•	•	•	•	•	•							•
6 Longview	45 25	•	•	•		•	•					•		•
7 Slough Creek	263 118	•	•	•	•	•	•					•		•
8 Perry			•	•	•	•	•	•					•	•

Pomona Lake

Pomona Lake, in east-central Kansas, is situated on the 110-Mile Creek west of Ottawa and about 35 miles south of Topeka. To reach the dam from Ottawa, travel 12 miles west on SH 68/268 to the dam access road. Project information is available from the visitor center on the south end of the dam.

Pomona State Park is on the south shore of the lake and is operated by the Kansas Department of Wildlife and Parks. The remaining recreation areas are operated by the Corps of Engineers. *Pomona State Park*

Kansas

has the largest number of campsites available for tent campers and RVers. The *Cedar* and *110-Mile* parks offer campers a more primitive setting. Those interested in hiking or horseback riding will find several trails throughout the project.

The 4,000-acre Pomona Lake, with 52 miles of shoreline, is stocked with largemouth bass, white bass, crappie, walleye, channel and flathead catfish, bluegill, and other sunfish. Fish attractors have been placed throughout the lake to improve fish habitat. The reservoir is noted for great crappie fishing and giant flathead catfish. The marinas in *Pomona State Park* and *Michigan Valley Park* offer a full range of fishing, boating and camping supplies and services.

Hunting is permitted in season on most of the land within the project. A hunting brochure is available at the information center. Hunters will find a variety of game including rabbit, dove, quail, deer, turkey and waterfowl.

At A Glance
- Auto Touring
- ✓ Biking
- ✓ Boating
- Climbing
- Cultural or Historic Sites
- ✓ Camping
- Educational Programs
- ✓ Fishing
- ✓ Groceries / Supplies
- ✓ Hiking
- ✓ Horseback Riding
- ✓ Hunting
- ✓ Lodging
- ✓ Off Highway Vehicles
- ✓ Visitor Center

Information: U.S. Army Corps of Engineers, Pomona Lake, 5260 Pomona Dam Rd., Vassar KS 66543 / 785-453-2201. Pomona State Park, RR 1 Box 118, Vassar KS 66543 / 785-828-4933.

Pomona Lake	⛺	🚐	🏕	🚻	🚰	🌳	🚿	🥾	🎣	🏊	🚶	⚓	🛶
1 Outlet Park	36	36	•	•	•	•	•			•	•		
2 Management Park				•	•	•	•						•
3 Pomona State Park	299	156	•	•	•	•	•	•	•	•	•	•	•
4 Carbolyn Park	32	29	•	•	•	•	•	•					•

continued next page

Pomona Lake *(continued)*	△	⛺	🚻	🚰	⛽	🚤	🏠	🔦	🏊	🏕	🚶	⚓	〰
5 Dragoon Access Area													•
6 110-Mile Park	30		•	•		•					•		•
7 Wolf Creek Park	119	44	•	•	•	•	•	•					•
8 Michigan Valley Park	98	60	•	•	•	•	•	•	•	•		•	•
9 Cedar Park	8				•	•							•

Toronto Lake

Toronto Lake is situated on the Verdigris River south of US 54 in southeast Kansas. The lake is set in the scenic cross-timbered Chautauqua Hills region of Kansas nearly 60 miles south of Emporia. Information is available from the project office on the west end of the dam.

At A Glance
- Auto Touring
- Biking
- ✓ Boating
- Climbing
- Cultural or Historic Sites
- ✓ Camping
- ✓ Educational Programs
- ✓ Fishing
- ✓ Groceries / Supplies
- ✓ Hiking
- Horseback Riding
- ✓ Hunting
- Lodging
- Off Highway Vehicles
- ✓ Visitor Center

All the recreation areas surrounding Toronto Lake are operated by the Kansas Department of Wildlife and Parks as units of Toronto State Park. Camping facilities are available in each of the state park areas. Three hiking trails wind through extensively wooded habitat teaming with a variety of wildlife; trail access is from *Toronto Point* and *Holiday Hill*. Special visitor programs are offered year-round such as interpretive programs, junior naturalist programs, and special recreational and cultural programs.

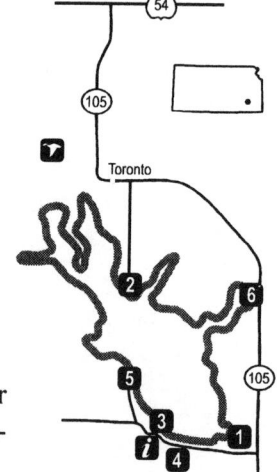

Toronto Lake offers the angler 2,800 acres of water and 51 miles of shoreline for pursuing their favorite pastime. Within the lake are largemouth bass, white bass, black and white crappie, channel catfish, flathead catfish, freshwater drum, bluegill, and other sunfish species. Bait, tackle, and other fishing supplies can be found near the lake.

Kansas

About 4,600 acres of land along the Verdigris River and Walnut Creek is open to the public for hunting. Wildlife inhabiting the area includes bobwhite quail, squirrel, cottontail rabbit, mourning dove, white-tailed deer, duck, goose, turkey, and greater prairie chicken.

Information: U.S. Army Corps of Engineers, Fall River - Toronto Project Office, P.O. Box 37, Fall River KS 67047 / 316-658-4445. Toronto State Park, RR 1 Box 44, Toronto KS 66777 / 316-637-2213.

Toronto Lake	▲	⌂	🚻	🚽	⛽	🍴	🏨	🎣	🏊	🚶	⚓	〰
1 Woodson Cove	•				•	•				•		
2 Toronto Point	200	47	•	•	•	•	•	•	•	•	•	•
3 Overlook					•					•		
4 East Spillway Area							•					
5 Holiday Hill	30	15	•	•		•	•			•		•
6 Manns Cove	20		•			•						•

Tuttle Creek Lake

Tuttle Creek Lake lies north of US 24 about six miles north of Manhattan and 60 miles west of Topeka. The lake is situated on the Big Blue River in the Flint Hills region of northeast Kansas. For additional information stop by the visitor center located below the west end of the dam.

At A Glance
✓ Auto Touring
✓ Biking
✓ Boating
Climbing
Cultural or Historic Sites
✓ Camping
Educational Programs
✓ Fishing
Groceries / Supplies
✓ Hiking
✓ Horseback Riding
✓ Hunting
Lodging
✓ Off Highway Vehicles
✓ Visitor Center

Visitors to Tuttle Creek Lake will find 11 public use areas within the project. Four areas, *River Pond, Spillway, Fancy Creek,* and *Randolph,* are operated as units of Tuttle Creek State Park. Camping facilities can be found in all but four of the project's recreation areas. With no designated camping sites in the *Spillway* and *Randolph* areas you are free to choose your own site.

Several trails are available throughout the area for your enjoyment. Nature Trails are located in the *Outlet* and *River Pond* areas while hiking and equestrian trails can be found in *Carnahan* and *Randolph*.

Hikers will also find a trail in the *Fancy Creek* recreation area. For the off-road vehicle enthusiast, two areas are designated for your sport. The *Tuttle Creek ORV* area is on the lake's western shore near the north end of the lake; the *Spillway Cycle* area is just east of the dam. For an enjoyable ride among tallgrass prairie, visitors will want to drive the Prairie Parkway; follow CR 43 east of the lake.

The 12,570-acre lake offers 104 miles of shoreline set among tallgrass prairie of the Flint Hills. Anglers will find Tuttle Creek Lake stocked with a variety of fish including walleye, white bass, crappie, catfish, and various sunfish. Fishing in the reservoir is especially good for crappie. The boat ramps in *Randolph* and *Fancy Creek* are only usable at high lake levels. A marina is located in the *Spillway* unit of Tuttle Creek State Park. Complete boating, fishing, and camping supplies can also be found in Manhattan.

Kansas Department of Wildlife and Parks manages 12,000 acres of land in the upper reaches of the project that is open to the public for hunting. Some of the wildlife species found here include quail, pheasant, squirrel, and rabbit. The lake attracts numerous waterfowl during the fall and spring migrations.

Information: U.S. Army Corps of Engineers, Tuttle Creek Lake, 5020 Tuttle Creek Blvd., Manhattan KS 66502 / 785-539-8511. Tuttle Creek State Park, 5020-B Tuttle Creek Blvd., Manhattan KS 66502 / 785-539-7941.

Kansas

Tuttle Creek Lake	▲	⌂	🚿	🚰	⛱	🏊	🚻	🛤	🎣	🗑	🚶	⚓	🛥
1 Outlet			•	•	•					•			
2 River Pond (State Park)	193	104	•	•	•	•	•	•	•	•	•		•
3 Spillway (State Park)	•			•	•		•	•				•	•
4 Carnahan Creek	3			•	•						•		•
5 Randolph (State Park)	•		•	•	•		•	•				•	•
6 Fancy Creek (State Park)	12	12		•	•						•		•
7 Tuttle Creek ORV											•		
8 Stockdale	13		•	•	•		•	•					•
9 Tuttle Creek Cove	30			•	•		•		•				•
10 Observation Point					•								
11 Spillway Cycle				•		•				•			

Wilson Lake

Wilson Lake is located on the Saline River in north-central Kansas 60 miles west of Salina and 30 miles east of Russell. The dam can be accessed by traveling seven miles north on SH 232 from the Wilson exit on I-70. Information about the project is available at the visitor center on the east end of the dam. Information is also available at the state park office in Wilson State Park.

The Kansas Department of Wildlife and Parks operates and maintains *Wilson State Park* and *Otoe Area*. More than 200 campsites for tent campers and RVers are available here. Hiking on the Dakota Trail, in the state park, offers an excellent view of the lake and native Kansas prairie. A new mountain bike trail, also in the state park, provides a great opportunity for bicyclists. Below the dam and adjacent to *Sylvan Park* is the Bur Oak Nature Trail. This ¾-mile interpretive trail has 23 stops that are described in a brochure available at the project office. The Rocktown Natural Area, located on the lake's north shore, has a rich diversity of mixed prairie grasses and other prairie plants. A three-mile loop trail here will take you through this Natural and Scientific Area.

At A Glance

- Auto Touring
- ✓ Biking
- ✓ Boating
- Climbing
- Cultural or Historic Sites
- ✓ Camping
- Educational Programs
- ✓ Fishing
- ✓ Groceries / Supplies
- ✓ Hiking
- Horseback Riding
- ✓ Hunting
- Lodging
- Off Highway Vehicles
- ✓ Visitor Center

Wilson Lake is one of the state's best fishing lakes and is especially known for excellent white bass and striped bass angling. Also found within the 9,000-acre lake are smallmouth bass, walleye, catfish, and various sunfish. Fishing and boating supplies are available at the marina in *Wilson State Park*.

Over 9,000 acres of land within the project is open to the public for hunting. Some game species include ring-necked pheasant, bobwhite quail, white-tailed deer, and cottontail rabbit. Waterfowl inhabit the lake area during spring and fall migrations.

Information: U.S. Army Corps of Engineers, Wilson Lake Project Office, Route 1 Box 241, Sylvan Grove KS 67481 / 785-658-2551. Wilson State Park, Rt. 1 Box 181, Sylvan Grove KS 67481 / 785-658-2465.

Wilson Lake	△	⌑	⌂	⊎	♨	⌇	⛺	⚐	⛰	⬛	⚲	⚓	⛵
1 Sylvan	15	9	•	•	•	•		•		•			
2 Lucas	103	62	•	•	•	•	•	•	•			•	•
3 Minooka	158	102	•	•	•	•	•	•	•	•			•
4 Wilson State Park	200	125	•	•	•	•	•	•	•			•	•
5 Otoe Area (SP)	•	27	•	•	•	•	•	•	•				•

Montana

1 Fort Peck Lake
2 Lake Koocanusa

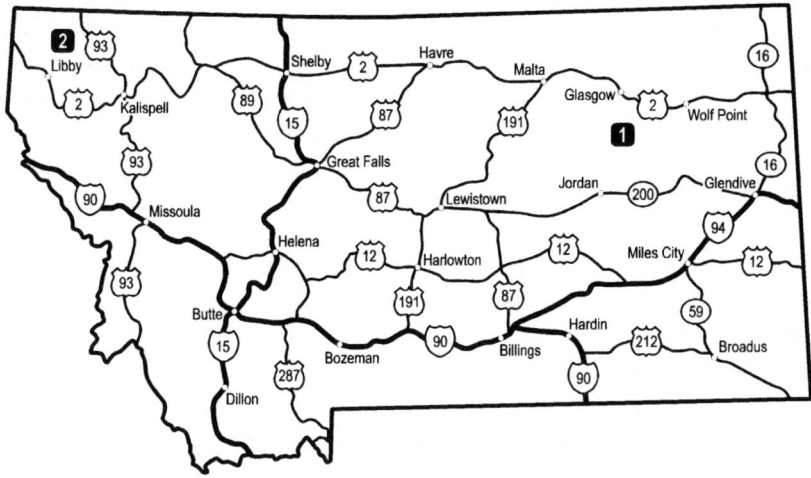

Montana Resources

- ***Travel Montana*** - 1424 9th Ave., Helena, MT 59620 / (800) 847-4868 or (406) 444-2654
- ***Montana Dept. of Fish, Wildlife & Parks*** - (406) 444-2535
- ***Road Condition Hotlines*** - (800) 332-6171 (recording) or (406) 444-6339 (recording)

Fort Peck Lake

Fort Peck Lake is in northeast Montana about 18 miles southeast of Glasgow. To reach the dam from Glasgow, follow SH 24; from Nashua, follow SH 117 south for about 11 miles. Information about the project and its recreation areas is available from the project office in Fort Peck located just north of the dam. Tours of the powerplant are given daily from Memorial Day to Labor Day.

At A Glance
- ✓ Auto Touring
- ✓ Biking
- ✓ Boating
-   Climbing
-   Cultural or Historic Sites
- ✓ Camping
- ✓ Educational Programs
- ✓ Fishing
- ✓ Groceries / Supplies
- ✓ Hiking
- ✓ Horseback Riding
-   Hunting
- ✓ Lodging
-   Off Highway Vehicles
- ✓ Visitor Center

Fort Peck Lake lies completely within the 1.1 million-acre Charles M. Russell National Wildlife Refuge. This vast wildlife area is home to pheasants, sage grouse, mule deer, pronghorns, elk, bighorn sheep, and white-tailed deer. The largest known fossil beds in the world can be found along a portion of the lake's southern shore.

There are 16 recreation areas located around the reservoir. The areas near and around the dam are more developed than those along the rest of the lake. The primitive areas are often accessed by gravel roads that may become impassable during inclement weather.

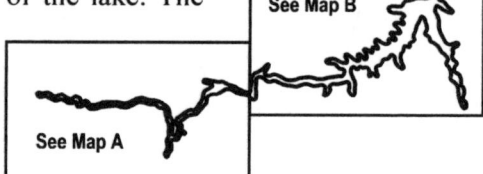

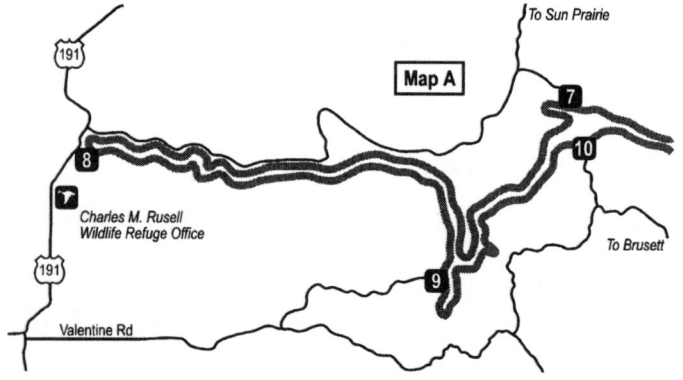

Montana

This 240,000-acre lake enjoys nationwide recognition as a hot spot for walleye fishing. Walleye in the 2- to 4-pound class is common, and 8- to 10-pounders are caught with increasing regularity. The 134-mile long lake with 1,520 miles of shoreline also offers excellent fishing for sauger, smallmouth bass, lake trout, chinook salmon, and northern pike. Fishing in the Missouri River below the dam can be good at any time of the year. Game fish include those caught in the lake, plus catfish, burbot and the prehistoric paddlefish. Today, paddlefish only survive in the Missouri River drainage and the Yangtze River drainage in China. Boating and fishing supplies are available at the marinas in *Fort Peck West*, *Crooked Creek*, *Hell Creek SRA*, and *Rock Creek*. Boat rentals are available at *Fort Peck West* and *Hell Creek SRA* areas.

Information: U.S. Army Corps of Engineers, Fort Peck Lake, P.O. Box 208, Fort Peck MT 59223 / 406-526-3411. Rock Creek State Park, Montana Fish Wildlife & Parks, 1420 E 6th Ave., Helena MT 59620 / 406-444-2535.

Fort Peck Lake	🏕	🚐	🚻	🥤	⛱	🎣	🏞	🚿	🥾	🛢	🚶	⚓	🌊
1 Dredge Cuts	9			•	•	•	•	•					•
2 Fort Peck West	21	13		•	•	•	•	•				•	•
3 Downstream	68	51	•	•	•	•	•	•		•	•		•
4 Flat Lake	5				•		•						•
5 The Pines	12			•	•	•	•				•		•
6 Bonetrail	9				•		•						•
7 Fourchette Bay	44				•		•						•
8 James Kipp	34		•	•	•		•						•
9 Crooked Creek	•				•		•					•	•

continued next page

Fort Peck Lake (continued)	⛺	🚐	🚻	🚰	🪑	🛥	🏚	🏔	🎣	🥫	🚶	⚓	〰
10 Devils Creek	5			•		•							•
11 Hell Creek SRA	40		•	•		•						•	•
12 Nelson Creek	30		•	•		•							•
13 McGuire Creek	8			•		•							
14 Rock Creek		•		•	•		•					•	•
15 Rock Creek State Park					•		•						•
16 Bear Creek	3			•		•							

Lake Koocanusa

Lake Koocanusa lies within the Kootenai National Forest in northwest Montana about 90 miles west of Kalispell. From US 2 in Libby, travel 17 miles east on SH 37 to reach the dam. A visitor center is located near the west end of the dam. It is open seven days a week from Memorial Day through Labor Day. Guided tours of the dam and powerhouse are offered daily during the summer.

At A Glance
✓ Auto Touring
✓ Biking
✓ Boating
✓ Climbing
Cultural or Historic Sites
✓ Camping
✓ Educational Programs
✓ Fishing
✓ Groceries / Supplies
✓ Hiking
Horseback Riding
✓ Hunting
Lodging
✓ Off Highway Vehicles
✓ Visitor Center

The 46,500-acre lake stretches some 90 miles along the Kootenai River with 42 miles extending into Canada. Along with excellent fishing, bird watchers enjoy sightings of the osprey and bald eagle. Rock climbers will want to visit a collection of rock faces known as Stone Hill. Kayaking and canoeing are popular activities on the Kootenai River below Libby Dam.

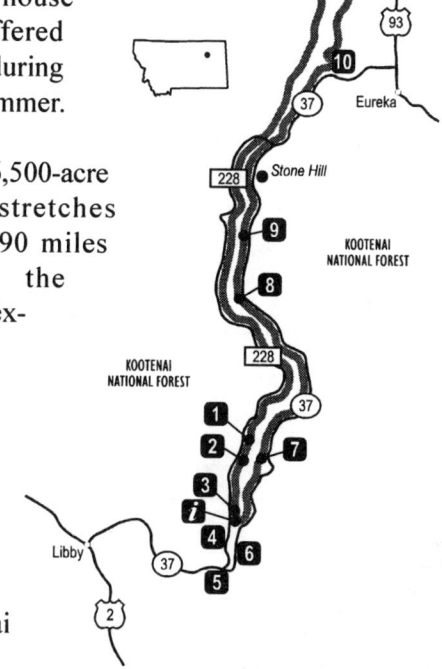

Lake Koocanusa is surrounded by the nearly two-million-acre Kootenai National Forest. The road following the lake's shore is officially designated a National Forest Scenic Byway.

The Kootenai River below Libby Dam is considered a blue ribbon fishery. Anglers will find the river and lake teaming with rainbow trout, west slope cutthroat, brook trout, kokanee salmon, ling (burbot), whitefish, and kamloops—a strain of rainbow trout. The past two state record rainbow trout were caught directly below the dam.

Information: U.S. Army Corps of Engineers, Libby Dam and Lake Koocanusa, 17115 SH 37, Libby MT 59923 / 406-293-7751, Visitor Center: 406-293-5577. Kootenai National Forest, 506 US Hwy 2 West, Libby MT 59923 / 406-293-6211.

Lake Koocanusa	Sites	🚐	🏕	🚻	⛱	🛌	🚿	🏢	♨	🗑	🚶	⚓	≋
1 Barron Creek		•											•
2 McGillivray	50			•	•		•		•				•
3 Souse Gulch					•	•	•	•				•	•
4 Alexander Creek		•				•							
5 Blackwell Flats		•				•							
6 Dunn Creek Flats		•				•							
7 Koocanusa Marina		•			•	•		•	•			•	•
8 Rocky Gorge	120				•	•							•
9 Peck Gulch	75				•	•							•
10 Rexford Bench	54	•	•	•		•		•		•		•	

NEBRASKA

1. Harlan County Lake
2. Papio Creek Watershed Projects
    a) Glenn Cunningham Lake
    b) Standing Bear Lake
    c) Wehrspann Lake
    d) Zorinsky Lake
3. Salt Valley Lakes
    a) Bluestem SRA
    b) Branched Oak SRA
    c) Conestoga SRA
    d) Olive Creek SRA
    e) Pawnee SRA
    f) Stagecoach SRA
    g) Twin Lakes WMA
    h) Wagon Train SRA
    i) Yankee Hill WMA

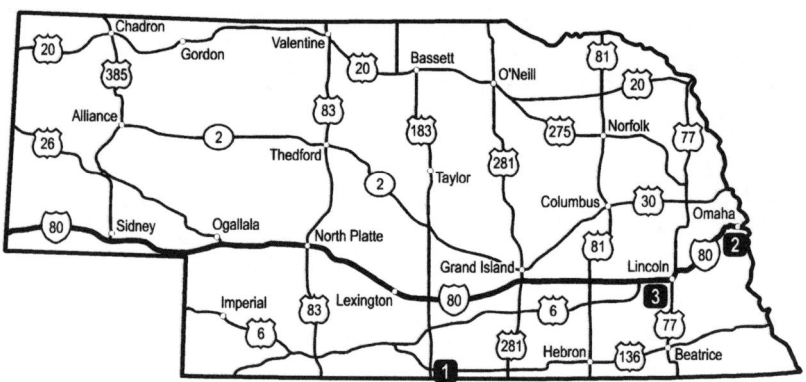

Nebraska Resources

- *Nebraska Travel & Tourism* - PO Box 98913, Lincoln, NE 68509 / (800) 228-4307
- *Nebraska Game & Parks Commission* - (800) 826-PARK or (402) 471-0641
- *Road Condition Hotlines* - (800) 906-9069 in state, 553-5000 Omaha area, or (402) 471-4533 out of state
- *Road Construction Hotline* - (402) 479-4512 weekdays

Harlan County Lake

Harlan County Lake is on the Republican River in south-central Nebraska about 180 miles southwest of Lincoln and 55 miles south of Kearney. The dam is accessed off US 136 in Republican City. Visitors will find the project office on the north end of the dam.

The Republican River Valley was once occupied by one of the greatest concentrations of buffalo on the Great Plains and was a favored hunting ground for the Pawnee, Sioux, Cheyenne and Arapaho Indian tribes. Today hunters will find a variety of game including pheasants, deer, quail, turkey, ducks, and Canada geese. Hunting is permitted on all government-owned land surrounding the lake with the exception of those areas that have been posted by the Corps. Additional information is available at the project office.

At A Glance
Auto Touring
Biking
✓ Boating
Climbing
Cultural or Historic Sites
✓ Camping
Educational Programs
✓ Fishing
✓ Groceries / Supplies
✓ Hiking
✓ Horseback Riding
✓ Hunting
✓ Lodging
✓ Off Highway Vehicles
✓ Visitor Center

The 13,250-acre Harlan County Lake, the second largest lake in Nebraska, is well known for its excellent spring walleye fishing. Other favorites with the angler include white bass, channel and flathead catfish, and northern pike. The angler will also find, in lesser numbers, wipers, largemouth bass, crappie and bluegill. Camping and fishing supplies as well as boat rentals and storage are available at the marinas in *Hunter Cove* and *Patterson Harbor*.

Information: U.S. Army Corps of Engineers, Harlan County Lake Project Office, Rt 1 Box 123A, Republican City NE 68971 / 308-799-2105.

Harlan County Lake	△	⌐⌐	🚻	🚰	🏕	🎣	⛺	🏖	🌊	🚶	⚓	〰
1 Alma City Park	42	34	•	•	•	•	•	•				•
2 Gremlin Cove	70			•	•	•	•		•			•
3 Hunter Cove	172	84	•	•	•	•	•	•		•		• •
4 North Cove						•						
5 Methodist Cove	159	48	•	•	•	•	•	•				•
6 Patterson Harbor	85			•	•		•		•		•	• •
7 Outlet North	30			•	•	•	•			•		
8 Outlet South	30				•		•					

Papio Creek Watershed Projects

This Corps of Engineers project consists of four small lakes in the Omaha metropolitan area: Glenn Cunningham Lake, Standing Bear Lake, Wehrspann Lake, and Zorinsky Lake. The recreation areas found at the lakes are operated by the City of Omaha except for Wehrspann Lake, which is operated by the Papio-Missouri River Natural Resources District. See each lake listing for location and directions.

The Nebraska Game and Parks Commission monitors fish populations in the four lakes and stocks thousands of game fish to provide quality fishing for all ages. Common game fish to the lakes include largemouth bass, crappie, walleye, bluegill, northern pike and catfish. Ice fishing is a popular winter activity on all four of the lakes. No-wake boating is permitted on all the lakes.

Information: For general information on the Papio Lakes contact: U.S. Army Corps of Engineers, Missouri River Projects Office, 9901 John J. Pershing Dr., Omaha NE 68112 / 402-453-0202. For specific information on Glenn Cunningham, Standing Bear or Zorinsky Lakes contact: City of Omaha Department of Parks Recreation and Public Property, 1819 Farnam St., Omaha NE 68102 / 402-444-5900. For information on Wehrspann Lake contact: Papio-Missouri River NRD, 8901 S. 154th St., Omaha NE 68138 / 402-444-6222.

Glenn Cunningham Lake

Located in north-central Omaha near the junction of SH 133 and I-680. The dam area is accessed via State Street. Glenn Cunningham Lake

Lake offers about 390 acres for boating and fishing. Visitors can also enjoy picnicking, hiking and bicycling on asphalt trails, and nature study opportunities. Horseback riding is permitted on designated trails. An archery range is found on the lake's northern end. Concessionaires near the east end of the dam, open during the summer, offer pop, snacks, and rentals for canoes, paddle boats, sailboats, and fishing boats. The angler will find good fishing conditions for bluegill, channel catfish, bullhead, largemouth, yellow and white bass. Snowmobiling, sledding, ice skating, and cross-country skiing are activities enjoyed during the winter months.

At A Glance
- Auto Touring
- ✓ Biking
- ✓ Boating
- Climbing
- Cultural or Historic Sites
- ✓ Camping
- Educational Programs
- ✓ Fishing
- ✓ Groceries / Supplies
- ✓ Hiking
- ✓ Horseback Riding
- Hunting
- Lodging
- Off Highway Vehicles
- Visitor Center

Standing Bear Lake

Standing Bear Lake is in northwest Omaha west of I-680. The dam area is accessed via 132nd Street. Standing Bear Lake is surrounded by 396 acres of park land. Visitors to the project find opportunities for picnicking, boating, fishing, hiking and bicycling. Horseback riding is allowed on designated trails. There is also a model-airplane field at the project. The lake has a surface area of 135 acres and a maximum depth of 24 feet.

At A Glance
- Auto Touring
- ✓ Biking
- ✓ Boating
- Climbing
- Cultural or Historic Sites
- Camping
- Educational Programs
- ✓ Fishing
- Groceries / Supplies
- ✓ Hiking
- ✓ Horseback Riding
- Hunting
- Lodging
- Off Highway Vehicles
- Visitor Center

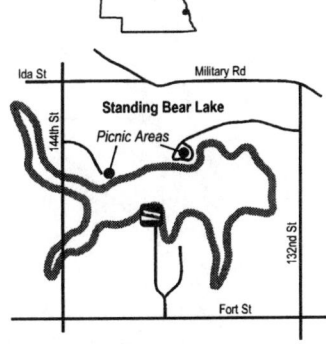

Fishing opportunities include bass, bluegill, catfish, crappie, drum, saugeye, trout, walleye, and yellow perch. The Nebraska Game and Parks Commission stocks the lake with rainbow trout every fall and winter. Sledding, ice skating, and cross-country skiing are popular activities in the winter months.

Wehrspann Lake

This lake is located in southwest Omaha west of I-80 and SH 50. The main entrance is off Giles Road. A visitor center in the Natural Resources Center is near the west end of the dam. The 246-acre lake is surrounded by the 940-acre Chalco Hills Recreation Area, a day-use only park. A 169-acre site south of SH 370 is allocated for wildlife management. Chalco Hills Recreation Area offers seven miles of biking and hiking trails, a nature trail, an arboretum, native prairie grasses and a bird-watching and waterfowl observation platform. Seven picnic areas are scattered throughout the park. Anglers come to Wehrspann Lake in search of bluegill, bullhead, channel catfish, crappie, largemouth bass, and walleye. A wheelchair-accessible fishing pier is on the east side of the lake off Cornhusker Road. Sledding, ice skating, and cross-country skiing are popular in the winter.

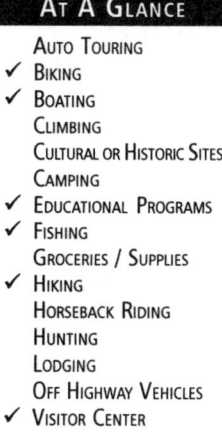

At A Glance	
	Auto Touring
✓	Biking
✓	Boating
	Climbing
	Cultural or Historic Sites
	Camping
✓	Educational Programs
✓	Fishing
	Groceries / Supplies
✓	Hiking
	Horseback Riding
	Hunting
	Lodging
	Off Highway Vehicles
✓	Visitor Center

Zorinsky Lake

Zorinsky Lake lies south of US 275 in west Omaha about six miles west of I-80 and five miles east of US 6. The dam area is reached via

Nebraska

At A Glance
- Auto Touring
- ✓ Biking
- ✓ Boating
- Climbing
- Cultural or Historic Sites
- Camping
- Educational Programs
- ✓ Fishing
- Groceries / Supplies
- ✓ Hiking
- ✓ Horseback Riding
- Hunting
- Lodging
- Off Highway Vehicles
- Visitor Center

156th Street south from West Center Road (US 275). Zorinsky Lake is a day-use only facility surrounded by 768 acres of park land. Nearly 200 acres of this land is dedicated to wildlife management. The project has one of the few native tall grass prairies remaining in eastern Nebraska. The 40-acre Bauermeister Prairie is home to numerous birds, animals, and 120 species of plants. Visitors to the park will find baseball diamonds, soccer fields, a football field, asphalt trails for hiking and bicycling and trails for horseback riding. Zorinsky Lake has a surface area of 255 acres and offers the angler bluegill, bullhead, channel catfish, crappie, largemouth bass, tiger muskie, and walleye. A fishing pier located near the dam and many other facilities around the park are accessible to the disabled. Winter time activities include sledding, ice skating, and cross-country skiing.

Papio Creek Watershed	▲	🚐	🏠	🚻	🍴	🚤	🍽	⛰	🎿	🛢	🚶	⚓	〰
1 Glenn Cunningham Lake	58	41	•	•	•		•	•			•	•	•
2 Standing Bear Lake				•	•	•	•					•	•
3 Wehrspann Lake				•	•	•	•					•	•
4 Zorinsky Lake				•	•	•	•					•	•

Salt Valley Lakes

The Salt Valley Lakes project consists of nine lakes constructed by the Corps of Engineers and managed by the Nebraska Game and Parks Commission. There are seven *state recreation areas* (SRA) and two *wildlife management areas* (WMA) scattered around the Lincoln area. See each lake description for location and directions. Since their construction in the 1960s, the Salt Valley Lakes have joined the ranks of the most popular outdoor recreation areas in the state. A park entry permit is required at the state recreation areas.

Camping is available year-round at all of the areas, however, only primitive camping is available at the wildlife management areas. Fees for camping in the developed campgrounds range from $3.00 to $10.00.

Information: U.S. Army Corps of Engineers, Missouri River Projects Office, 9901 John J. Pershing Dr., Omaha NE 68112 / 402-453-0202. Nebraska Game and Parks Commission, Metro Information Officer, 1212 Deer Park Blvd., Omaha NE 68108 / 402-595-2144.

At A Glance
Auto Touring
✓ Biking
✓ Boating
Climbing
Cultural or Historic Sites
✓ Camping
Educational Programs
✓ Fishing
✓ Groceries / Supplies
✓ Hiking
✓ Horseback Riding
✓ Hunting
Lodging
Off Highway Vehicles
Visitor Center

Bluestem SRA

This 742-acre area is located about 20 miles southwest of Lincoln and 2½ miles west of Sprague. The dam area is off West Sprague Road near the junction of SW 58th Street. The 325-acre lake offers diverse

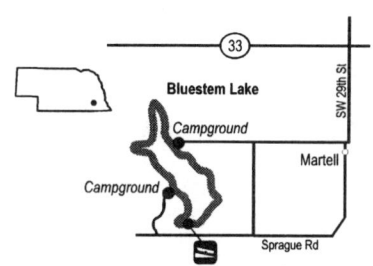

action for anglers of all abilities. Opportunity awaits the angler with largemouth bass, bluegill, crappie, flathead and channel catfish, walleye, saugeye, northern pike, and wipers occupying the lake. There are three boat ramps around the lake; one in each campground and another near the south end of the dam. Campers will find over 200 campsites to choose from. There is also an archery range for those wishing to sharpen their skills. Hunting is permitted on the 417 acres of land surrounding the lake. Species of wildlife include pheasant, quail, cottontail, squirrel, dove, waterfowl, and deer.

Branched Oak SRA

This project is 15 miles northwest of Lincoln and three miles north of Malcolm. With over 5,700 acres for boating, fishing, camping and outdoor recreation, Branched Oak is the largest of the Salt Valley Lakes.

Unique to Branched Oak, the 800-acre dog trial area draws championship events from across the nation every year. The Nebraska Game and Parks Commission has established an arboretum there, with over 100 species of trees and shrubs. Anglers will find the 1,800-acre lake offers ample opportunities for landing largemouth bass, walleye, bluegill, bullhead, white perch, wiper, northern pike, crappie, carp, channel and flathead catfish. There are five boat ramps scattered around the lake and nearly 200 campsites, many with electrical hook-ups. 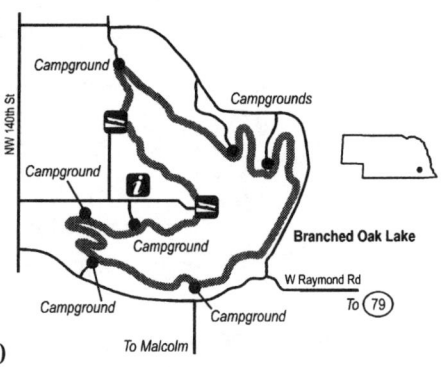 A handicapped accessible fishing pier, food and basic supplies are found in the northeast area of the lake. Hunting is permitted in season on the nearly 4,000 acres of land within the project. Wildlife species include pheasant, quail, cottontail, squirrel, waterfowl, and deer.

Conestoga SRA

The 716-acre Conestoga SRA is located near Denton off SH 55A about 20 miles west of Lincoln. The dam and campground are located about one mile west of SH 55A along West Pioneers Boulevard. For the angler, the 230-acre lake offers largemouth bass, bluegill, channel catfish, walleye, saugeye, wiper, and crappie. A boat ramp and fish cleaning station are adjacent to the campground on the lake's northern shore. Nearly 500 acres of land is open to the public for hunting. Wildlife species include  pheasant, quail, cottontail rabbit, squirrel, dove, and deer. Waterfowl hunting is not permitted within this project.

Olive Creek SRA

This 612-acre area is located 30 miles southwest of downtown Lincoln and three miles southeast of Kramer. Although small, the 175-acre lake supports a variety of fish. Fishing is good for largemouth bass, crappie, bluegill, carp, channel and flathead catfish. The only boat ramp can be found in the campground on the lake's western shore. The two campgrounds offer a total of 50 campsites. No hook-ups are available at either campground. More than 400 acres of land surrounding the lake is open to the public for hunting. Wildlife species include pheasant, quail, cottontail rabbit, squirrel, dove, deer, and waterfowl.

Pawnee SRA

The 2,544-acre Pawnee SRA is about 12 miles west of downtown Lincoln and three miles northwest of Emerald. Take exit #388 from I-80 to reach this and the Twin Lakes WMA. This 740-acre lake is the second largest in the Salt Valley Lakes project. Anglers will find sauger, largemouth and white bass, bluegill, walleye, drum, crappie, carp, channel and flathead catfish. Two campgrounds on the northern end of the lake provide facilities for tent campers and RVers. Nearly 300 campsites are available, some with hook-ups. Two boat ramps are near the southern portion of the lake. There is just over 1,800 acres of land open to the public for hunting. Wildlife found in the area includes pheasant, quail, cottontail rabbit, squirrel, waterfowl, and deer.

Stagecoach SRA

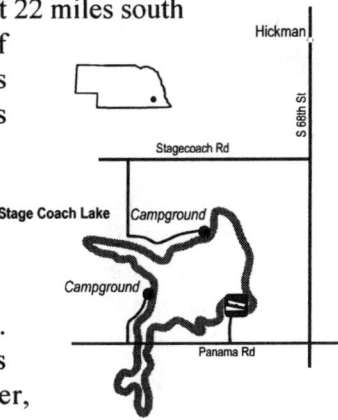

The 607-acre Stage Coach SRA is about 22 miles south of Lincoln and two miles southwest of Hickman. There are two campgrounds around the lake with a total of 50 sites for tents and recreational vehicles. Anglers will find largemouth bass, bluegill, channel catfish, crappie, and northern pike in the 195-acre lake. Surrounding the lake is 412 acres of land open to the public for hunting. Wildlife found in the region includes pheasant, quail, cottontail rabbit, deer, squirrel, and waterfowl.

Twin Lakes WMA

Twin Lakes WMA is about 14 miles west of Lincoln and three miles north of Pleasant Dale. Refer to the map shown for Pawnee SRA. The two lakes, East Twin and West Twin, offer a total of 255 acres. Only non-motorized boating is permitted on the lakes. Anglers will find walleye, largemouth bass, bluegill, channel catfish, tiger muskie, bullhead and crappie in the 210-acre East Twin Lake. The 60-acre West Twin Lake is very shallow and offers limited fishing opportunities. There is 1,015 acres of land that is open to the public for hunting. Wildlife inhabiting the area includes pheasant, quail, dove, cottontail rabbit, squirrel, and deer. Waterfowl hunting is not permitted.

Wagon Train SRA

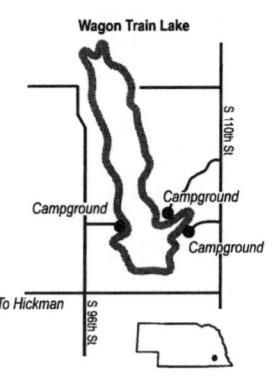

This 1,060-acre recreation area is located 21 miles south of Lincoln and two miles east of Hickman. Three camping areas surround the lake; two are on the eastern shore off 110th Street. The 315-acre lake tempts anglers with year-round fishing opportunities for walleye, largemouth bass, northern pike, bluegill, carp, redear sunfish, channel catfish, and crappie. There is 745 acres of land within the project that is open to the public for hunting. Wildlife inhabiting the area includes pheasant, quail, cottontail rabbit, squirrel, deer, dove, and waterfowl.

Yankee Hill WMA

The 930-acre Yankee Hill WMA is located 12 miles southwest of Lincoln and three miles southeast of Denton. Anglers will find a variety of fish within the 210-acre lake including largemouth bass, bluegill, bullhead, channel catfish, crappie, and walleye. Only non-motorized boating is allowed on the lake. Over 700 acres of land surrounding the lake is open to the public for hunting. Wildlife species include pheasant, quail, cottontail rabbit, squirrel, deer, waterfowl, and dove.

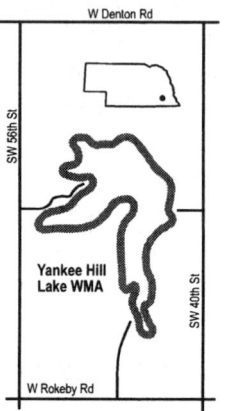

Salt Valley Lakes			▲	🚐	🏠	🚻	⛽	🍴	🍽	🚿	🐟	📦	🚶	⚓	〰
1	Bluestem SRA	219	19	•	•	•	•	•			•				•
2	Branched Oak SRA	195	114	•	•	•	•	•	•	•			•	•	•
3	Conestoga SRA	30			•	•	•		•					•	•
4	Olive Creek SRA	50				•	•		•						•
5	Pawnee SRA	275	68	•	•	•	•	•	•	•			•	•	•
6	Stagecoach SRA	50				•	•		•						•
7	Twin Lakes WMA	•						•							•
8	Wagon Train SRA	70		•	•	•	•	•		•					•
9	Yankee Hill WMA	•					•								•

New Mexico

1 Abiquiu Reservoir
2 Cochiti Lake
3 Conchas Lake
4 Santa Rosa Lake

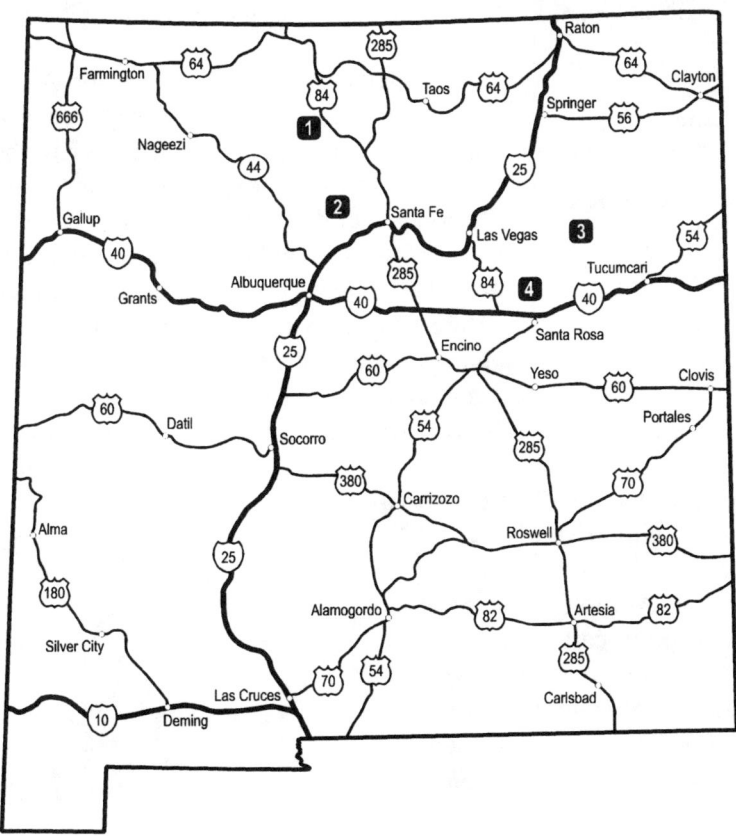

New Mexico Resources

- *New Mexico Travel and Tourism Department* - PO Box 20003, Santa Fe NM 87503 / (800) 733-6396
- *New Mexico Dept. of Game & Fish* - (505) 827-7911 or (800)-ASK-FISH (recorded message)
- *Road Condition Hotlines* - (505) 827-5154 (recording) or (800) 432-4269 (NM only; recording)

Abiquiu Reservoir

Abiquiu Reservoir is located in north-central New Mexico about 55 miles northwest of Santa Fe. To reach the lake from Espanola, travel 30 miles west on US 84 and then two miles south on SH 96. The project office is near the north end of the dam; information about the project is available here.

At A Glance
- Auto Touring
- Biking
- ✓ Boating
- Climbing
- ✓ Cultural or Historic Sites
- ✓ Camping
- Educational Programs
- ✓ Fishing
- Groceries / Supplies
- ✓ Hiking
- Horseback Riding
- Hunting
- Lodging
- Off Highway Vehicles
- ✓ Visitor Center

Constructed on the Rio Chama River, Abiquiu Reservoir is a popular spot for boating and water skiing. Three recreation areas have been developed on the lake just west of the dam. Camping facilities for tents and recreational vehicles are available in the *Riana* recreation area. The *Overlook* provides an excellent view of the lake from the bluff area and a wheelchair-accessible picnic site. The *Cerrito* recreation area provides the only access to the lake for boaters; the area also has a fishing pier.

Fishing at the 4,029-acre reservoir is good with several cold and warm water species inhabiting the lake. Anglers most often seek crappie, catfish, rainbow trout, smallmouth bass, walleye, and kokanee salmon. German brown trout are usually found downstream from the dam. Summer and fall months are very good for channel catfish.

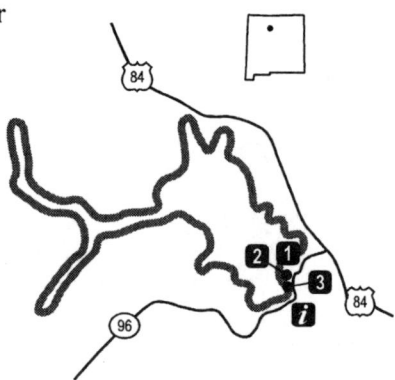

Information: U.S. Army Corps of Engineers, Abiquiu Lake Project Office, P.O. Box 290, Abiquiu NM 87510 / 505-685-4371.

Abiquiu Reservoir	△	🚐	🏠	🍴	🎣	🏛	🥾	🏊	🛶	🚶	⚓	〰
1 Cerrito				•	•	•						•
2 Riana		53		•	•	•	•	•	•		•	•
3 Overlook				•	•		•					

Cochiti Lake

Cochiti Lake is in north-central New Mexico about 50 miles from Albuquerque. To reach the lake from Albuquerque, follow I-25 north to exit #259 and then follow SH 22 north for 14 miles. A visitor center is located on the west side of the lake. A nature trail departs from the visitor center.

At A Glance
Auto Touring
Biking
✓ Boating
Climbing
Cultural or Historic Sites
✓ Camping
Educational Programs
✓ Fishing
Groceries / Supplies
✓ Hiking
Horseback Riding
Hunting
Lodging
Off Highway Vehicles
✓ Visitor Center

Cochiti Lake, constructed on the Rio Grande, lies within the boundaries of the Pueblo de Cochiti Indian Reservation. Please observe all Pueblo regulations and do not trespass on lands closed to the public. There are two recreation areas on the lake that offer camping facilities for tents and recreational vehicles. The *Cochiti* recreation area is on the western shore of the lake near the visitor center. *Tetilla Peak* recreation area is on the lake's eastern shore and is reached via a ten-mile paved road from SH 16, look for signs. Swimming is allowed in the lake, however, there is no designated swimming beach.

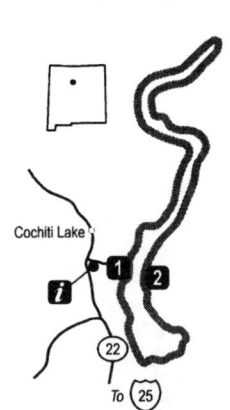

The 1,200-acre lake hosts a variety of game fish. Anglers will find rainbow trout, catfish, largemouth bass, bluegill, and crappie. An occasional walleye and kokanee salmon have been caught. Fishing is at its best from late March through May; the best places to fish are along the lake's eastern shore and the dam area. The stretch of river below the dam is also a favorite spot among anglers. The marina in *Cochiti* is operated by the Cochiti Community Development Corporation (CCDC) and provides basic necessities. For boat rental information, contact the CCDC at 505-465-2219.

Information: U.S. Army Corps of Engineers, Cochiti Lake Project, 82 Dam Crest Rd., Pena Blanca NM 87041 / 505-465-0307.

Cochiti Lake	⛺	🏠	🚻	🚰	🪑	💧	👥	⛰	🏊	♨	🚶	⚓	〰
1 Cochiti	55	38	•	•	•	•	•	•			•	•	•
2 Tetilla Peak	69	39	•	•	•		•	•					•

Conchas Lake

Conchas Lake is located in northeast New Mexico about 50 miles northeast of Santa Rosa and 32 miles northwest of Tucumcari. To reach the dam from Tucumcari, follow SH 104. Information is available from the Corps at the information center north of the dam or from the Conchas Lake State Park headquarters also north of the dam.

At A Glance
- Auto Touring
- ✓ Biking
- ✓ Boating
- Climbing
- ✓ Cultural or Historic Sites
- ✓ Camping
- ✓ Educational Programs
- ✓ Fishing
- ✓ Groceries / Supplies
- ✓ Hiking
- Horseback Riding
- Hunting
- ✓ Lodging
- ✓ Off Highway Vehicles
- ✓ Visitor Center

The *Overlook, North Side* and *Central Recreation Areas* are leased to the state of New Mexico as units of Conchas Lake State Park. The *South Conchas Recreation Area* is leased to private operators, phone 505-868-2988. Camping facilities are found in three of the four recreation areas. The *North Side Recreation Area* includes a store, lounge, marina, and cabin rentals. *South Conchas Recreation Area* includes a restaurant, lodge, store, and gas station. A nine-hole golf course can be found off SH 104 near the *South Conchas Recreation Area*

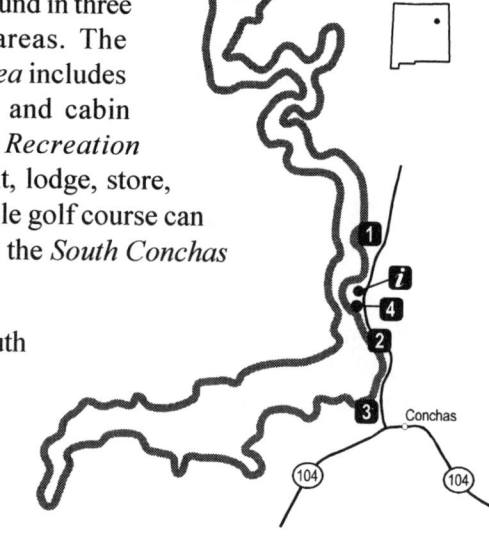

Conchas Dam is on the South Canadian River, just below its confluence with the Conchas River. The lake extends about 11 miles southwest along the Conchas River and northwest along the South Canadian River for approximately 14 miles. Anglers will find a variety of fish within the lake including walleye, channel catfish, bluegill, crappie, and largemouth bass. The project's marina and stores provide bait and tackle supplies, boat and motor services, food and refreshments.

Information: U.S. Army Corps of Engineers, Conchas Lake Visitors Center, P.O. Box 1008, Conchas Dam NM 88416 / 505-868-2221. Conchas Lake State Park, P.O. Box 976, Conchas Dam NM 88416 / 505-868-2270. A recorded message with general information is available by calling 505-868-2961.

Conchas Lake	▲	🚻	🅿	🛥	⚓	🏊	🏕	🥾	🏇	🍴	🚶	⚓	🎣
1 North Side Recreation Area	75	40	•	•	•		•	•				•	•
2 Central Recreation Area	•				•		•						
3 South Conchas Rec. Area	66	28	•	•	•	•	•	•					•
4 Overlook					•	•	•	•					

Santa Rosa Lake

Santa Rosa Lake is on the Pecos River in east-central New Mexico about 120 miles east of Albuquerque and seven miles north of Santa Rosa. To reach the lake from Santa Rosa go north on Second Street, east on Eddy Avenue, and then north on Eighth Street. Visitor information is available from the project office on the west side of the dam.

At A Glance
Auto Touring
Biking
✓ Boating
Climbing
Cultural or Historic Sites
✓ Camping
Educational Programs
✓ Fishing
Groceries / Supplies
✓ Hiking
Horseback Riding
✓ Hunting
Lodging
Off Highway Vehicles
✓ Visitor Center

The New Mexico State Park and Recreation Division operates the two recreation areas at this project. Camping facilities for tents and RV's have been developed on either side of the dam. The Corps operates and maintains an overlook and paved trail near the dam. The one-half-mile trail, accessible to the disabled, is just east of the dam and follows a bluff overlooking the reservoir. Several hiking trails have been developed around the lake. Please note that archeological sites may be encountered by the hiker and it is illegal to damage or remove any of the remains.

The water level at Santa Rosa Lake varies with irrigation usage and spring runoff, causing fishing conditions to vary. At normal water levels, fishing for black bass, walleye, catfish and panfish can be good to excellent. In the winter months, walleye fishing in the control tower area can be really good. During low water levels, fishing can be a losing proposition. Public access downstream along the Pecos River is now permitted, however, fishing beyond the Corps boundary fence requires permission of the landowner.

Information: U.S. Army Corps of Engineers, Santa Rosa Dam and Lake, P.O. Box 345, Santa Rosa NM 88435 / 505-472-3115. Santa Rosa Lake State Park, New Mexico Park and Recreation Division, P.O. Box 1147, Santa Fe NM 87504 / 505-827-7465

Santa Rosa Lake	▲	🚐	🚻	🚰	🌳	🍽	🚿	🔥	🏞	🥾	⚓	〰
1 Rocky Point	49	23	•	•	•		•	•				
2 Juniper Park	26	2	•	•	•		•					•

NORTH DAKOTA

1 Lake Ashtabula
2 Bowman-Haley Lake
3 Homme Lake
4 Pipestem Lake
5 Lake Sakakawea

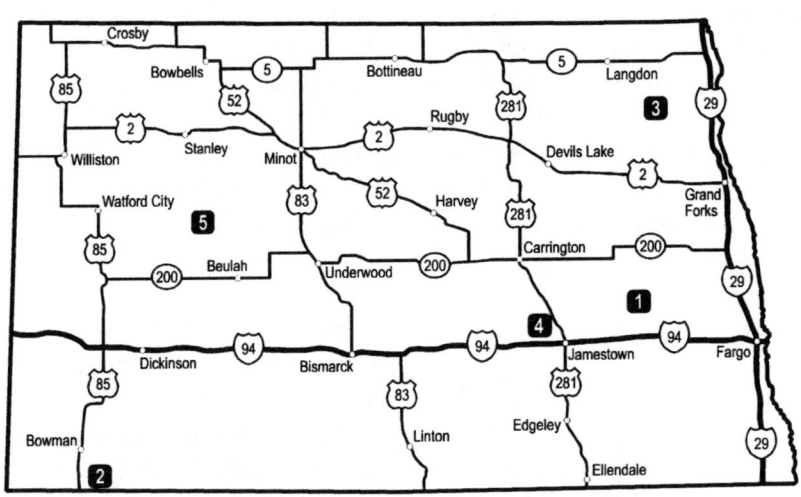

North Dakota Resources

- *North Dakota Tourism Department* - 604 East Boulevard Avenue, Bismarck ND 58505 / (800) 435-5663 or (701) 328-2525
- *North Dakota State Game & Fish Dept.* - (701) 328-6300
- *Road Condition Hotlines* - (800) 472-2686 (ND only) (recording) or (701) 328-7623 (recording)
- *Road Construction Hotline* - (701) 328-4418 weekdays

Lake Ashtabula

Lake Ashtabula and Baldhill Dam are located on the Sheyenne River in east-central North Dakota. The lake lies north of I-94 about 40 miles east of Jamestown. To reach the dam from I-94, take the Valley City exit #292 and follow signs to CR 19 (River Road). Follow CR 19 north for about 12 miles. Information about the lake is available from the project office located on the west side of the dam.

Lake Ashtabula is situated in one of the most scenic river valleys in the region. The 2,500 acres of gently rolling landscape, dotted with wooded areas and shrub lands, provides habitat for a wide variety of wildlife. The lake is along the central flyway for migrating birds and hosts a great number of ducks and geese each fall. Snowmobiling, cross-country skiing, and ice fishing are popular winter time activities.

At A Glance
Auto Touring
Biking
✓ Boating
Climbing
Cultural or Historic Sites
✓ Camping
✓ Educational Programs
✓ Fishing
✓ Groceries / Supplies
✓ Hiking
Horseback Riding
✓ Hunting
✓ Lodging
Off Highway Vehicles
✓ Visitor Center

The name "Ashtabula," an Indian word meaning "fish river," hints at the opportunities for the angler. The 5,234-acre lake is home to an abundant population of such game fish as yellow perch, walleye, white bass, northern pike, and black bullheads. The lake is periodically stocked with fingerlings of walleye and northern pike by the U.S. Fish and Wildlife Service. Fishing supplies are available at the marina in *Ashtabula Crossing* and *Eggert's Landing*.

The Corps of Engineers manages 13 separate wildlife areas at Lake Ashtabula. These areas are open to the public for hunting. Contact the North Dakota Game and Fish Department for seasons, restrictions and licenses.

Information: U.S. Army Corps of Engineers, Baldhill Dam - Lake Ashtabula, 2630 114th Ave. SE, Valley City ND 58072 / 701-845-2970.

Lake Ashtabula	▲	🚐	🏠	🚻	⛲	💧	🏕	🎣	🐟	🥫	🚶	⚓	🏊
1 Mel Reiman	21	10	•	•	•	•	•	•					•
2 Sundstrom's Landing				•	•	•	•						•
3 Eggert's Landing	42	37	•	•	•	•	•		•			•	•
4 Ashtabula Crossing	78	52	•	•	•	•	•	•	•			•	•
5 Sibley Crossing					•		•					•	•
6 Katie Olson's Landing					•	•	•	•					•

Bowman-Haley Lake

Bowman-Haley Lake is in southwestern North Dakota about 24 miles southeast of Bowman near the South Dakota state line. To reach the dam from Bowman, follow US 85 south for 12 miles and then travel east on county roads for another 11 miles.

At Bowman-Haley Lake, 6,720 acres of prairie creeks and rolling upland provide a home to a wide variety of wildlife and waterfowl. This natural setting has been enhanced by selective planting of more than 120 acres of trees around the lake. Creating wetland areas and reintroducing native vegetation have contributed to the healthy wildlife and waterfowl populations found at the project.

At A Glance
Auto Touring
Biking
✓ Boating
Climbing
Cultural or Historic Sites
✓ Camping
✓ Educational Programs
✓ Fishing
Groceries / Supplies
Hiking
Horseback Riding
✓ Hunting
Lodging
Off Highway Vehicles
Visitor Center

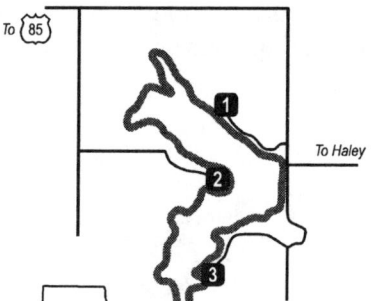

The 1,732-acre V-shaped Bowman-Haley Lake was formed at the confluence of Spring Creek, Alkali Creek, and North Fork of the Grand River. The lake has 17 miles of shoreline and an average depth of 39 feet. Bowman-Haley Lake provides year-round fishing opportunities for the angler. Walleye and northern pike are among the species found in the lake.

Information: U.S. Army Corps of Engineers, Bowman-Haley Lake, P.O. Box 527, Riverdale ND 58565 / 701-654-7411. Park Manager, Corps of Engineers, P.O. Box 1752, Jamestown ND 58402 / 701-252-7666. Bowman County Water Resource District, Box 156, Bowman ND 58623 / 701-523-3629.

Bowman Haley Lake											
1 North Shore	8	8	•	•	•		•				•
2 Point Area							•				
3 South Shore	2			•	•						•

Homme Lake

Homme Lake is located in the northeast corner of North Dakota about 60 miles northwest of Grand Forks and 19 miles west of Grafton. To reach the dam from Grand Forks, travel north on US 81 for 40 miles and then west on SH 17 for 19 miles.

At A Glance	
	Auto Touring
	Biking
✓	Boating
	Climbing
	Cultural or Historic Sites
✓	Camping
	Educational Programs
✓	Fishing
✓	Groceries / Supplies
✓	Hiking
	Horseback Riding
✓	Hunting
	Lodging
	Off Highway Vehicles
✓	Visitor Center

The Walsh County Park Board operates and maintains the project's only recreation area, which is located near the dam. The park is open April through November and has facilities for boat launching, picnicking and camping. A nominal fee is charged for entry into the park. The 200 acres of land surrounding the project is managed by the Corps of Engineers and is open to hunting, hiking, cross-country skiing and snowmobiling.

This small, picturesque lake on the South Branch of Park River provides a quiet, peaceful get-a-way in the middle of the prairie. Four miles of shoreline surround the 194-acre lake, providing the

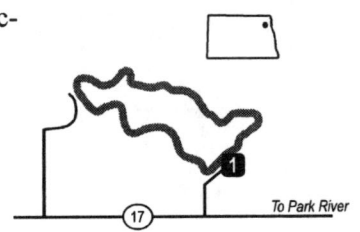

fisherman with opportunities for landing largemouth bass, walleye, crappie, saugeye, muskie, bullhead, or northern pike.

Information: U.S. Army Corps of Engineers, Homme Lake, 2630 114th Ave. SE, Valley City ND 58072 / 701-845-2970.

Homme Lake													
1 County Park	19	13	•	•	•	•	•						•

Pipestem Lake

Pipestem Lake is located in east-central North Dakota north of Jamestown. To reach the dam from Jamestown, travel five miles north on US 52/281. Visitor information and a scenic overlook are located at the project office on the east side of the dam.

At Pipestem Lake, 4,200 acres of creek valley and rolling upland is home to a wide variety of wildlife and waterfowl. This natural setting has been enhanced by selective planting of more than a quarter of a million trees around the lake. The area offers a quiet and peaceful retreat for camping, fishing, wildlife viewing, and photography. Birdwatching has also become a popular activity at the lake. *Parkhurst,* the project's most developed recreation area, is operated and maintained by the Stutsman County Park Board. Several undeveloped areas around the lake provide additional opportunities for fishing, boating, and hunting. A rifle range is located west of the dam area.

At A Glance
Auto Touring
Biking
✓ Boating
Climbing
Cultural or Historic Sites
✓ Camping
✓ Educational Programs
✓ Fishing
Groceries / Supplies
Hiking
Horseback Riding
✓ Hunting
Lodging
Off Highway Vehicles
✓ Visitor Center

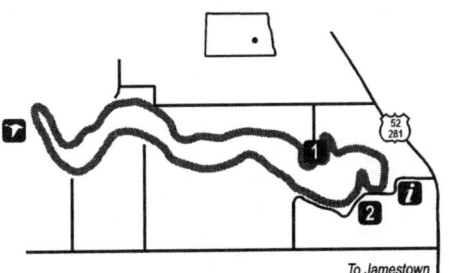
To Jamestown

The 840-acre lake, constructed on Pipestem Creek, is nearly six miles long with 14 miles of shoreline. Anglers enjoy year-round fishing opportunities for walleye, pike, bluegill, crappie, muskie, perch, and smallmouth bass. Although there is no marina at Pipestem Lake, fishermen will find that all the necessary supplies for a successful outing are available in Jamestown.

Information: U.S. Army Corps of Engineers, Pipestem Lake Project Office, P.O. Box 1752, Jamestown ND 58402 / 701-252-7666.

Pipestem Lake												
1 Parkhurst	16		•		•						•	
2 Public Use Area			•	•		•						

Lake Sakakawea

Lake Sakakawea was formed by the construction of Garrison Dam on the Missouri River. Construction of the dam, one of the largest rolled earth-fill dams in the world, began in 1947 and was completed in 1953.

At A Glance
- Auto Touring
- ✓ Biking
- ✓ Boating
- Climbing
- ✓ Cultural or Historic Sites
- ✓ Camping
- ✓ Educational Programs
- ✓ Fishing
- ✓ Groceries / Supplies
- ✓ Hiking
- ✓ Horseback Riding
- ✓ Hunting
- ✓ Lodging
- ✓ Off Highway Vehicles
- ✓ Visitor Center

The lake is located in west-central North Dakota about 60 miles northwest of Bismarck. To reach the dam from Bismarck, follow US 83 north to SH 200 and then head west for ten miles. Exhibits in the lobby of the power plant feature displays on the construction and operation of the dam. Information about the lake and its recreation areas is also available here and in the visitor center located in the project office. Tours of the power plant are given daily during the summer months.

Lake Sakakawea is one of the largest man-made lakes in the United States. Named for Lewis and Clark's Shoshone Indian guide, the lake extends from Riverdale to Trenton, North Dakota. The lake extends 178 miles up the Missouri River and has 1,340 miles of picturesque shoreline. The Missouri River Valley domi-

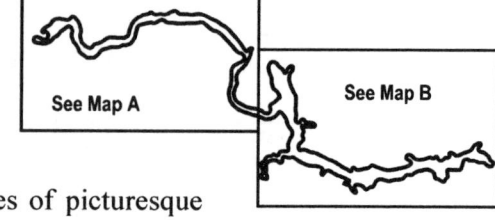

nates the landscape surrounding the 368,000-acre lake. Rolling prairie, split by woody draws, can be seen for miles along the shoreline. The North Dakota Badlands in the southwest part of the project were formed by the Little Missouri River, which carved a colorful wonderland of towering buttes and eroded hills. Sites of early Indian culture and of trading and Army posts are located in the area.

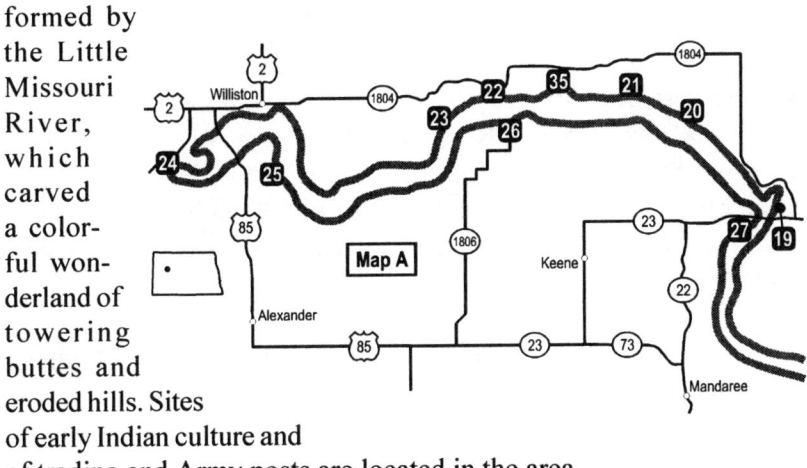

Lake Sakakawea is a birdwatcher's paradise. Thousands of geese, ducks, and shore birds migrate through or nest at the lake. Bald eagles are a wintertime resident around the dam. Other wildlife inhabiting the region includes pronghorn antelope, white-tailed deer and mule deer. Elk use the badlands as a wintering area. Coyote, beaver, porcupine, squirrel, prairie dog, fox, and badger also inhabit the area.

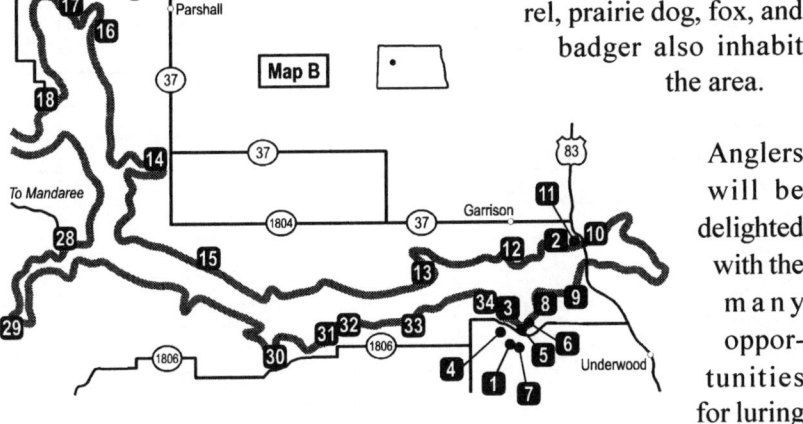

Anglers will be delighted with the many opportunities for luring trophy walleye, sauger, saugeye, smallmouth bass, northern pike, chinook salmon and a variety of trout. Catfish and yellow perch are found in the shallow areas of the lake. The true enthusiast can enjoy year-round fishing in the open tailwaters of the dam. Fishing and boating supplies as well as boat rentals are available from the marinas and concession services around the lake.

Information: U.S. Army Corps of Engineers, Lake Manager - Lake Sakakawea, P.O. Box 527, Riverdale ND 58565 / 701-654-7411. Fort Stevenson State Park, RR1 Box 262, Garrison ND 58540 / 701-337-5576. Lewis & Clark State Park, 4904 119th Road NW, Epping ND 58843 / 701-859-3071. Lake Sakakawea State Park, Box 732, Riverdale ND 58565 / 701-487-3315.

Lake Sakakawea	Tent	RV	🚽	💧	🍴	⛺	🏠	🏊	🎣	🛢	🚶	⚓	🌊
1 Downstream Campground	117	101	•	•			•	•	•		•	•		•
2 Sportsmen's Centennial Park	113	18				•		•					•	•
3 Intake Picnic Area						•		•						
4 Tailwaters								•						•
5 Spillway Overlook						•		•						
6 Riverdale Overlook						•								
7 Spillway Pond					•	•	•	•		•				•
8 Government Bay								•						•
9 Wolf Creek	93				•	•	•	•						•
10 East Totton Trail	40	30	•	•	•			•						•
11 West Totton Trail								•						•
12 Ft. Stevenson State Park	145	100	•	•	•	•	•	•	•	•	•	•	•	•
13 Douglas Creek	17				•	•		•						•
14 Deepwater Creek	30				•	•		•						•
15 Indian Hills	45	29	•	•	•		•	•					•	•
16 Parshall Bay	50	22	•	•	•	•	•	•					•	•
17 Van Hook	44	30	•	•	•	•	•	•					•	•
18 Pouch Point	20	10	•	•	•	•	•	•					•	•
19 New Town	15	15	•	•	•	•	•	•	•				•	•
20 White Earth Bay	6	6		•	•		•							•
21 Little Beaver Bay	6				•		•							•
22 White Tail Bay (Lund's Lndng)	3			•	•		•						•	•
23 Lewis & Clark State Park	78	58	•	•	•	•	•	•		•		•	•	•
24 Lake Trenton	18			•	•	•	•						•	•
25 American Legion Post 37	20	20		•	•	•							•	•

continued next page

North Dakota

Lake Sakakawea (continued)	▲	🚐	🍴	🥤	⛱	🎣	🚻	🎆	🚣	🛢	🚶	⚓	🌊
26 Tobacco Gardens	20	10		•	•		•					•	•
27 Four Bears						•							•
28 McKenzie Bay	42	42	•	•	•	•	•					•	•
29 Little Missouri Bay	80	50	•	•	•	•	•	•				•	•
30 Beaver Creek Bay	11				•		•						•
31 Lake Shore Park (Dakota Wtrs)	47	35		•	•	•	•	•				•	•
32 Beulah Bay	38	32	•	•	•	•	•	•					•
33 Hazen Bay	48	7		•	•		•	•				•	•
34 Lake Sakakawea State Park	300	150	•	•	•	•	•	•	•	•	•	•	•
35 Little Egypt				•			•						

Oklahoma

1. Arcadia Lake
2. Birch Lake
3. Broken Bow Lake
4. Canton Lake
5. Chouteau Lock & Dam
6. Copan Lake
7. Eufaula Lake
8. Fort Gibson Lake
9. Fort Supply Lake
10. Great Salt Plains Lake
11. Heyburn Lake
12. Hugo Lake
13. Hulah Lake
14. J.W. Trimble Lock & Dam
15. Kaw Lake
16. Keystone Lake
17. Newt Graham Lock & Dam
18. Oologah Lake
19. Optima Lake
20. Pine Creek Lake
21. Robert S. Kerr Reservoir
22. Sardis Lake
23. Skiatook Lake
24. Tenkiller Ferry Lake
25. Lake Texoma
26. W.D. Mayo Lock & Dam
27. Waurika Lake
28. Webbers Falls Lock & Dam
29. Wister Lake

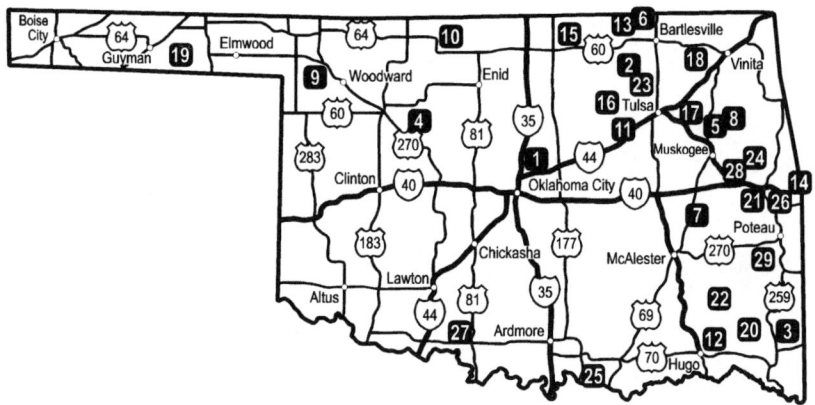

Oklahoma Resources

- **Oklahoma Dept. of Tourism and Recreation** - PO Box 60789, Oklahoma City OK 73146-0789 / (800) 652-6552 (lower 48 states) or (405) 521-2409
- **Oklahoma Dept. of Wildlife Conservation** - (405) 521-3855 or (800) 275-3474, (405) 521-3721 (current fishing report)
- **Road Condition Hotline** - (405) 425-2385, press 6
- **Road Construction Hotline** - (405) 521-2554 (weekdays)

Arcadia Lake

Arcadia Lake is on the Deep Fork River in central Oklahoma just east of Edmond and northeast of Oklahoma City. To reach the lake from Oklahoma City, follow I-35 north about 15 miles to Exit 141. The project office is located near the north end of the dam approximately three miles east of I-35.

Arcadia Lake rests in a part of Oklahoma called the Cross Timbers. It is a unique environment where grasslands intersect with forest on a bed of red soil. Family recreation and environmental education programs are offered throughout the summer in *Central State Park*. Hiking and bicycle trails can be found throughout all four parks at Arcadia Lake. For a unique round of golf, try the 36-hole disc golf course located in *Spring Creek Park*.

At A Glance
Auto Touring
✓ Biking
✓ Boating
Climbing
Cultural or Historic Sites
✓ Camping
✓ Educational Programs
✓ Fishing
Groceries / Supplies
✓ Hiking
✓ Horseback Riding
Hunting
Lodging
Off Highway Vehicles
Visitor Center

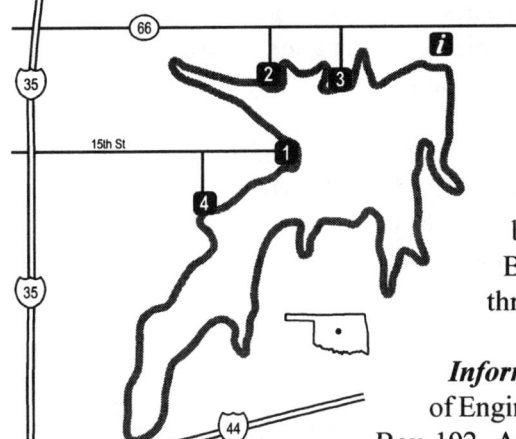

Twenty-six miles of shoreline surround this 1,820-acre lake. For the angler, the lake thrives with large populations of bluegill, bass, and catfish. Boat ramps are located in three parks.

Information: U.S. Army Corps of Engineers, Arcadia Lake, P.O. Box 192, Arcadia OK 73007 / 405-396-8026. City of Edmond, Arcadia Lake, 9000 East Second St., Arcadia OK 73007 / 405-359-4570.

Arcadia Lake		🅰	🚐	🏠	🚽	🚻	🍴	🏨	🚿	⛵	⛺	🚶	⚓	〰️
1 Spring Creek Park						•	•		•		•		•		•
2 Edmond Park	23					•	•	•	•		•		•		•

continued next page

Arcadia Lake (continued)													
3 Central State Park	80	44	•	•	•	•	•	•	•			•	•
4 Scissortail Campground	38	38	•	•			•	•				•	

Birch Lake

Located in northeastern Oklahoma about 20 miles southwest of Bartlesville and 35 miles northwest of Tulsa. The project office is located on the north end of the dam and can be reached by traveling two miles south of Barnsdall off SH 11.

At A Glance
Auto Touring
Biking
✓ Boating
Climbing
Cultural or Historic Sites
✓ Camping
Educational Programs
✓ Fishing
Groceries / Supplies
✓ Hiking
✓ Horseback Riding
✓ Hunting
Lodging
Off Highway Vehicles
Visitor Center

Birch Lake is cradled in valleys surrounded by rolling, forested hills that provide a perfect setting for nature lovers and outdoor enthusiasts. The small lake's shoreline ranges from gentle to steep slopes with numerous rock outcrops. The hilltops and upper slopes are forested with small hardwood trees. The principal game species on project lands for hunting include bobwhite quail, mourning dove, deer, squirrel, and rabbit.

The 1,137-acre lake on Birch Creek, a tributary of Bird Creek, offers excellent year-round opportunities for the angler. Fish species include largemouth bass, walleye, spotted bass, black and white crappie, channel and flathead catfish, and various species of sunfish. Fishermen will find a fishing dock in *Birch Cove*.

Information: U.S. Army Corps of Engineers, Birch Lake, HC 67 Box 135, Skiatook OK 74070 / 918-396-3107.

Oklahoma

Birch Lake	⛺	🚻	🅿	🚽	🛣	🍴	🏛	⛽	🏞	🗑	🚶	⚓	🏊
1 Birch Cove	84	84	•	•			•	•	•	•			•
2 Outlet Park							•						
3 Twin Cove Point	11		•	•	•	•			•		•		•

Broken Bow Lake

Broken Bow Lake lies in the southeast corner of Oklahoma north of Broken Bow. To reach the dam from Broken Bow, travel seven miles north on US 259 and then two miles east on SH 259A.

At A Glance
- ✓ Auto Touring
- ✓ Biking
- ✓ Boating
-   Climbing
-   Cultural or Historic Sites
- ✓ Camping
- ✓ Educational Programs
- ✓ Fishing
- ✓ Groceries / Supplies
- ✓ Hiking
- ✓ Horseback Riding
- ✓ Hunting
- ✓ Lodging
-   Off Highway Vehicles
- ✓ Visitor Center

Broken Bow Lake is highly developed with most of the recreation areas operated by the State of Oklahoma. For hikers there are several nature trails around the lake. The Big Oak Nature Trail is a short ¼-mile walk that is suitable for all ages. The rugged and beautiful Beaver Lodge Nature Trail, located near the *River Bend* area, winds along a clear stream through a valley surrounded by pine-covered hills. The state park areas offer many facilities and recreational opportunities. Some of the attractions include the 18-mile David Boren Hiking Trail, a 40-room lodge and 47 cabins, bicycle and boat rentals, restaurant, miniature golf, train rides, horseback riding, and an 18-hole

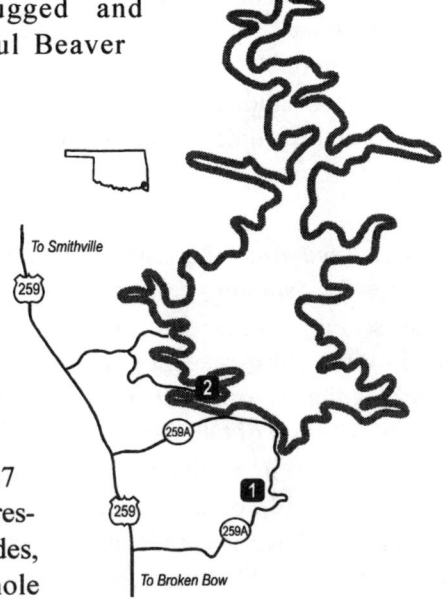

golf course. Several festivals are also held throughout the year.

The 14,240-acre lake is on the Mountain Fork River, a tributary of the Little River. Broken Bow Lake stretches 22 miles into the scenic Ouachita mountain country. The climate at Broken Bow offers excellent opportunities for year-round angling. Fly fishing clinics are available November through April.

Information: U.S. Army Corps of Engineers, Broken Bow Lake, Route 1 Box 400, Valliant OK 74764 / 580-933-4239. Beavers Bend State Park, P.O. Box 10, Broken Bow OK 74728 / 580-494-6450. Hochatown State Park, c/o Beavers Bend State Park, P.O. Box 10, Broken Bow OK 74728 / 580-494-6452.

Broken Bow Lake													
1 Beaver's Bend State Park	238	52	•	•	•			•	•		•	•	•
2 Hochatown State Park	231	51	•	•	•			•	•				•

Canton Lake

Canton Lake is located in the high plains of western Oklahoma about 75 miles northwest of Oklahoma City. From Fairview travel 13 miles south on SH 58 and then two miles west on SH 58A. Additional information is available from the project office near the south end of the dam.

At A Glance
✓ Auto Touring
Biking
✓ Boating
Climbing
Cultural or Historic Sites
✓ Camping
Educational Programs
✓ Fishing
✓ Groceries / Supplies
✓ Hiking
Horseback Riding
✓ Hunting
✓ Lodging
Off Highway Vehicles
✓ Visitor Center

Canton Lake offers the visitor plenty of opportunities for camping, fishing, picnicking, and sight-seeing. All the recreation areas are operated by the Corps except *Cheyenne-Arapaho Park*, which is operated by the Cheyenne-Arapaho Tribes of Oklahoma. Camping facilities are found in all but one of the parks. A major attraction for the hunter is the 14,862-acre public hunting area that is open year-round and managed by the Oklahoma Department of Wildlife Conservation. The area primarily offers hunting for bobwhite quail, deer, waterfowl, squirrel, wild turkey, and dove. A rifle range is also located off Thunder Road north of the *Sandy Cove* recreation area.

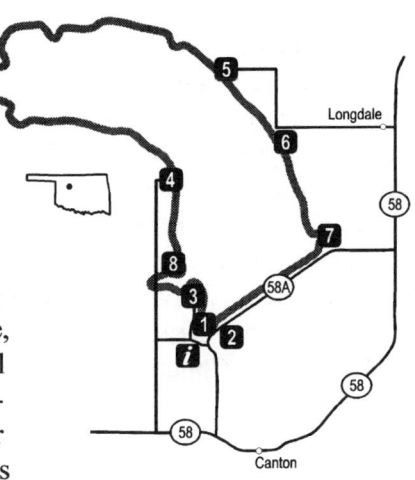

The 7,910-acre lake on the North Canadian River is Oklahoma's leading fisherman's paradise. Anglers will find crappie, white bass, hybrid bass, channel catfish, and largemouth bass. Canton Lake is also widely known for an abundance of walleye and hosts an annual Walleye Rodeo fishing derby in May. In addition to the developed recreation areas, three pullouts with fishing jetties are located on the dam. Services and supplies are available on access roads leading to the project areas and at commercial concessions on the lake.

Information: U.S. Army Corps of Engineers, Canton Lake, P.O. Box 69, Canton OK 73724 / 580-886-2989.

CANTON LAKE													
1 Overlook				•		•							
2 Blaine Park	16			•		•	•				•		•
3 Canadian	130 122	•	•	•	•	•	•			•			•
4 Big Bend	115 96	•	•	•	•	•	•						•
5 Fairview Group Camp	1			•			•						
6 Longdale	37			•	•	•							•
7 Sandy Cove	37 37			•	•	•	•	•					•
8 Cheyenne-Arapaho Park	21												•

Chouteau Lock and Dam

Chouteau Lock and Dam, part of the McClellan-Kerr Arkansas River Navigation System, is located in northeastern Oklahoma about 45 miles southeast of Tulsa. From Muskogee head north on US 69 for seven miles and then southeast on an access road.

The lock and dam was named for Col. Auguste P. Chouteau whose father built a shipyard on the river bank to build keelboats for the fur trade. Four recreation areas surround the project. Camping is only available in *Afton Landing*. Most of the campsites in this park have hookups for RVs. Information and maps on hunting, fishing, boating, and the 64-mile Jean Pierre Chouteau National Recreation Trail can be obtained from the lockmasters. Portions of the Jean Pierre Chouteau NRT are open for equestrian use.

At A Glance	
	Auto Touring
	Biking
✓	Boating
	Climbing
	Cultural or Historic Sites
✓	Camping
	Educational Programs
✓	Fishing
	Groceries / Supplies
✓	Hiking
✓	Horseback Riding
✓	Hunting
	Lodging
	Off Highway Vehicles
	Visitor Center

About 1,990 acres of land and water have been designated a wildlife management area. Public hunting is allowed here as well as in the timbered cutoff loops along the navigation system. Principal game species include deer, dove, quail, squirrel, rabbit, turkey and several migratory waterfowl species.

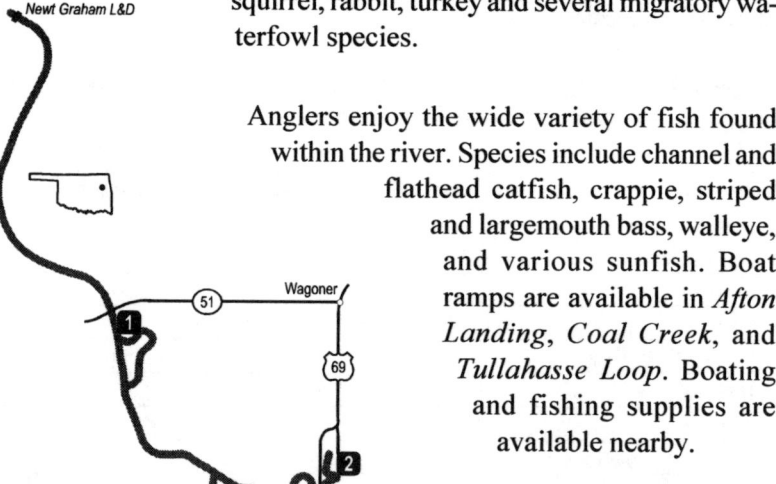

Anglers enjoy the wide variety of fish found within the river. Species include channel and flathead catfish, crappie, striped and largemouth bass, walleye, and various sunfish. Boat ramps are available in *Afton Landing*, *Coal Creek*, and *Tullahasse Loop*. Boating and fishing supplies are available nearby.

Information: U.S. Army Corps of Engineers, Chouteau Lock & Dam 17, Route 2 Box 21, Gore OK 74435 / 918-489-5541.

Oklahoma

Chouteau Lock & Dam													
1 Afton Landing	22	20	•	•			•	•					•
2 Coal Creek													•
3 Pecan Park	N	O	F	A	C	I	L	I	T	I	E	S	
4 Tullahasse Loop													•

Copan Lake

Copan Lake lies west of US 75 in northeast Oklahoma about 60 miles north of Tulsa. A small portion of the project's land extends into southeast Kansas. From Bartlesville, Oklahoma travel 15 miles north on US 75 and then west on SH 10 to the dam. Additional information is available from the project office near the dam.

At A Glance
Auto Touring
Biking
✓ Boating
Climbing
Cultural or Historic Sites
✓ Camping
Educational Programs
✓ Fishing
Groceries / Supplies
✓ Hiking
✓ Horseback Riding
✓ Hunting
Lodging
Off Highway Vehicles
Visitor Center

Visitors to the project will find five developed recreation areas surrounding the lake. The largest campground is *Washington Cove*, located along the eastern shore of the lake. An equestrian trail can be accessed in *Washington Cove*. Lake access for the handicapped is available in *Washington Cove* and *Copan Point*.

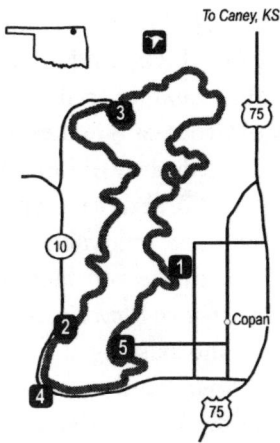

A large portion of the project land has been set aside for wildlife management. Wildlife inhabiting the area includes deer, wild turkey, cottontail rabbit, squirrel, mourning dove, bobwhite quail, and a variety of waterfowl.

Nearly 5,000 acres of water is impounded behind the dam built on the Little Caney River. Anglers find excellent opportunities for hooking largemouth bass, white crappie, channel and flathead catfish, and various species of sunfish. The lake also includes an experimental stocking of the hybrid cross between the white bass and striped bass, more commonly called the "wiper."

Information: U.S. Army Corps of Engineers, Copan Lake Office, Route 1 Box 260, Copan OK 74022 / 918-532-4334.

Copan Lake	🅰	🚐	🍽	🗑	⛺	⛲	🚻	🚿	🏊	🍴	🚶	⚓	🎣
1 Washington Cove	101	101	•	•		•	•	•			•		•
2 Post Oak Park	20	20	•	•			•	•					
3 Osage Plains													•
4 Angler's Point							•						
5 Copan Point				•	•		•		•	•			•

Eufaula Lake

Eufaula Lake, constructed on the Canadian River, is in east-central Oklahoma about 30 miles south of Muskogee. The dam can be reached from Eufaula by traveling 16 miles east on SH 9 and then north on SH 71 for six miles. Information is available from the project office near the south end of the dam.

> **At A Glance**
> Auto Touring
> Biking
> ✓ Boating
> Climbing
> Cultural or Historic Sites
> ✓ Camping
> Educational Programs
> ✓ Fishing
> ✓ Groceries / Supplies
> ✓ Hiking
> ✓ Horseback Riding
> ✓ Hunting
> Lodging
> ✓ Off Highway Vehicles
> ✓ Visitor Center

There are 29 developed recreation areas surrounding the lake including 15 campgrounds. Twenty-five areas are operated and maintained by the Corps of Engineers. The state of Oklahoma operates the *Arrowhead* and *Fountainhead State Parks*, which provide covered fishing docks, stables, nature trails, and golf courses. The City of Crowder operates the *Crowder City Park* area and the city of Eufaula manages the *Eufaula Cove North* day use area. Three nature trails provide an enjoyable and scenic walk through some of the surrounding countryside. The Dogwood Trail, located in *Belle Starr Park South*, is a one-mile path winding over soft, sandy soil and passing through heavily wooded areas. Located in the *Dam Site South* park is the Terrapin Trail. This ¾-mile trail traverses through the woods above the swimming beach.

Visitors in autumn will be treated to a collage of colors as the surrounding hills provide unparalleled beauty of fall foliage. Numerous commercial concessions around the lake provide supplies as well as dining, lodging and recreational opportunities.

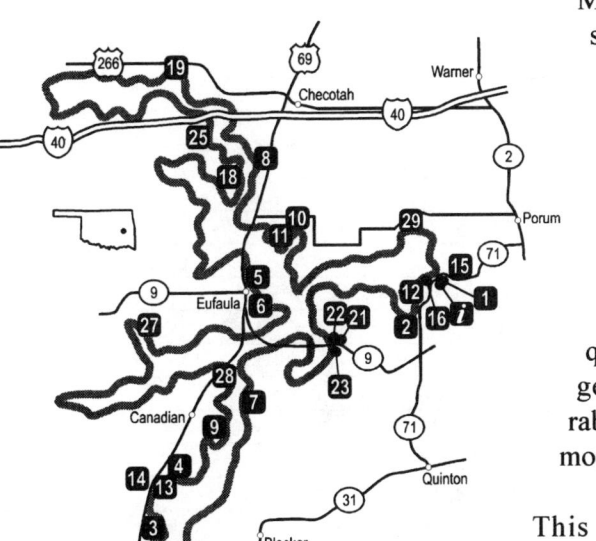

Much of the land surrounding the lake is open to the public for hunting. Maps are available at the project office. Wildlife species include bobwhite quail, deer, duck, geese, cottontail rabbit, squirrel, and mourning dove.

This large 102,200-acre lake provides more than 600 miles of shoreline with numerous arms and coves. Eufaula Lake has long been recognized for its outstanding fishery. Crappie, sand bass, catfish and black bass in the lake reach record size. Below the dam, striped bass reaching over 40 pounds have been caught in the tailwaters. Fishing is good year-round but spring and fall are the best times of the year. Anglers will find stripped bass, largemouth bass, white bass, crappie, catfish, walleye, and a variety of sunfish. Fishing, camping, and boating supplies are available from the seven marinas located around the lake. Boaters traveling through the Standing Rock area can admire the same beauty observed by Spanish explorers.

Information: U.S. Army Corps of Engineers, Eufaula Project Office, Route 4 Box 5500, Stigler OK 74462 / 918-484-5135. Arrowhead State Park, HC 67 Box 57, Canadian OK 73439 / 918-339-2204.

Fountainhead State Park, HC 60 Box 1340, Checotah OK 74426 / 918-689-5311.

Eufaula Lake			1	2	3	4	5	6	7	8	9	10	11	12
1 Ben O. Carroll Overlook						•		•						
2 Brooken Cove South														•
3 Cardinal Point						•	•							•
4 Crowder City Park						•	•	•	•					•
5 Eufaula Cove North						•		•		•			•	•
6 Eufaula Cove South														•
7 Gaines Creek														•
8 Onapa Cove														•
9 Arrowhead State Park	207	85	•	•	•		•	•				•	•	•
10 Belle Starr Park North	13	13												•
11 Belle Starr Park South	•	•	•	•	•	•	•	•	•	•		•	•	•
12 Brooken Cove North	81	69	•	•	•	•	•	•	•	•		•		•
13 Crowder Point East														•
14 Crowder Point West														•
15 Damsite East Outlet	10	10		•			•							
16 Damsite South	75	75	•	•	•	•	•	•	•			•	•	•
17 Elm Point	17	14		•			•							•
18 Fountainhead State Park	234	84	•	•	•		•	•	•			•	•	•
19 Gentry Creek Cove	40	14	•	•			•	•						•
20 Hickory Point														•
21 Hwy. 9 Landing East	18	14		•			•							•
22 Hwy. 9 Landing North	35	33	•	•	•	•	•	•	•				•	•
23 Hwy. 9 Landing South	30	27		•			•	•						•
24 Highway 31 Landing														•
25 Holiday Cove														•
26 Juniper Point														•
27 Mill Creek Bay	12				•	•								•
28 Oak Ridge	13	8		•			•							•
29 Porum Landing	53	37	•	•	•	•	•	•	•				•	•

Fort Gibson Lake

Fort Gibson Lake is located in northeast Oklahoma about five miles north of the town of Fort Gibson. The dam can be reached from Fort Gibson by following SH 80 north. Fort Gibson Lake is the third project of a three-lake system on the lower Neosho River. Additional information is available from the resident office located on the west side of the dam.

Two of the 24 recreation areas on the lake, *Sequoyah* and *Sequoyah Bay State Parks*, are operated by the state of Oklahoma. Both state parks offer a full range of facilities. The city of Pryor manages a golf course on the north end of the lake. About 21,800 acres of land surrounding the lake is licensed to the Oklahoma Department of Wildlife Conservation. Of this public land, 17,300 acres are managed for hunting and the rest as a waterfowl refuge. Maps are available from the resident office.

At A Glance
Auto Touring
Biking
✓ Boating
Climbing
✓ Cultural or Historic Sites
✓ Camping
Educational Programs
✓ Fishing
✓ Groceries / Supplies
✓ Hiking
✓ Horseback Riding
✓ Hunting
✓ Lodging
Off Highway Vehicles
✓ Visitor Center

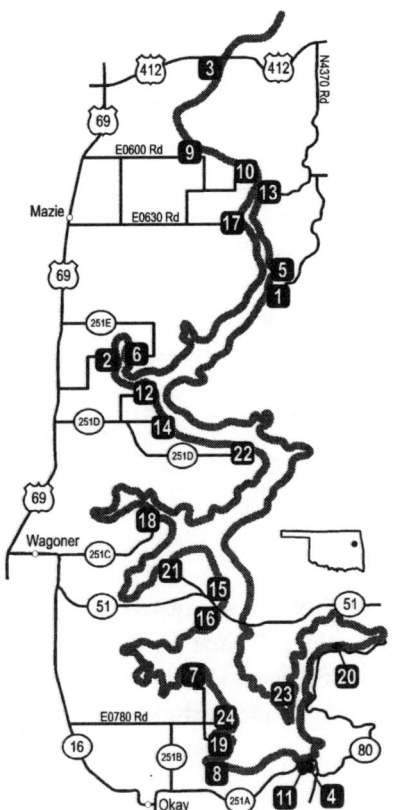

Wildlife inhabiting the area includes white-tailed deer, bobwhite quail, mourning dove, duck, geese, cottontail rabbit and squirrel. The Fort Gibson Stockade, a restored frontier fort, is located near the lake.

Species of fish found in Fort Gibson Lake include black bass, white bass, crappie, and several varieties of catfish and sunfish. Three heated fishing docks provide winter fun for crappie fishing. Fishing supplies and boat rentals are available from the concession services located around this 19,900-acre lake.

Information: U.S. Army Corps of Engineers, Fort

Gibson Resident Office, Route 1 Box 3900, Fort Gibson OK 74434 / 918-682-4314. Sequoyah Bay State Park, Route 2 Box 252, Wagoner OK 74477 / 918-683-0878. Sequoyah State Park, P.O. Box 509, Wagoner OK 74477 / 918-772-2046.

Fort Gibson Lake	△	🚐	🍴	🥤	🚻	?	🏠	?	🛢	🚶	⚓	🚤
1 Big Hollow												•
2 Blue Bill Point	43	35	•	•	•		•	•				•
3 Chouteau Bend	20	20	•	•		•				•	•	
4 Damsite	47	47	•	•	•		•	•				•
5 Earbob Ferry												•
6 Flat Rock Creek	46	36	•	•	•		•	•		•	•	
7 Jackson Bay					•					•	•	
8 Mallard Bay												•
9 Mazie Landing				•	•		•					•
10 Mission Bend	•				•							•
11 Overlook					•		•					
12 Rocky Point	63	57	•	•	•		•	•	•			•
13 Spring Creek												•
14 Snug Harbor												•
15 Taylor Ferry North					•		•				•	•
16 Taylor Ferry South	102	95	•	•	•		•	•				•
17 Three Finger Bay					•							•
18 Wagoner Park												•
19 Wahoo Bay	16					•	•					•
20 Wildwood	30	30	•	•	•		•	•				•
21 Long Bay Landing	28	12	•	•		•					•	•
22 Whitehorn Cove	16	16	•	•	•		•		•		•	•
23 Sequoyah State Park	357	179	•	•	•	•	•	•	•	•	•	•
24 Sequoyah Bay State Park	187	77	•	•	•		•	•	•		•	•

Fort Supply Lake

Fort Supply Lake, constructed on Wolf Creek, is about 13 miles northwest of Woodward in northwest Oklahoma. Information about the area is available from the visitor center near the west side of the dam. The visitor center features exhibits of Indian arts and crafts, a wildlife display, and Fred the prairie dog.

Fort Supply Lake encompasses about eight miles of Wolf Creek. The lake has a shoreline that is comparatively regular and unbroken by the entrance of tributary streams and is dotted with some of the whitest natural sand beaches this side of the Gulf. A major attraction for campers is the numerous campsites situated on the water's edge, providing easy access to the lake. Swimming and sunbathing opportunities abound at the designated swim beach, or the sand dunes that are on the east side of the lake. Some original buildings from Fort Supply, used as a base by Lt. Col. George Custer's 7th Cavalry, are located nearby on the Western State Hospital grounds east of Fort Supply, Oklahoma.

At A Glance
Auto Touring
Biking
✓ Boating
Climbing
✓ Cultural or Historic Sites
✓ Camping
Educational Programs
✓ Fishing
Groceries / Supplies
Hiking
Horseback Riding
✓ Hunting
Lodging
Off Highway Vehicles
✓ Visitor Center

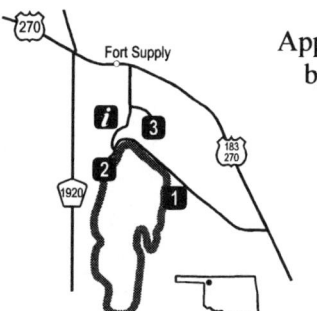

Approximately 6,000 acres of land is managed by the Corps of Engineers and the Oklahoma Department of Wildlife Conservation for hunting. Maps showing these areas are available at the project office. Wildlife commonly found in the area includes deer, bobwhite quail, wild turkey, pheasant, dove, squirrel, and rabbit. There are also two maintained shooting ranges at the lake.

Although the 1,820-acre lake is one of the oldest impounds in the state, fishing is still considered remarkably good by fishing enthusiasts. Anglers can try their luck with largemouth bass, crappie, white bass, walleye and several species of catfish. A fishing berm is located in the *Supply Park* recreation area. There are three handicap-accessible fishing piers on the lake and plenty of open shoreline for bank fishing.

Information: U.S. Army Corps of Engineers, Fort Supply Project Office, P.O. Box 248, Fort Supply OK 73841 / 580-766-2701.

Fort Supply Lake	⛺	🚐	🚻	🍴	🚰	👥	🏠	⛽	🛥	🚶	⚓	〰
1 Beaver Point	16								•			•
2 Supply Park	110	82	•	•	•	•	•	•	•			•
3 Wolf Creek				•		•						

Great Salt Plains Lake

Great Salt Plains Lake is in northern Oklahoma about 40 miles northwest of Enid and eight miles north of Jet. The lake was constructed on the Salt Fork of the Arkansas River. To reach the dam from Jet, follow SH 38 north. Information about the area is available from the state park office located near the southern end of the dam.

At A Glance
- ✓ Auto Touring
- Biking
- ✓ Boating
- Climbing
- Cultural or Historic Sites
- ✓ Camping
- Educational Programs
- ✓ Fishing
- Groceries / Supplies
- ✓ Hiking
- Horseback Riding
- Hunting
- ✓ Lodging
- Off Highway Vehicles
- ✓ Visitor Center

This lake sits in a basin bordered by salt plains on the west with red shale bluffs and sandy beaches nearer the dam. The salt plains are a unique geological feature. Concentrated saline water combines with gypsum to promote growth of a crystal with an hourglass shaped sand inclusion. This is the only documented area in the world where they are found. The Selenite Crystal Digging Area is managed by the US Fish and Wildlife Service. Crystal digging is permitted during daylight hours from April 1 to October 15.

Six recreation areas surround the lake and are operated by the state as units of the Great Salt Plains State Park. A total of 171 designated campsites is available for tent campers and RVers. The state park also has six cabins available for rent year-round. Bordering the lake is the 32,000-acre Salt Plains National Wildlife Refuge. Located on the central flyway, the refuge provides habitat for approximately 300 species of birds and 30 species of mammals. The refuge offers a self-guided nature trail for viewing shorebirds and the salt flats, a children's fishing pond, and a self-guided auto tour route.

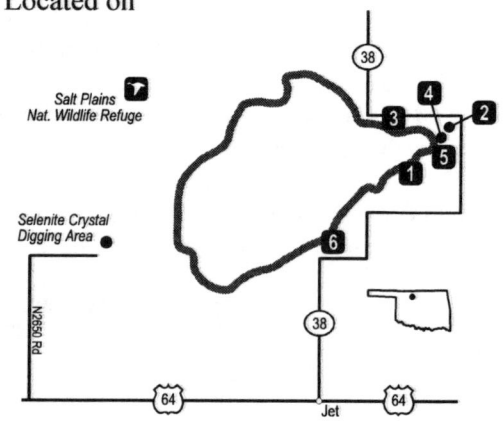

Great Salt Plains Lake provides 8,700 acres for boating and fishing. The lake is known for excellent channel cat fishing. Bass and saugeye also inhabit the lake. An annual saugeye fishing derby is held in late winter. Fishing is most popular in the area of the spillway. Many areas around the lake are closed to fishing from mid-October through April. Fishing is permitted year-round in the area around the dam.

Information: U.S. Army Corps of Engineers, Great Salt Plains Lake, P.O. Box 69, Canton OK 73724 / 580-886-2989. Great Salt Plains State Park, Route 1 Box 28, Jet OK 73749 / 580-626-4731. Salt Plains National Wildlife Refuge, Route 1 Box 76, Jet OK 73749 / 580-626-4794.

GREAT SALT PLAINS	△	⌂	🚻	🚽	🛣	🚤	🏨	⛺	🏞	🛢	🚶	⚓	〰
1 SOUTH RECREATION AREA				•	•		•						•
2 RIVER ROAD		•	•		•	•			•	•		•	
3 SANDY BEACH		•	•		•	•		•	•	•			•
4 NORTH SPILLWAY		•			•	•		•					
5 SOUTH SPILLWAY		•			•	•		•					
6 JET RECREATION AREA		•			•	•		•					•

Heyburn Lake

Heyburn Lake is on Polecat Creek in central Oklahoma about 20 miles southwest of Tulsa and five miles west of Kellyville. To reach the dam from Kellyville, follow E0740 Road west. Information on the area is available from the project office located on the east end of the dam.

Heyburn Lake lies in a picturesque setting of rolling grassland and gently sloping, wooded hills. In the spring, flowering wild plum and redbud trees add color to the green landscape. Four recreation areas have been constructed around the lake. *Sheppard Point* and *Rocky Point* are operated by the state of Oklahoma.

AT A GLANCE
AUTO TOURING
BIKING
✓ BOATING
CLIMBING
CULTURAL OR HISTORIC SITES
✓ CAMPING
EDUCATIONAL PROGRAMS
✓ FISHING
GROCERIES / SUPPLIES
✓ HIKING
HORSEBACK RIDING
✓ HUNTING
LODGING
OFF HIGHWAY VEHICLES
VISITOR CENTER

For the angler, the 920-acre lake is known for good catfish fishing. Flatheads of 15 to 30 pounds are not uncommon. Also in the lake,

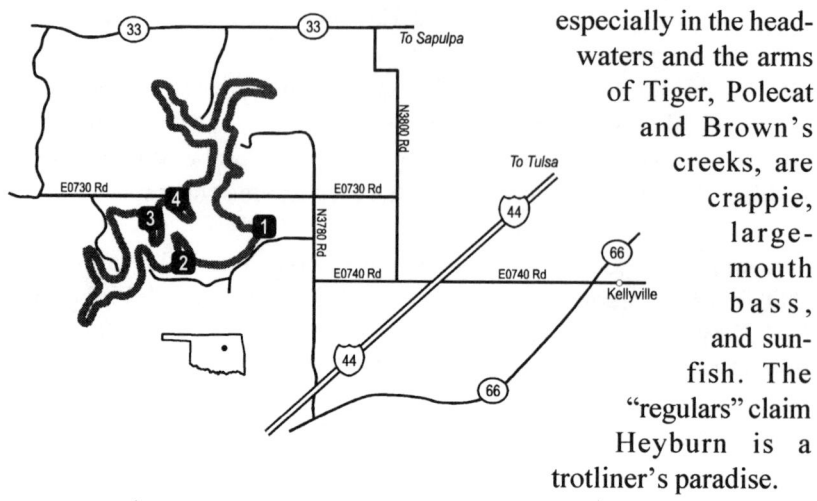

especially in the headwaters and the arms of Tiger, Polecat and Brown's creeks, are crappie, largemouth bass, and sunfish. The "regulars" claim Heyburn is a trotliner's paradise.

Information: U.S. Army Corps of Engineers, Heyburn Lake, Route 2 Box 140, Kellyville OK 74039 / 918-247-6391.

Heyburn Lake														
1 Sunset Bay	14			•			•	•						•
2 Heyburn Park	60	45	•	•	•	•	•	•	•					•
3 Sheppard Point	88	53	•	•	•	•	•	•			•			•
4 Rocky Point	37	20		•	•		•	•						

Hugo Lake

Hugo Lake is in southeast Oklahoma about seven miles east of Hugo and 30 miles north of Paris, Texas. The lake was constructed on the Kiamichi River. Information is available from the project office located near the west end of the dam.

Hugo Lake is set in a narrow valley with densely wooded hills rising sharply on all sides. A variety of flowering shrubs, native grasses and wildflowers add a variety of colors each season. The Oklahoma Department of Wildlife Conservation manages over 18,000 acres of

At A Glance
Auto Touring
✓ Biking
✓ Boating
Climbing
Cultural or Historic Sites
✓ Camping
Educational Programs
✓ Fishing
Groceries / Supplies
✓ Hiking
Horseback Riding
✓ Hunting
Lodging
Off Highway Vehicles
Visitor Center

Oklahoma

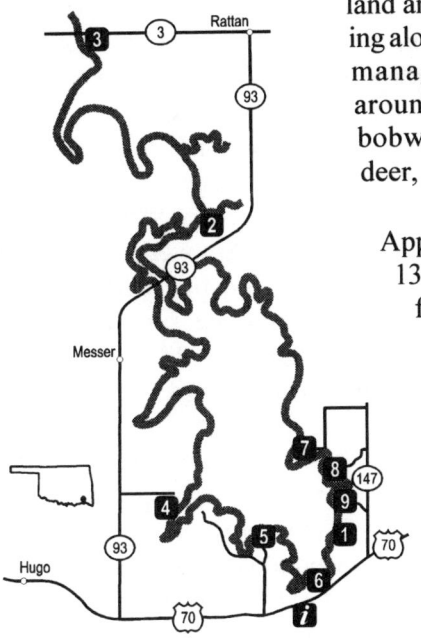

land and water, which is open to hunting along with an additional 8,000 acres managed by the Corps. Wildlife around the lake includes waterfowl, bobwhite quail, dove, white-tailed deer, and beaver.

Approximately 5,000 acres of the 13,250-acre lake remains uncleared for anglers to enjoy without the intrusion of skiers. Boating lanes have been provided through the uncleared northern half of the lake. Anglers will find a wide variety of fish including channel and flathead catfish, drum, carp, buffalo, bluegill, sunfish, crappie, and largemouth, spotted and white, bass.

Information: U.S. Army Corps of Engineers, Hugo Project Office, P.O. Box 99, Sawyer OK 74756 / 580-326-3345.

Hugo Lake	🛖	🏕	🚻	🚰	🛣	🚤	🏛	🚿	🗄	🚶	⚓	🏊
1 Sawyer Bluff							•					•
2 Frazier Point												•
3 Rattan Landing	10	10		•	•		•					•
4 Salt Creek Cove							•					
5 Kiamichi Park	88	88	•	•		•	•	•	•		•	•
6 Bridge View				•			•					
7 Group Camp	4	4	•	•		•	•	•	•			
8 Virgil Point	52	52	•	•			•	•				•
9 Wilson Point				•	•		•		•			•

Hulah Lake

Hulah Lake is situated on the Caney River in northeast Oklahoma. The lake lies about 20 miles north of Bartlesville. To reach the dam from

Bartlesville, follow US 75 north for eight miles and then travel west on SH 10 for about 12 miles. Additional information is available from the project office near the dam.

> **AT A GLANCE**
>
> AUTO TOURING
> BIKING
> ✓ BOATING
> CLIMBING
> CULTURAL OR HISTORIC SITES
> ✓ CAMPING
> EDUCATIONAL PROGRAMS
> ✓ FISHING
> GROCERIES / SUPPLIES
> HIKING
> HORSEBACK RIDING
> ✓ HUNTING
> LODGING
> OFF HIGHWAY VEHICLES
> VISITOR CENTER

Hulah Lake lies in the upper reaches of the Osage Hills in a farming and ranching community where grazing cattle and working cowboys are familiar sights. Oil discoveries here made the Osage Indian tribe the wealthiest in America. All recreation areas at Hulah Lake are operated by the state of Oklahoma as units of the Wah-Sha-She State Park.

Nearly 9,000 acres of land surrounding the lake have been made available to the Oklahoma Department of Wildlife Conservation for wildlife management. Two thousand acres of this land has been set aside as a waterfowl refuge. The remaining acreage is managed for upland game and white-tailed deer and is open to the public for hunting. Game species prevalent include deer, morning dove, waterfowl, squirrel, rabbit, prairie chicken and wild turkey.

Hulah Lake provides 3,570 surface acres and 62 miles of shoreline for the angler. The lake is known for big catfish, as well as excellent bass and crappie fishing. The lake also supports various species of sunfish.

Information: U.S. Army Corps of Engineers, Hulah Lake, Route 1 Box 260, Copan OK 74022 / 918-532-4334. Wah-Sha-She State Park, Route 1 Box 301, Copan OK 74022 / 918-532-4627.

HULAH LAKE													
1 WA-SHA-SHE S P	158	46	•	•	•	•	•	•	•				•

J.W. Trimble Lock and Dam

The J.W. Trimble Lock and Dam is located three miles east of Fort Smith, Arkansas near Barling. The lake formed by the construction of the dam on the Arkansas River extends to the W.D. Mayo Lock and Dam in Oklahoma. The dam is reached by way of SH 59 from either Barling or Van Buren, Arkansas.

At A Glance
Auto Touring
Biking
✓ Boating
Climbing
Cultural or Historic Sites
✓ Camping
Educational Programs
✓ Fishing
Groceries / Supplies
Hiking
Horseback Riding
✓ Hunting
Lodging
Off Highway Vehicles
Visitor Center

This lock and dam structure is the last unit on the Arkansas portion of the McClellan-Kerr Arkansas River Navigation System. There are four developed recreation areas along the river. Camping facilities for tents and recreational vehicles are available in *Damsite*, *Lee Creek*, and *Arkoma*. The *Arkoma* park is situated along the Poteau River, a tributary of the Arkansas River. Visitors to the project in fall are treated to the vibrant colors of blackjack oak, post oak, red oak, and other hardwoods. During the spring, wild plum, redbud, and dogwood display their colors. White-tailed deer, mourning dove, and wild turkeys are among the wildlife inhabiting the region.

Among the fish inhabiting the Arkansas River are largemouth bass, channel and flathead catfish, crappie, striped bass, walleye, and various sunfish. The impoundment of the Arkansas River by J.W. Trimble Lock

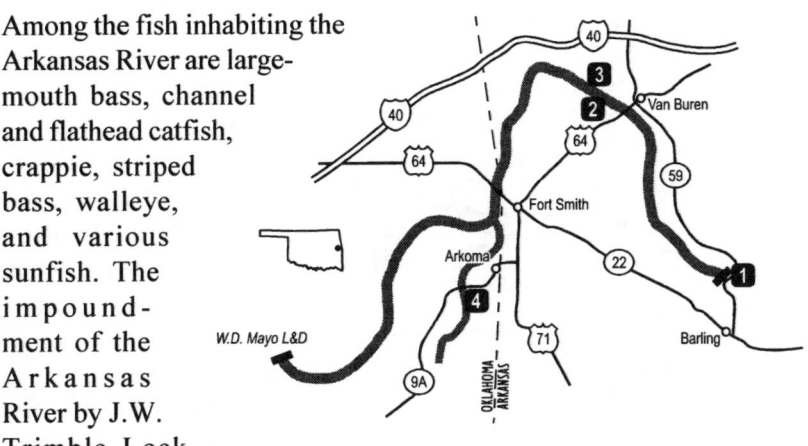

and Dam stretches 27 miles to the W.D. Mayo Lock and Dam. Boat ramps are located in all four recreation areas. Complete fishing and boating supplies may be found in Fort Smith.

Information: U.S. Army Corps of Engineers, J.W. Trimble Lock and Dam, Route 2 Box 21, Gore OK 74435 / 918-489-5541.

J.W. TRIMBLE LOCK & DAM	△	🚐	🚻	🚰	⛱	🍴	🏛	📚	🎣	🥫	🚶	⚓	〰
1 DAMSITE	•	•	•	•	•	•	•	•	•			•	•
2 FORT SMITH			•	•		•							•
3 LEE CREEK	•		•	•	•	•		•	•				•
4 ARKOMA	•			•	•		•						•

Kaw Lake

Located on the Arkansas River, Kaw Lake lies north of US 60 in northern Oklahoma near Ponca City. From Ponca City travel about ten miles east on US 60, then north on the dam access road. The uppermost portion of the project extends into Kansas. Information about the area is available from the project office located near the west end of the dam.

AT A GLANCE
AUTO TOURING
✓ BIKING
✓ BOATING
CLIMBING
✓ CULTURAL OR HISTORIC SITES
✓ CAMPING
EDUCATIONAL PROGRAMS
✓ FISHING
✓ GROCERIES / SUPPLIES
✓ HIKING
✓ HORSEBACK RIDING
✓ HUNTING
✓ LODGING
✓ OFF HIGHWAY VEHICLES
✓ VISITOR CENTER

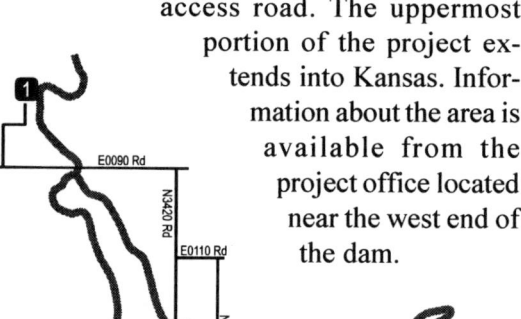

One of Kaw Lake's most popular winter attractions is the bald eagle. Peak viewing usually occurs shortly after the first of the year and lasts throughout January. Other wildlife inhabiting the project area includes white-tailed deer, wild turkey, quail, cottontail rabbit, and squirrel. In fall the lake attracts large numbers of migrating waterfowl. Of historical interest is the Deer Creek archaeological site located near *Traders Bend*. This site, listed on the National Register of Historic Places, is believed to represent an early French trading post and Indian village.

A variety of recreational opportunities await the visitor to Kaw Lake. An off road vehicle area is located in *Sarge Creek Cove*. The Eagle View Hiking Trail, about 12 miles long, runs from *Osage Cove* to Burbank Landing. An equestrian trail, the Five Fingers Equestrian Trail, extends from Burbank Landing to *Sarge Creek Cove*. There are seven parks surrounding the lake that have camping facilities for tents and recreational vehicles.

With 168 miles of shoreline and 17,000 acres of water, Kaw Lake offers an abundance of opportunities for the angler. Kaw Lake and the Arkansas River have long been known for producing some of Oklahoma's largest catfish. The lake supports such species as channel catfish, flathead catfish, crappie, white, black and stripped bass, and walleye. Boating and fishing supplies are available from the two full-service marinas.

Information: U.S. Army Corps of Engineers, Kaw Lake Project Office, 9400 Lake Road, Ponca City OK 74604 / 580-762-5611.

Kaw Lake			⛺	🚐	🚻	💧	🪑	🎣	🏕	🥾	🏊	🚶	⚓	🛟
1 Traders Bend														•
2 Coon Creek Cove	66	54	•	•	•		•	•						•
3 McFadden Cove	15	15		•	•		•						•	•
4 Fisherman's Bend				•	•		•							
5 Sandy Park	12	12		•	•		•		•					•
6 Osage Cove	94	94	•	•	•	•	•	•			•	•		•
7 Pioneer Park				•	•		•		•			•		•
8 Sarge Creek Cove	51	51	•	•	•	•	•	•			•	•		•
9 Washunga Bay	20	20	•	•	•		•	•						•
10 Bear Creek Cove	22	22	•	•			•	•						•

Keystone Lake

Located in north-central Oklahoma 19 miles west of Tulsa. Keystone Dam, on the Arkansas River, can be reached from US 412/64 (Keystone Expressway) or from SH 51. Information is available from the project office located on the north end of the dam.

Keystone Lake's blue-green water is set among the natural beauty of its wooded shoreline, sandy beaches, high bluffs, grassland, and low rolling hills. The recreation areas provide access to miles of sandy beaches, five short-distance trails, two off-road vehicle areas, a waterfowl refuge, and three seasonal green-tree reservoirs. *Keystone State Park* offers 21 cabins that are available for rent. Boat rentals are available at two area marinas. Bicycle rentals are also available in the state park.

At A Glance
Auto Touring
✓ Biking
✓ Boating
Climbing
Cultural or Historic Sites
✓ Camping
Educational Programs
✓ Fishing
✓ Groceries / Supplies
✓ Hiking
✓ Horseback Riding
✓ Hunting
✓ Lodging
✓ Off Highway Vehicles
✓ Visitor Center

Approximately 17,000 acres of land surrounding the lake is open to the public for hunting. Wildlife found in the region includes white-tailed deer, bobwhite quail,

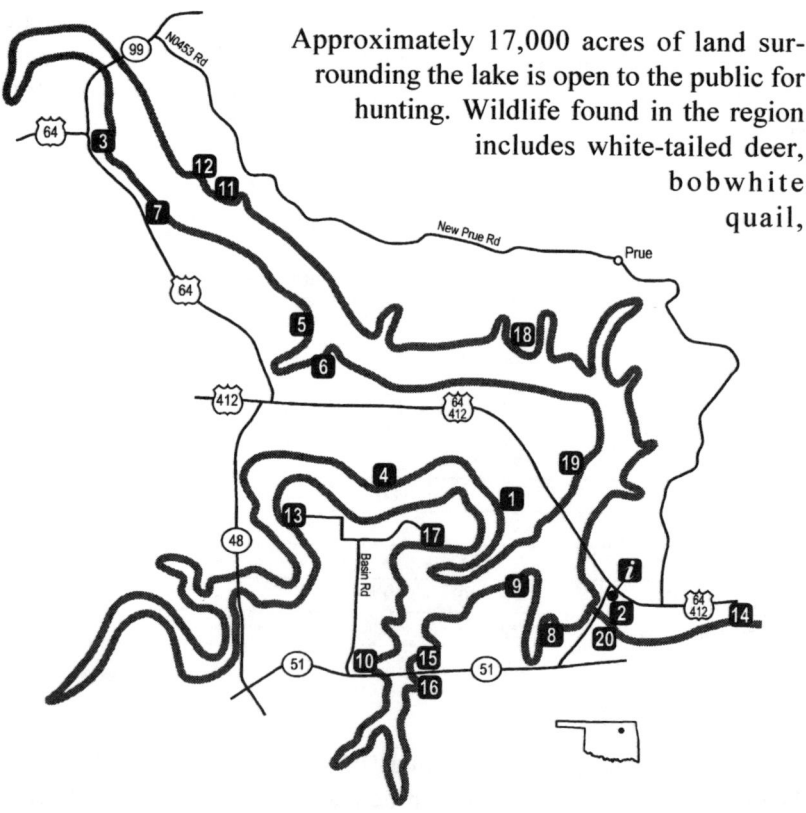

mourning dove, ducks, geese, cottontail rabbit, and squirrel. Maps of the hunting areas are available from the project office.

The 26,000-acre Keystone Lake meanders into small valleys, creating many arms and land fingers along its 330 miles of shore. The lake is known locally as "the new home of the striped bass." It is believed that with the initial stocking and natural spawns over the past several years, some 40+ pounders are lurking in the waters. White and black bass, crappie, and catfish are also abundant. Downstream fisheries are accessible from *Whitewater* and *Brush Creek* parks. Supplies and services are available from concessionaire services around the lake as well as the surrounding communities.

Information: U.S. Army Corps of Engineers, Keystone Project Office, Route 1 Box 100, Sand Springs OK 74063 / 918-865-2621. Keystone State Park, P.O. Box 147, Mannford OK 74044 / 918-865-4477 park office, or 918-865-4991 cabin office and reservations. Walnut Creek State Park, P.O. Box 26, New Prue OK 74060 / 918-242-3362.

Keystone Lake													
1 Appalachia Bay	18			•	•		•	•	•		•		•
2 Brush Creek	20	20		•	•								
3 Cedar Creek Bay													•
4 Cimarron Park							•						
5 Cowskin Bay North													•
6 Cowskin Bay South	30			•	•		•					•	•
7 Feyodi Creek	•	•	•	•	•		•	•					
8 Keystone State Park	141	80	•	•	•	•	•	•		•	•	•	•
9 Keystone Ramp					•		•		•				•
10 New Mannford Ramp	46	38	•	•	•		•	•					•
11 Osage Point	•			•	•		•	•					•
12 Osage Ramp													•
13 Pawnee Cove North													•
14 River City Park				•	•		•						•
15 Salt Creek Cove North	119	112	•	•	•	•	•	•	•		•	•	•
16 Salt Creek Cove South	N	O	F	A	C	I	L	I	T	I	E	S	
17 Sandy Park							•						
18 Walnut Creek State Park	172	88	•	•	•	•	•	•	•	•	•	•	•
19 Washington Irving Cove S.	40	38	•	•	•	•	•	•		•	•	•	•
20 Whitewater Park							•						

Newt Graham Lock and Dam

The Newt Graham Lock and Dam is located in northeast Oklahoma about 33 miles east of Tulsa. To reach the dam from Tulsa, follow US 412 east for 25 miles to N 4200 Road just west of Inola. Follow N 4200 Road south for seven miles to the dam. Information about the project is available from the lockmasters.

Newt Grahm Lock and Dam is part of the McClellan-Kerr Navigation System on the Arkansas River. Visitors to the project have an opportunity to enjoy the outdoors year-round. Spring offers the vivid pinks of redbud; the crispy white of dogwood trees bring life to the grays of winter. Summer is alive with vibrant greens of oak, hickory, pecan, hackberry, sycamore and walnut trees. Nature lovers will enjoy the numerous birds and animals of the area. Wildlife inhabiting the area includes quail, dove, wild turkey, white-tailed deer, mourning dove, cottontail rabbit, and squirrel.

At A Glance
Auto Touring
Biking
✓ Boating
Climbing
Cultural or Historic Sites
✓ Camping
Educational Programs
✓ Fishing
Groceries / Supplies
✓ Hiking
✓ Horseback Riding
✓ Hunting
Lodging
Off Highway Vehicles
Visitor Center

Of interest to the hiker is the Jean Pierre Chouteau National Recreation Trail, which extends 64 miles from *Rogers Point* to Fort Gibson Park on the Webbers Falls project. Portions of the trail are open for equestrian use. Maps showing the location and features of the trail are available from the lockmasters.

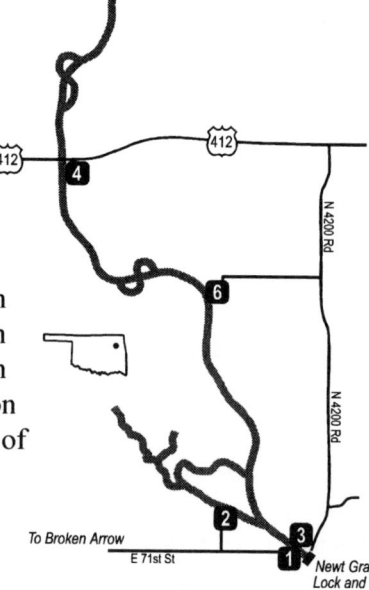

Species of fish inhabiting the river include channel and flathead catfish, crappie, largemouth and striped bass, walleye, and various sunfish. A heated fishing dock is located in the *Highway 33 Landing* recreation area. Fishing supplies are available on access roads leading to the project.

Information: U.S. Army Corps of Engineers, Newt Graham Lock & Dam 18, Route 2 Box 21, Gore OK 74435 / 918-489-5541.

Newt Graham Lock & Dam													
1 Blue Gill Point	N	O		F		A	C		L	I	T	I	E	S
2 Bluff Landing	21	21	•	•	•			•	•					•
3 Goodhope Ramp					•							•		•
4 Highway 33 Landing								•				•		•
5 Rocky Point	•				•			•	•			•		•
6 Rogers Point	•			•	•			•						•

Oologah Lake

Oologah Lake is on the Verdigris River in northeast Oklahoma. To reach the dam from Tulsa, travel 30 miles north on US 169 and then three miles east on SH 88. More information about the lake is available from the project office located near the west end of the dam.

With over 50,000 acres of land and water, Oologah Lake provides a great getaway for a sunny afternoon. Wide stretches of water, perfect for catching the wind, make it one of the most popular lakes in the area for sailing. Those interested in horseback riding will find a trail in the *Blue Creek Ramp* area. The Skull Hollow Nature Trail in *Hawthorn Bluff* offers three routes: short loop, long loop and a hiking trail. The trek ranges from a third of a mile to a little more than one mile. For the more adventurous hiker or horseback rider, the Will Rogers Centennial Trail winds 12 miles alongside the lake from *Blue Creek Park* to the spillway area.

At A Glance

Auto Touring
✓ Biking
✓ Boating
Climbing
✓ Cultural or Historic Sites
✓ Camping
Educational Programs
✓ Fishing
✓ Groceries / Supplies
✓ Hiking
✓ Horseback Riding
✓ Hunting
Lodging
Off Highway Vehicles
Visitor Center

Over 19,000 acres of land is open to the public for hunting. Wildlife found in the region includes white-tailed deer, quail, fox, turkey, squirrel and rabbit. Maps of the hunting areas are available from the Corps project office.

The 29,500-acre lake offers the angler over 209 miles of shoreline. Standing timber, brush piles, and millet planted on exposed mud flats enhances the fishing experience. The lake and its tailwaters are stocked with a variety of fish, including sand bass, catfish, hybrid striped bass, crappie, and walleye. Fishing docks, heated and otherwise, can be found in *Red Bud Bay*. Fishing and camping supplies are available at the marina.

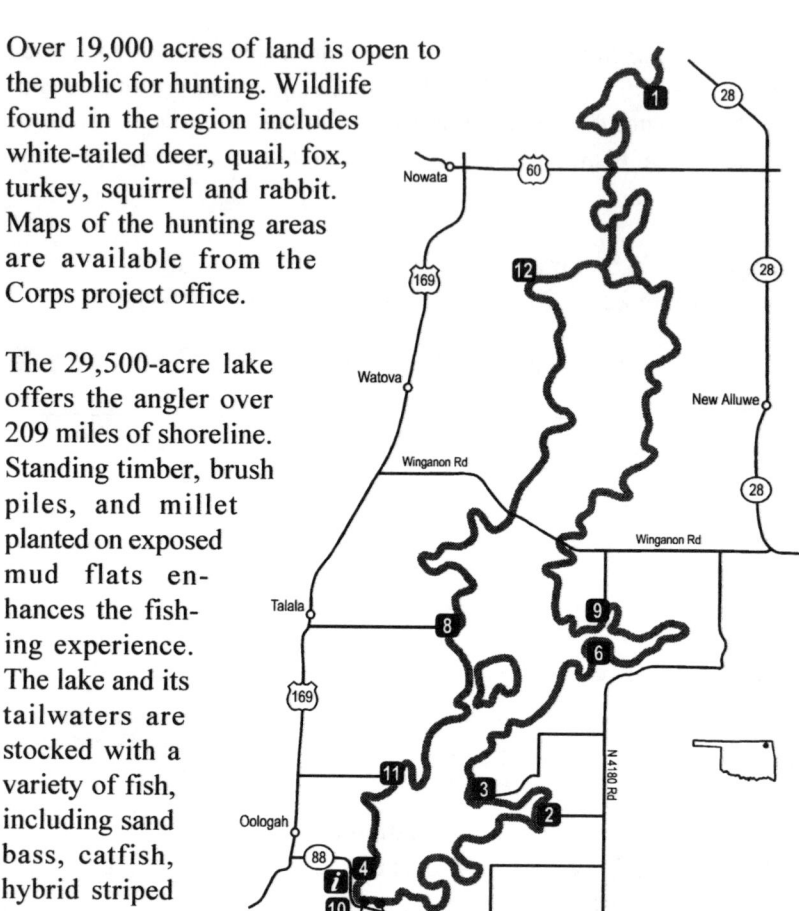

Information: U.S. Army Corps of Engineers, Oologah Resident Office, P.O. Box 700, Oologah OK 74053 / 918-443-2250.

OOLOGAH LAKE	▲	⌐	🚻	🚰	🏕	⛱	🏛	🏊	⛽	🚶	⚓	≈
1 BIG CREEK PARK	16				•		•					•
2 BLUE CREEK PARK	60	22	•	•	•	•	•	•			•	•
3 CLERMONT PARK	5				•							•

continued next page

Oklahoma

Oologah Lake *(continued)*	⛺	🚐	🚽	🚰	🏕	🎣	🍴	🚿	🏊	🛶	🚶	⚓	🐟
4 Hawthorne Bluff	89	65	•	•	•	•	•	•	•	•		•	•
5 Overlook				•	•		•						
6 Spencer Creek Cove	86	30	•	•	•	•	•	•	•	•			•
7 Red Bud Bay	12	12		•	•		•					•	•
8 Sunnyside Park	8												•
9 Winganon Park													•
10 Verdigris River Park	10			•			•						•
11 Will Rogers Birthplace					•		•						
12 Double Creek Park	20	14	•	•	•			•	•				•

Optima Lake

Optima Lake is in the panhandle of Oklahoma about 25 miles east of Guymon. The lake lies north of US 412/SH 3 near the town of Hardesty. Information is available from the Fort Supply Lake office.

Optima Lake is set in an area of sand hills, rock outcrops, and rolling grassland. Visitors will find the developed recreation area below the lake. Camping facilities are designed for tents and recreational vehicles. The campground is closed November through October. About 8,000 acres of land surrounding the lake is managed by the Oklahoma Department of Wildlife Conservation and another 4,300 acres by the U.S. Fish and Wildlife Service as the Optima National Wildlife Refuge. Wildlife inhabiting the area includes bobwhite quail, cottontail rabbit, deer, mourning dove, pheasant, and wild turkey. A variety of migrating waterfowl also visit the lake.

At A Glance
- Auto Touring
- Biking
- Boating
- Climbing
- ✓ Cultural or Historic Sites
- ✓ Camping
- Educational Programs
- ✓ Fishing
- Groceries / Supplies
- ✓ Hiking
- Horseback Riding
- ✓ Hunting
- Lodging
- Off Highway Vehicles
- Visitor Center

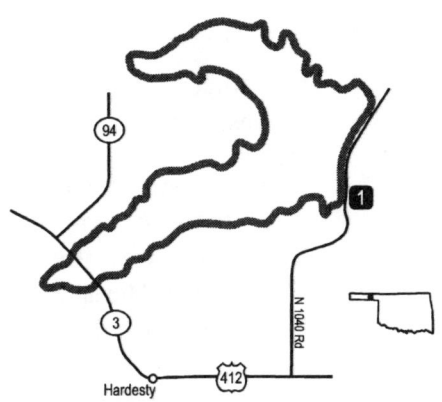

When full, the lake will have 5,340 acres and 38 miles of shoreline. A variety of fish may be found in the lake. Species include largemouth bass, bluegill, catfish, crappie, and walleye. The Beaver River and Coldwater Creek arms of the lake remain uncleared and provide excellent fishing spots. Camping and fishing supplies can be found in nearby Guymon.

Information: U.S. Army Corps of Engineers, Fort Supply Lake Office, P.O. Box 248, Fort Supply OK 73841 / 580-766-2701.

Optima Lake														
1 Angler Point	20	20	•	•	•		•				•			

Pine Creek Lake

Pine Creek Lake is in southeast Oklahoma about 25 miles northwest of Idabel and eight miles north of Valliant. To reach the dam from Idabel, follow US 70 west for 18 miles to SH 98. Follow SH 98 north two miles and then Pine Creek Road eight miles to the dam. Information about the lake is available from the project office on the west end of the dam.

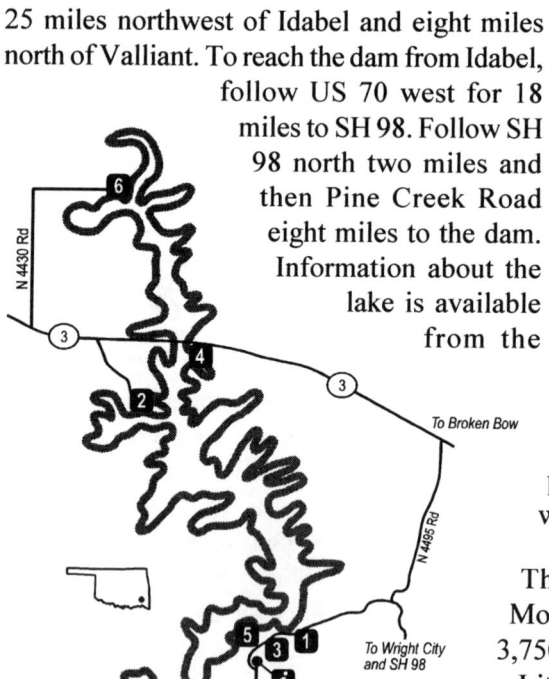

At A Glance
Auto Touring
✓ Biking
✓ Boating
Climbing
Cultural or Historic Sites
✓ Camping
Educational Programs
✓ Fishing
Groceries / Supplies
✓ Hiking
✓ Horseback Riding
✓ Hunting
Lodging
Off Highway Vehicles
Visitor Center

The forested Kiamichi Mountains surround this 3,750-acre lake constructed on Little River. The lake provides 74 miles of shoreline that form a series of long, deep coves around the main body of water.

There are six developed parks on the lake; four have camping facilities for tents and recreational vehicles. Numerous side roads invite visitors that wish to explore the area on foot or horse. The Oklahoma Department of Wildlife Conservation manages over 10,000 acres of land for wildlife.

The high ratio of shoreline length to water area at Pine Creek Lake is conducive to good fishing. Anglers will find largemouth bass, channel and flathead catfish, crappie, black bass, saugeye, and various sunfish. The old Highway 7 bridge at the upper end of the lake has been converted into a fishing pier that extends out into the lake. Boat ramps are located in four of the parks.

Information: U.S. Army Corps of Engineers, Pine Creek Lake, Route 1 Box 400, Valliant OK 74764 / 580-933-4239.

Pine Creek Lake														
1 Billy Bell Shoals							•							
2 Little River Park	88	62	•	•				•	•	•	•	•		•
3 Lost Ferry							•							
4 Lost Rapids Park	30	16	•	•	•		•							•
5 Pine Creek Cove	41	40	•	•	•	•	•	•	•	•				•
6 Turkey Creek Landing	34	10					•	•						•

Robert S. Kerr Reservoir

The Robert S. Kerr Reservoir, part of the McClellan-Kerr Navigation System, is on the Arkansas River in eastern Oklahoma. The lake is 60 miles southeast of Muskogee and eight miles south of Sallisaw. To reach the dam from Sallisaw, follow US 59 south.

Completed in 1970, Kerr Reservoir offers a variety of outdoor recreation opportunities. Thirteen parks have been constructed on the lake; eight of these have camping facilities for tents and recreational vehicles. Sun-seekers and swimmers will find four parks with developed

At A Glance
Auto Touring
Biking
✓ Boating
Climbing
Cultural or Historic Sites
✓ Camping
Educational Programs
✓ Fishing
✓ Groceries / Supplies
✓ Hiking
Horseback Riding
✓ Hunting
Lodging
Off Highway Vehicles
Visitor Center

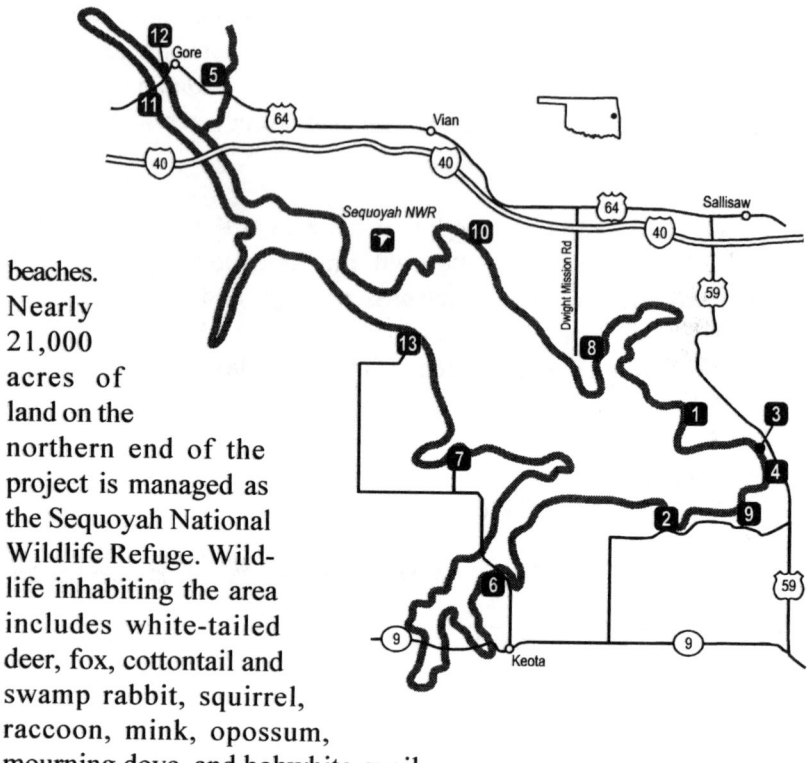

beaches. Nearly 21,000 acres of land on the northern end of the project is managed as the Sequoyah National Wildlife Refuge. Wildlife inhabiting the area includes white-tailed deer, fox, cottontail and swamp rabbit, squirrel, raccoon, mink, opossum, mourning dove, and bobwhite quail.

Robert S. Kerr Reservoir provides 250 miles of shoreline and 43,800 acres of water for boating and fishing. Principal species of fish include channel catfish, flathead catfish, white crappie, largemouth bass, striped bass, walleye and various sunfish. Boat ramps are located in all but two of the recreation areas. Supplies and boat rentals are available from the *Applegate Cove Marina* and on access roads around the project.

Information: U.S. Army Corps of Engineers, Robert S. Kerr Lock & Dam 15, Route 2 Box 21, Gore OK 74435 / 918-489-5541.

Robert S. Kerr Reservoir	🏕	🚐	🚻	🚰	🔥	🛶	🏚	🚿	🏊	🛢	🚶	⚓	🎣	🏪
1 Applegate Cove	27	27	•	•	•		•	•			•		•	•
2 Cowlington Point	56	28	•	•	•		•		•					•
3 Damsite			•	•			•		•					

continued next page

Robert S. Kerr (continued)	⛺	🚐	🚻	🚰	⛽	🍴	🏠	🎣	🏞	🗑	🚶	⚓	〰
4 Fisherman's Landing									•				
5 Gore Landing	24												•
6 Keota Landing	32	32	•	•	•		•		•				•
7 Little Sansbois Creek													•
8 Sallisaw Creek	39	11	•	•	•		•						•
9 Short Mountain Cove	48	26	•	•	•		•						•
10 Vian Creek													•
11 Webbers Falls City Park			•			•	•	•					•
12 Summers Ferry			•		•	•	•						•
13 Tamaha			•			•	•						•

Sardis Lake

Sardis Lake is on the Jackfork Creek, a tributary of the Kiamichi River, in southeast Oklahoma. The lake lies in the foothills of the Ouachita Mountains about 46 miles southeast of McAlester. The dam can be reached by following SH 270 east for 15 miles to SH 2 and then south for nearly ten miles. The project office is located off SH 2 near the northeast end of the dam.

The Jackfork Creek Basin in which Sardis Lake lies is enclosed by the Jackfork Mountains to the west, Winding Stair Mountains to the north, and the Potato Hills to the northeast. A wide variety of vegetation offers a panorama of color each season. A nature trail, the Lost Buffalo Trail, winds nearly one mile through a forested area connecting *Potato Hills Park Central* to *Potato Hills Park South*. Campsites suitable for tents and RVs are available in three parks.

At A Glance
Auto Touring
Biking
✓ Boating
Climbing
Cultural or Historic Sites
✓ Camping
Educational Programs
✓ Fishing
Groceries / Supplies
✓ Hiking
Horseback Riding
✓ Hunting
Lodging
Off Highway Vehicles
Visitor Center

Sardis Lake offers the angler 14,360 surface acres and 117 miles of shoreline. Large areas of timber and brush left standing provide excellent fishing spots. Sardis Lake is known for producing several of Oklahoma's largest bass. The lake also supports crappie, walleye, and catfish. The Oklahoma Department of Wildlife Conservation has stocked the lake with channel and blue catfish, largemouth and small-

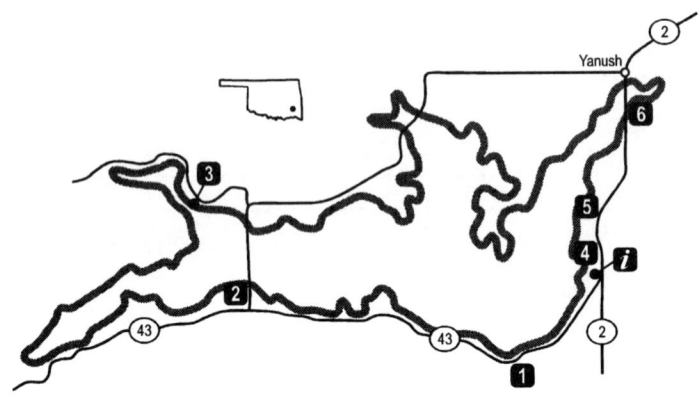

mouth bass, threadfin shad, and bluegill. Fishing docks are located in *Potato Hills Park Central* and *South* areas.

Information: U.S. Army Corps of Engineers, Sardis Lake Office, HC 60 Box 175, Clayton OK 74536 / 918-569-4131.

Sardis Lake												
1 Mathies Park						•		•				
2 Sardis Cove	45	22	•	•		•						•
3 The Narrows							•					•
4 Potato Hills Park South	18				•	•	•	•		•	•	•
5 Potato Hills Park Central	80	80	•	•		•	•	•		•		
6 Potato Hills Park North						•						

Skiatook Lake

Skiatook Lake is located in northern Oklahoma about 20 miles northwest of Tulsa. Reaching the dam from Tulsa is by way of SH 11 north, then five miles west on SH 20. Information about the area is available from the project office located near the west end of the dam.

Rolling hills of blackjack and post oak interspersed with tall grass prairie surround Skiatook Lake. Visitors to the project will find eight recreation areas for camping, picnicking, and swimming. *Tall Chief Cove* and *Twin Points* have campgrounds open from April through October. Electric hookups are available at all of the campsites. *Bull*

Oklahoma

Creek Peninsula is open year-round and offers a more primitive setting for the camper.

Nearly 8,000 acres of land within the project is open to the public for hunting. White-tailed deer, cottontail rabbit, and bobwhite quail are among the species of wildlife inhabiting the area. Check with the project office for more information.

At A Glance
Auto Touring
Biking
✓ Boating
Climbing
Cultural or Historic Sites
✓ Camping
Educational Programs
✓ Fishing
✓ Groceries / Supplies
Hiking
Horseback Riding
✓ Hunting
Lodging
Off Highway Vehicles
✓ Visitor Center

Skiatook Lake, constructed on Hominy Creek, is 10,500 acres and has 160 miles of meandering shoreline. Skiatook Lake supports a variety of sport fish including black and white crappie, largemouth bass, channel catfish, and numerous species of sunfish. A fishing dock is located in the *Hominy Landing* recreation area. Boat ramps are located in all but one of the recreation areas.

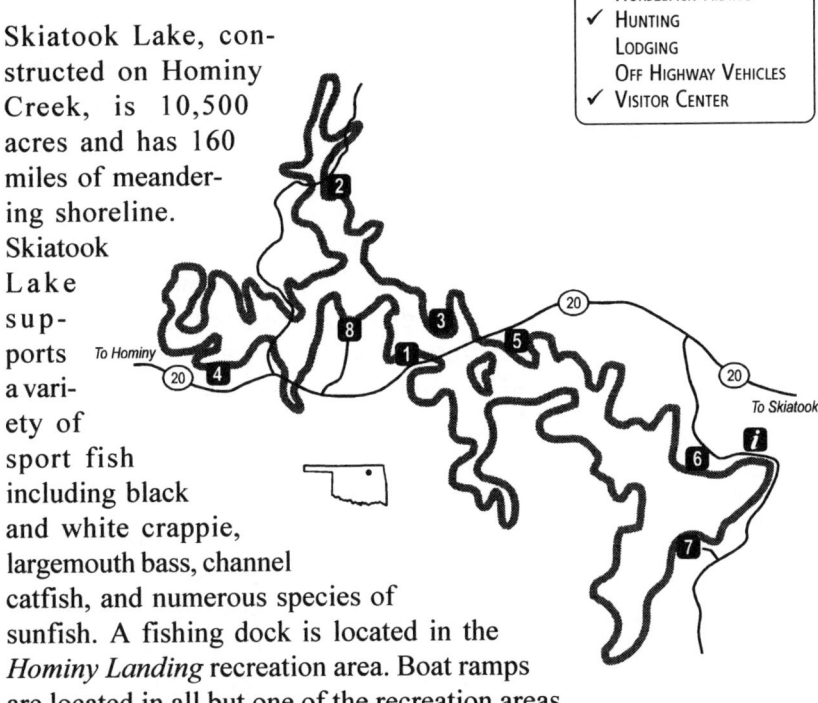

Information: U.S. Army Corps of Engineers, Skiatook Project Office, HC 67 Box 135, Skiatook OK 74070 / 918-396-3170.

Skiatook Lake												
1 Black Dog												•
2 Bull Creek Peninsula	26				•	•						•
3 Gouin Point	N	O		F	A	C	I	L	I	T	I	E	S

continued next page

Skiatook Lake *(continued)*	🅰 🚐 🚻 🚰 ⛽ 🚤 🏕 🚿 ⛴ 🏞 🚶 ⚓ 🛥													
4 Hominy Landing														•
5 Osage Park														•
6 Skiatook Point														•
7 Tall Chief Cove	57	57	•	•	•	•	•	•	•	•	•	•	•	•
8 Twin Points	54	54						•	•					•

Tenkiller Ferry Lake

Tenkiller Ferry Dam, on the Illinois River, is nestled in the Cookson Hills of eastern Oklahoma. The lake is 22 miles southeast of Muskogee and about seven miles northeast of Gore. The dam is reached from Gore by following SH 100. The project office is on the west end of the dam.

At A Glance
- Auto Touring
- Biking
- ✓ Boating
- Climbing
- ✓ Cultural or Historic Sites
- ✓ Camping
- Educational Programs
- ✓ Fishing
- ✓ Groceries / Supplies
- ✓ Hiking
- Horseback Riding
- ✓ Hunting
- ✓ Lodging
- Off Highway Vehicles
- ✓ Visitor Center

Tenkiller Lake is known by many as "Oklahoma's Clear Water Wonderland." The lake is known by fishermen, pleasure boaters and scuba divers as the best place for water-based activities. The project offers ten marinas and 15 campgrounds operated by the Corps, the state of Oklahoma, and concessionaires. Within the project are three nature trails ranging in length from 1¼ miles to over two miles. *Tenkiller State Park* has 40 cabins available for rent plus scuba diving, a nature center, marina with house and fishing boat rentals, and a restaurant and gift shop. Near the northern end of the lake is Tsa-La-Gi, an authentic recreation of a 1700's Cherokee village. The Trail of Tears drama is presented here.

Much of the land surrounding the lake is open to the public for hunting. Principal species of wildlife include white-tailed deer, wild turkey, bobwhite quail, mourning dove, duck, geese, cottontail rabbit and squirrel. A map of the hunting areas is available from the project office.

The 12,900-acre lake and every inch of the 130-mile shoreline is publicly owned; the boater is free to go ashore anywhere he wishes. The lake provides good year-round fishing for black bass, white bass, striped bass, crappie, catfish, bream and walleye. Rainbow trout is stocked in the Illinois River below the dam. There are five heated fishing docks offering winter fun for crappie fishing. Complete supplies and boat rentals are available at the numerous marinas located along the lake.

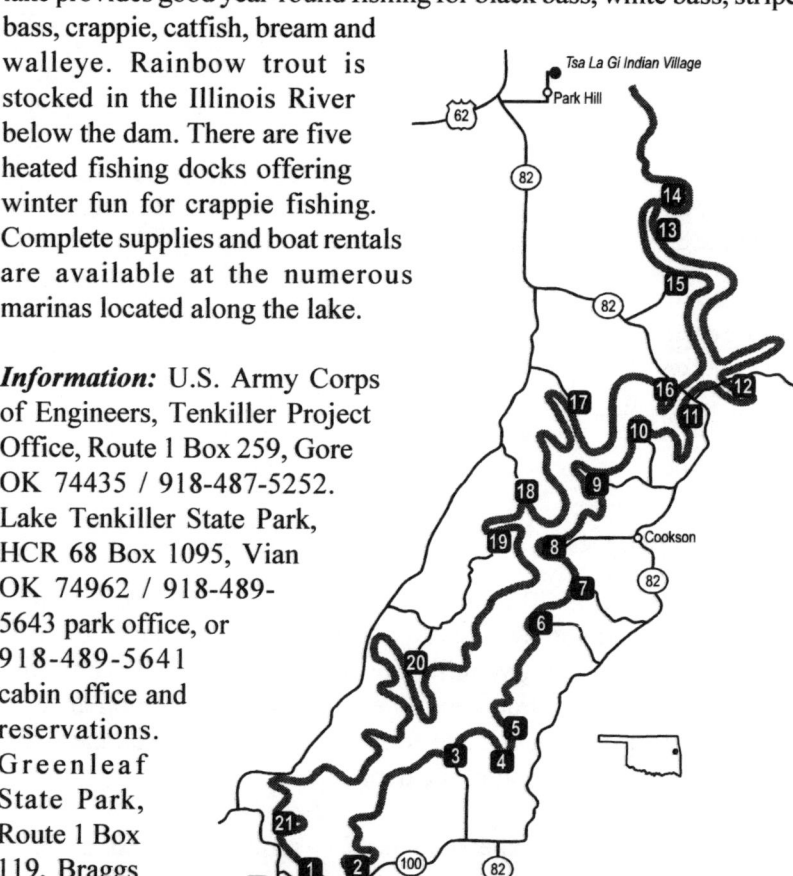

Information: U.S. Army Corps of Engineers, Tenkiller Project Office, Route 1 Box 259, Gore OK 74435 / 918-487-5252. Lake Tenkiller State Park, HCR 68 Box 1095, Vian OK 74962 / 918-489-5643 park office, or 918-489-5641 cabin office and reservations. Greenleaf State Park, Route 1 Box 119, Braggs OK 74423 / 918-487-5196.

Tenkiller Ferry Lake													
1 Overlook					•	•	•				•		
2 Tenkiller State Park	259	87	•	•	•	•	•	•	•			•	•
3 Blackgum Landing													•
4 Cato Creek Landing	•					•	•				•		•
5 Snake Creek Cove	44	12	•	•	•		•	•	•			•	•
6 Chicken Creek	101	59	•	•	•		•	•	•				•
7 Sixshooter	1	1					•					•	•

continued next page

Lake Texoma

Tenkiller Ferry (continued)														
8 Cookson Bend	105	66	•	•	•		•	•				•		•
9 Carlile Cove														•
10 Standing Rock Landing	10			•	•		•				•			
11 Elk Creek Landing	41	17	•	•	•		•		•				•	•
12 Caney Ridge				•	•		•						•	•
13 Etta Bend														•
14 Horshoe Bend							•		•					•
15 Carters Landing	31													•
16 Cherokee Landing	145	92	•	•	•		•	•	•					•
17 Pettit Bay	91	70	•	•	•		•	•	•				•	•
18 Sizemore Landing	32				•	•		•						•
19 Sizemore Cove	•	•	•	•			•						•	•
20 Burnt Cabin	•	•			•	•		•	•					
21 Strayhorn Landing	42	42	•	•	•		•	•	•				•	•
22 Trout Stream							•							

Lake Texoma

Denison Dam and Lake Texoma are located on the Red River in southern Oklahoma and northern Texas. The dam is about 15 miles south of Durant, Oklahoma and five miles north of Denison, Texas. Information about the lake and its recreation areas is available from the project office on the south end of the dam.

At A Glance
- Auto Touring
- ✓ Biking
- ✓ Boating
- Climbing
- ✓ Cultural or Historic Sites
- ✓ Camping
- ✓ Educational Programs
- ✓ Fishing
- ✓ Groceries / Supplies
- ✓ Hiking
- ✓ Horseback Riding
- ✓ Hunting
- ✓ Lodging
- Off Highway Vehicles
- ✓ Visitor Center

Lake Texoma, "Playground of the Southwest," offers a multitude of amenities for anyone who enjoys the outdoors. The horseback rider is treated to more than 40 miles of trails. For the hiker there is the Cross Timbers trail that winds 14 miles above the lake on rocky ledges through blackjack oak woodland. *Eisenhower State Park* provides nature/environment programs, a lighted fishing pier, 10-acre mini-bike area, 4½-mile hiking and nature study trail, and a Texas state park store. *Texoma State Park* in Oklahoma offers a 100-room resort, 67 cottages, 20-room lodge and lake huts. Visitors will also find a restaurant, waterfront lounge, nature center, indoor fitness & recreation center, horseback riding, hayrides, go-cart track, 18-hole golf course, bicycle rentals, and bumper boats. *Pennington Creek* park is operated by the city of Tishomingo. More than 20 additional parks on the lake are operated by private concession. Information about these areas is available from the Lake Texoma Association, phone 580-564-2334.

Wildlife enthusiasts will enjoy the two national wildlife refuges that have locations in both Oklahoma and Texas. Each year thousands of Canada and snow geese, various shorebirds, several species of ducks, and bald eagles migrate to the refuges.

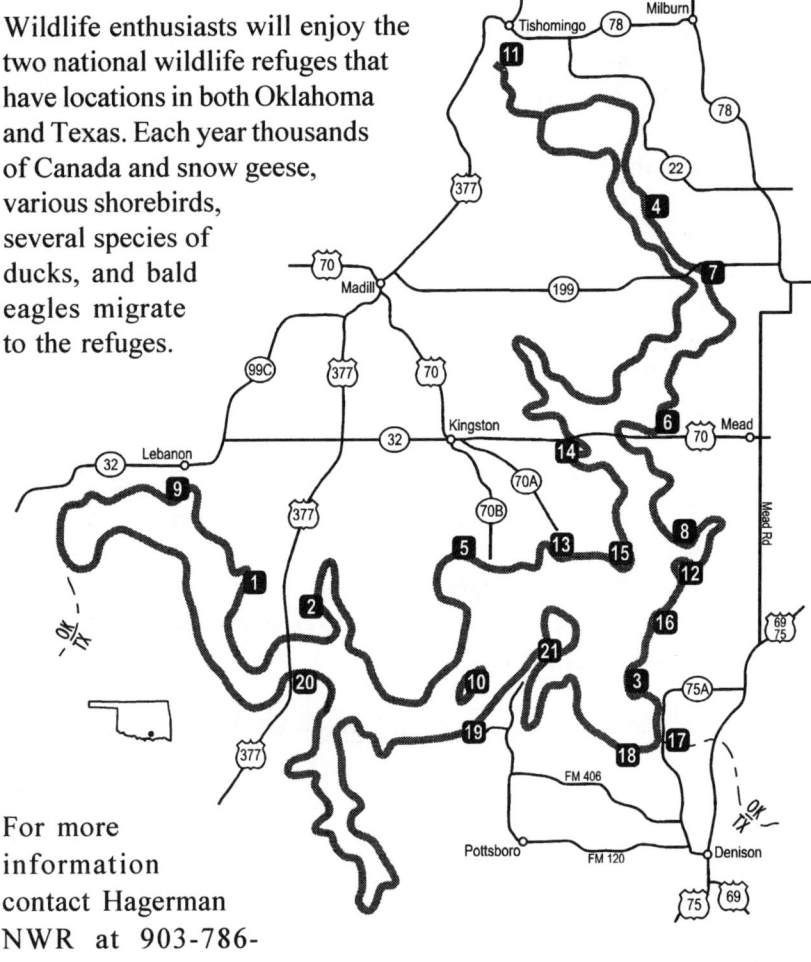

For more information contact Hagerman NWR at 903-786-2826 and the Tishomingo NWR at 580-371-2402.

About 80,000 acres of land within the project is open to the public for hunting. Wildlife inhabiting the area includes white-tailed deer, bobwhite quail, mourning dove, ducks, geese, cottontail rabbits, and squirrel. Maps showing the areas open for hunting are available from the project office. Hunters should note that a separate license is needed for each state, they are not reciprocal.

The 93,000-acre Lake Texoma with 580 miles of shoreline is the second most popular Corps lake in the country. It offers some of the best fishing in the nation as well. The lake is known as the "Striper Capital of the World" and is one of the few reservoirs in the nation where striped bass reproduce naturally. The striped bass was first introduced to the lake in 1969. Today, striped bass in excess of 25 pounds are being caught in the lake and tailwater below the dam. This anglers' paradise also offers channel and blue catfish, largemouth and smallmouth bass, white bass, white crappie, black crappie, and various sunfish. Complete camping, fishing, and boating supplies and services are available at the many marinas and concession services scattered around the lake. Striper and sand bass festivals are held in June. The boat ramp in *Preston Bend* is available for use only by those staying in the campground.

Information: U.S. Army Corps of Engineers, Lake Texoma Project Office, 351 Corps Rd., Denison TX 75020 / 903-465-4990. Lake Texoma State Park, Box 248, Kingston OK 73439 / 580-564-2311 resort lodge, 580-564-2566 park office. Eisenhower State Park, 50 Park Road 20, Denison TX 75020 / 903-465-1956. For information on private resorts, contact the Lake Texoma Association at 580-564-2334.

LAKE TEXOMA (OKLAHOMA)	△	▦	🚻	🚰	🪑	⛺	🏕	🚿	🏞	🎣	🚶	⚓	🏊
1 BRIAR CREEK	N	O	F	A	C	I	L	I	T	I	E	S	
2 BUNCOMBE CREEK	53	53	•	•			•	•					•
3 BURNS RUN	194	172	•	•	•	•	•	•	•		•		•
4 BUTCHER PEN	N	O	F	A	C	I	L	I	T	I	E	S	
5 CANEY CREEK	52	42	•	•	•	•	•	•			•		•
6 JOHNSON CREEK	55	55	•	•	•	•	•	•		•	•		•
7 KANSAS CREEK	N	O	F	A	C	I	L	I	T	I	E	S	
8 LAKESIDE	126	122	•	•	•	•	•	•			•		•
9 LEBANON	20	12					•						•
10 NORTH ISLAND						•							

continued next page

Oklahoma

LAKE TEXOMA OK *(continued)*	▲	🚐	🚻	🚰	⛱	🎣	🏪	🏊	⛵	🚶	⚓	〰
11 PENNINGTON CREEK	36	30	•	•	•		•	•				•	•
12 PLATTER FLATS	83	44	•	•	•		•					•		•
13 ROADS END													•
14 TEXOMA STATE PARK	927	697	•	•	•	•	•	•	•	•	•		•	•
15 WASHITA POINT													•
16 WILLAFA WOODS													•

LAKE TEXOMA (TEXAS)	▲	🚐	🚻	🚰	⛱	🎣	🏪	🏊	⛵	🚶	⚓	〰
17 DAMSITE AREA	28	20	•	•	•		•	•				•	•
18 EISENHOWER STATE PARK	143	95	•	•	•	•	•	•	•	•	•		•	•
19 HIGHPORT													•
20 JUNIPER POINT	70	44	•	•			•	•				•	•
21 PRESTON BEND REC. AREA	38	26	•	•			•	•					•

W.D. Mayo Lock and Dam

The W.D. Mayo Lock and Dam is in east-central Oklahoma about 75 miles southeast of Muskogee and 15 miles west of Fort Smith, Arkansas. The dam is reached from Spiro, Oklahoma by following SH 9/US 271 east a few miles and then north on CR N4750. Additional information is available from the lockmaster.

AT A GLANCE
AUTO TOURING
BIKING
✓ BOATING
CLIMBING
CULTURAL OR HISTORIC SITES
✓ CAMPING
EDUCATIONAL PROGRAMS
✓ FISHING
GROCERIES / SUPPLIES
HIKING
HORSEBACK RIDING
✓ HUNTING
LODGING
OFF HIGHWAY VEHICLES
VISITOR CENTER

This lock and dam structure is the first unit in the Oklahoma portion of the McClellan-Kerr Arkansas River Navigation System. The lake formed behind this dam extends 16 miles to the Robert S. Kerr Lock and Dam. It has a surface area of 1,050 acres. Two recreation areas have been developed near the dam. On the north bank is *Wilson's Rock*, a day-use area. *LeFlore Landing* is on the south bank of the river and has camping facilities for tents and RVs.

Principal species of fish include channel and flathead catfish, largemouth bass, crappie, striped bass, walleye, and various sunfish. Boat ramps are available in both parks. Boating and fishing supplies can be found in Spiro.

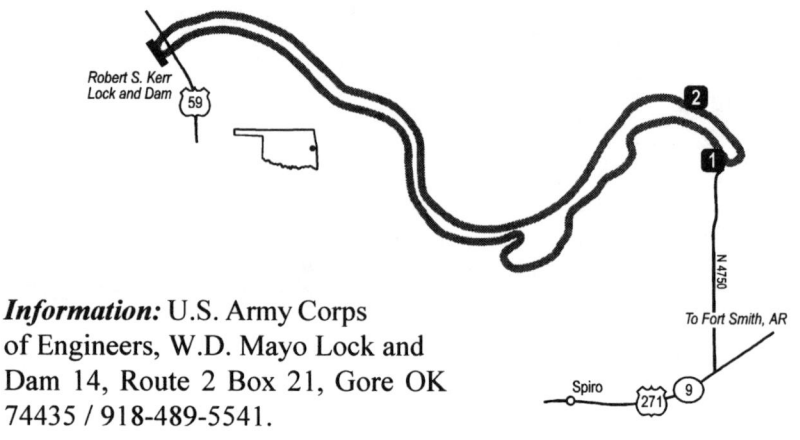

Information: U.S. Army Corps of Engineers, W.D. Mayo Lock and Dam 14, Route 2 Box 21, Gore OK 74435 / 918-489-5541.

W.D. Mayo Lock & Dam	🔺	🚐	🚻	🚰	🛣	🛶	🏨	🍴	🏊	🛢	🚶	⚓	〰
1 LeFlore Landing	•		•	•	•		•	•					•
2 Wilson's Rock				•	•		•						•

Waurika Lake

Waurika Lake lies in southwest Oklahoma six miles north of Waurika and 18 miles south of Duncan. Follow SH 5 from Waurika to reach the dam. Information about the project is available from the project office on the east end of the dam.

The dam forming Waurika Lake was constructed on Beaver Creek, a tributary of the Red River. The lake is set among rolling prairie interspersed with cropland and wooded areas. Boating and skiing enthusiasts enjoy the lake's large open areas of water. Six developed parks around the lake provide such facilities as campgrounds, picnic areas, showers, and swimming beaches. Campgrounds are located in all but one of the parks.

Over 6,000 acres of land within the project is managed for wildlife by the Oklahoma Department of Wildlife Conservation. This land is open

At A Glance	
	Auto Touring
✓	Biking
✓	Boating
	Climbing
	Cultural or Historic Sites
✓	Camping
	Educational Programs
✓	Fishing
✓	Groceries / Supplies
✓	Hiking
✓	Horseback Riding
✓	Hunting
✓	Lodging
	Off Highway Vehicles
✓	Visitor Center

to the public for hunting. Wildlife found in the area includes whitetailed deer, bobwhite quail, mourning dove, cottontail rabbit, wild turkey, and various waterfowl. Maps are available from the project office showing the location of the public hunting areas.

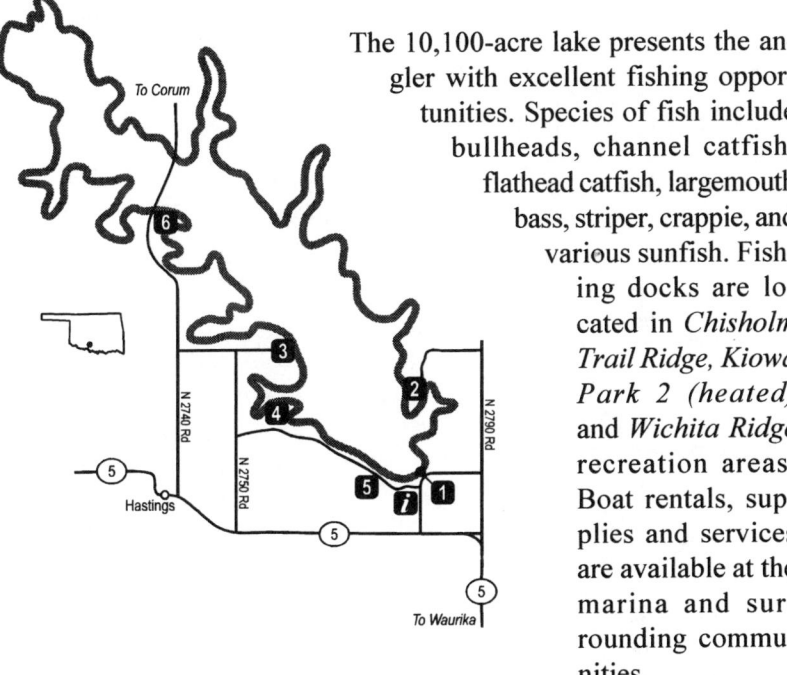

The 10,100-acre lake presents the angler with excellent fishing opportunities. Species of fish include bullheads, channel catfish, flathead catfish, largemouth bass, striper, crappie, and various sunfish. Fishing docks are located in *Chisholm Trail Ridge, Kiowa Park 2 (heated)* and *Wichita Ridge* recreation areas. Boat rentals, supplies and services are available at the marina and surrounding communities.

Information: U.S. Army Corps of Engineers, Waurika Lake Project Office, P.O. Box 29, Waurika OK 73573 / 580-963-2111.

Waurika Lake													
1 Beaver Creek Landing								•					•
2 Chisholm Trail Ridge	95	95	•	•	•	•	•	•	•				•
3 Kiowa Park 1	180	180	•	•	•	•	•	•	•	•			•
4 Kiowa Park 2	19	19		•	•		•				•	•	
5 Moneka Park	38			•	•		•			•			
6 Wichita Ridge	27	10		•	•		•			•			•

Webbers Falls Lock and Dam

Webbers Falls Lock and Dam is in east-central Oklahoma about 27 miles southeast of Muskogee. The project is a unit in the McClellan-Kerr Arkansas River Navigation System. To reach the dam from Muskogee, travel 20 miles south on Muskogee Turnpike, then five miles east on US 64 and north two miles on SH 10. Information is available from the project office located near the east end of the lock and dam.

Near the lock and dam is an observation platform where visitors can watch the lock in operation. On a bluff above the powerhouse is a scenic overlook that offers a view of the lock and dam and a large area of the lake. Those interested in hiking can access the Jean Pierre Chouteau National Recreation Trail in *Fort Gibson* park. This trail is 64 miles long and extends from *Fort Gibson* park to Rogers Point in the Newt Graham project. The trail runs through several recreation areas that provide hikers a place to camp. Wildlife common to the area includes white-tailed deer, bobwhite quail, mourning dove, rabbit, squirrel, and opossum.

The lock and dam constructed on the Arkansas River forms a 10,500 acre lake encompassing 28 miles of the river.

At A Glance	
	Auto Touring
	Biking
✓	Boating
	Climbing
	Cultural or Historic Sites
✓	Camping
	Educational Programs
✓	Fishing
	Groceries / Supplies
✓	Hiking
	Horseback Riding
✓	Hunting
	Lodging
	Off Highway Vehicles
	Visitor Center

The project offers year-round fishing opportunities. Fish species include catfish, white and black bass, crappie, bream, walleye, sauger, buffalo, carp, and a rapidly growing population of striped bass. Bait, tackle, and boat rentals are available near the project.

Information: U.S. Army Corps of Engineers, Webbers Falls Lock and Dam 16, Route 2 Box 21, Gore OK 74435 / 918-489-5541.

Webber's Falls Lock & Dam	▲	🚐	🚻	🚿	🛣	🍴	🏛	🗼	🏊	🚶	⚓	〰
1 Lock & Dam Area					•	•						
2 Brewer Bend	39	31	•	•	•			•	•	•		•
3 Spaniard Creek	32	32	•	•	•			•	•			•
4 Hopewell Park	•		•	•	•			•	•			•
5 Arrowhead Point	•		•	•	•			•	•			•
6 Fort Gibson Park	•		•	•	•			•			•	•
7 Canyon Road	•	•	•	•	•			•	•			•
8 Three Forks Ramp				•	•			•				•
9 Greenleaf Cove					•	•						

Wister Lake

Wister Lake is in the San Bois Mountains of east-central Oklahoma about 65 miles east of McAlester. To reach the dam from Wister, follow US 270 southeast for two miles. The project office is on the south end of the dam.

Construction of Wister Lake began in 1946 and was placed in full operation in 1949. The project is listed on the National Register of Historic Places. Surrounding the lake are wooded areas of dogwood, redbud, wild cherry, northern spruce, and ponderosa pine. Organized groups come from all over to view the area's vibrant fall colors. The Ouachita National Forest lies to the south of the project.

At A Glance
- Auto Touring
- ✓ Biking
- ✓ Boating
- Climbing
- ✓ Cultural or Historic Sites
- ✓ Camping
- Educational Programs
- ✓ Fishing
- ✓ Groceries / Supplies
- ✓ Hiking
- ✓ Horseback Riding
- ✓ Hunting
- ✓ Lodging
- Off Highway Vehicles
- ✓ Visitor Center

Nine recreation areas surround the lake. The parks are managed by the state as units of *Lake Wister State Park*. Nearly 200 campsites in four parks accommodate tents and recreational vehicles. Approximately 100 campsites have hookups for RVs. In addition to camping facilities, 15 cabins are available for rent. The state park also offers a gift shop, bicycle rentals, miniature golf, a family activity center, and hiking and bicycling trails. *Lake Wister State Park* is open year-round.

The Oklahoma Department of Wildlife Conservation manages more than 33,000 acres for wildlife. Most of this land is open to the public for hunting. Maps of the hunting areas are available from the project office. Wildlife found in the region includes bobwhite quail, wild turkey, white-tailed deer, mourning dove, and a variety of waterfowl.

Wister Lake is on the Poteau River, a tributary of the Arkansas River. It is the only river in Oklahoma that flows northward. Wister Lake is fairly shallow and covers approximately 7,300 surface acres. Species of fish found in the lake include channel catfish, flathead catfish, sand bass, small and largemouth bass, crappie, and various sunfish. Services and supplies are available at the concession operations and on lake access roads.

Information: U.S. Army Corps of Engineers, Wister Lake Office, Route 3 Box 100, Wister OK 74966 / 918-655-7206. Lake Wister State Park, Route 3 Box 70, Wister OK 74966 / 918-655-7756 park office, 918-655-7212 cabin reservations. For information on private resorts call the Wister Lake Association at 918-655-7217.

Oklahoma

Wister Lake	⛺	🚐	🚻	🥤	🛣	🛶	🍽	🚿	🛢	🚶	⚓	〰
1 Overlook												•
2 Fanny Creek	N	O		F	A	C	I	L	I	T	I	E S
3 Potts Mountain												•
4 Conser Crossing												•
5 Heavener Landing	N	O		F	A	C	I	L	I	T	I	E S
6 Victor Area	•	•	•	•	•	•	•	•		•		•
7 Wards Landing	•			•	•		•	•		•	•	•
8 Quarry Island	•	•	•	•	•	•	•	•	•		•	•
9 Damsite	•	•		•	•	•	•					•

OREGON

1. Applegate Lake
2. Blue River Lake
3. Lake Bonneville
4. Lake Celilo
5. Cottage Grove Lake
6. Cougar Lake
7. Detroit Lake
8. Dorena Lake
9. Fall Creek Lake
10. Fern Ridge Lake
11. Foster & Green Peter Lakes
12. Hills Creek Lake
13. Lookout Point & Dexter Lakes
14. Lost Creek Lake
15. Lake Umatilla
16. Lake Wallula

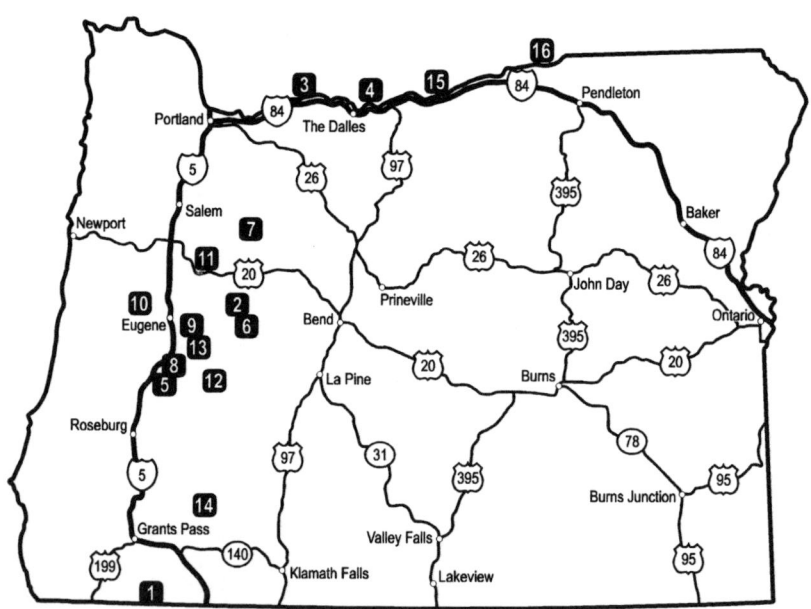

Oregon Resources

- ***Oregon Tourism Commission*** - 775 Summer St. NE, Salem OR 97310 / (800) 547-7842 or (503) 986-0000
- ***Oregon Department of Fish & Wildlife*** - (503) 872-5268
- ***Road Condition Hotline*** - (800) 977-6368 or (541) 889-3999 (recording)

Applegate Lake

Applegate Lake is located in southwest Oregon, 23 miles southwest of Medford in the Rogue River National Forest. To reach the lake from Medford, follow SH 238 west to the town of Ruch and then south on Applegate Street.

At A Glance
Auto Touring
✓ Biking
✓ Boating
Climbing
Cultural or Historic Sites
✓ Camping
Educational Programs
✓ Fishing
✓ Groceries / Supplies
✓ Hiking
✓ Horseback Riding
Hunting
Lodging
Off Highway Vehicles
Visitor Center

The forested slopes and often snow-covered peaks of the Siskiyou Mountains are reflected in the clear blue waters of Applegate Lake. It is in this scenic setting that the U.S. Forest Service operates the hike-in campgrounds and lakeside recreation areas surrounding the lake. Applegate Lake extends to the California border and offers a hiking trail that follows the 18-mile shoreline. Several other trails are around the project for hiking, horseback riding, mountain biking, and limited motorcycle riding. Development at most of the recreation areas is minimal and most of the lakeshore has been maintained in a natural state.

At full pool, which is usually around May or June, Applegate Lake covers 988 acres and is over four miles long. Fishing is good below the dam for steelhead trout. Catches in the lake include smallmouth bass, catfish, crappie, and an occasional steelhead or coho salmon. Fishing for trout and salmon is best in the fall and spring. From spring until just after Labor Day, *Hart-tish* offers a small store with food and fishing supplies.

Fishermen should note that just after Labor Day the level of the lake is dropped steadily until it reaches low pool, around 205 acres.

Information: U.S. Army Corps of Engineers, Applegate Lake, Rogue River Basin Projects, 100 Cole M Rivers Drive, Trail OR 97541 / 541-878-2255. U.S. Forest Service, Rogue River National Forest, Applegate Ranger District, 6941 Upper Applegate Rd., Jacksonville OR 97530 / 541-899-1812.

APPLEGATE LAKE	🏕	🚐	🚻	🚰	⛱	🛶	🚽	🛣	🔥	🗑	🚶	⚓	🏊
1 CARBERRY	•		•		•								
2 WATKINS	•		•		•					•			
3 HART-TISH	•		•	•	•			•			•	•	
4 SWAYNE VIEWPOINT			•	•	•					•			
5 FRENCH GULCH	•		•		•					•			•
6 COPPER BOAT RAMP							•						•
7 STRINGTOWN	7		•	•	•			•					
8 HARR POINT	5				•			•					
9 LATGAWA COVE	5				•			•					
10 TIPSU-TYEE	5				•			•					
11 FRENCH GULCH BOAT RAMP							•						•
12 SEATTLE BAR		•	•		•			•		•			
13 LAKE ACCESS				•									

Blue River Lake

Blue River Lake is located in west-central Oregon 40 miles east of Eugene. To reach the dam from Eugene, follow SH 126 east to the community of Blue River.

The recreation areas on Blue River Lake lie within the Willamette National Forest at the foothills of the Cascade Mountains. The sites are operated and maintained by the U.S. Forest Service. *Mona Campground* has camping facilities with 23 sites suitable for tents and recreation vehicles. *Lookout Creek* area has open-meadow type camping allowing for group camping.

AT A GLANCE
✓ AUTO TOURING
BIKING
✓ BOATING
CLIMBING
CULTURAL OR HISTORIC SITES
✓ CAMPING
EDUCATIONAL PROGRAMS
✓ FISHING
GROCERIES / SUPPLIES
HIKING
HORSEBACK RIDING
✓ HUNTING
LODGING
OFF HIGHWAY VEHICLES
VISITOR CENTER

Nearby is the Robert Aufderheide Memorial Drive, an officially designated National Forest Scenic Byway. This scenic drive follows FSR 19

Oregon

south for 65 miles to the town of Westfir. A free audio cassette of the tour is available from the ranger station in Blue River. The drive skirts the shore of Cougar Lake, another Corps of Engineers project.

Blue River Lake is a scenic 1,420-acre lake with many miles of forested shoreline. Fishing below the dam yields steelhead trout. The lake offers anglers smallmouth bass, catfish, crappie and an occasional steelhead or coho salmon. Fishing for trout and salmon is best in the fall and spring. Boat ramps are located in two recreation areas.

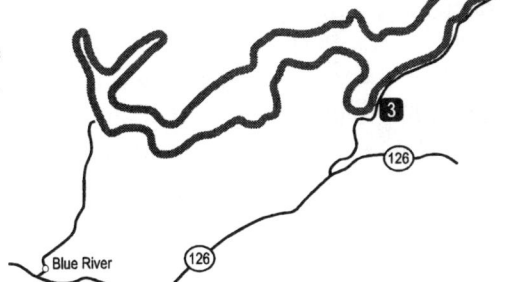

Principal game for the hunter includes waterfowl, quail, deer, rabbit, and osprey. Maps of public hunting areas are available from the national forest ranger station in Blue River.

Information: U.S. Army Corps of Engineers, Blue River Lake, P.O. Box 429, Lowell OR 97452 / 541-937-2131. U.S. Forest Service, Willamette National Forest, Blue River Ranger District, Blue River OR 97413 / 541-822-3317.

Blue River Lake												
1 Mona Campground	23		•		•							
2 Lookout Creek Ramp	50		•	•	•							•
3 Saddle Dam					•							•

Lake Bonneville

Located in the Columbia River Gorge National Scenic Area 40 miles east of Portland, Oregon and Vancouver, Washington. To reach the Bonneville Dam from Portland, follow I-84 east to Exit 40; from Vancouver, follow SH 14 east to milepost 40.

At A Glance
- ✓ Auto Touring
- ✓ Biking
- ✓ Boating
-   Climbing
- ✓ Cultural or Historic Sites
- ✓ Camping
- ✓ Educational Programs
- ✓ Fishing
- ✓ Groceries / Supplies
- ✓ Hiking
-   Horseback Riding
- ✓ Hunting
-   Lodging
-   Off Highway Vehicles
- ✓ Visitor Center

Bonneville Lock and Dam, a National Historic Landmark, spans the Columbia River linking Oregon and Washington. With one of the largest public viewing facilities in the Corps of Engineers, visitors have lots to see and learn at Bonneville. Three visitor centers, two in Oregon, are open all year except on major holidays. The Bridge of the Gods, a toll bridge about three miles upstream in Cascade Locks, Oregon, provides easy access between the Oregon and Washington visitor centers.

Those interested in camping will find four recreation areas along the lake. *Eagle Creek* and *Wyeth* campgrounds are operated and maintained by the U.S. Forest Service. These offer a more primitive setting than the two state parks, *Viento* and *Memaloose*. A hiking trail chiseled into the cliffs above Eagle Creek begins in the park with the same name. The trail passes Metalko, Punch Bowl, Loowit, and Tunnel Falls before joining the Pacific Crest National Scenic Trail.

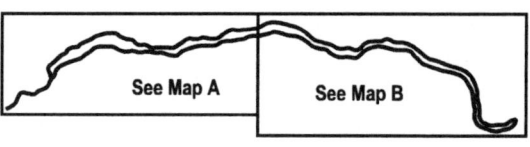

Fort Cascades park, on the Washington side, is a National Historic Site. The 59-acre area includes a hiking trail, portions of the old portage railroad, a Chinook Indian village, and one of the three military forts near the Cascades Rapids.

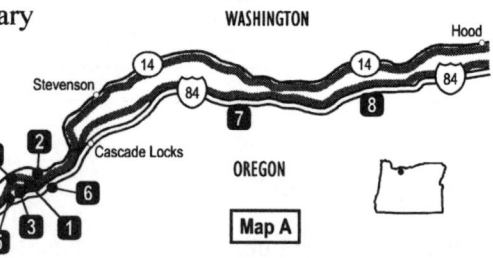

Rugged rock walls of the Columbia River Gorge rise to 2,000 feet above this 48 mile long reservoir. The angler will find many good spots to drop a line. Fishing the waters produce chinook, coho, and sockeye salmon,

Oregon

steelhead trout, smallmouth bass, walleye, shad, and sturgeon. Fishing for trout and salmon is best in the fall and spring.

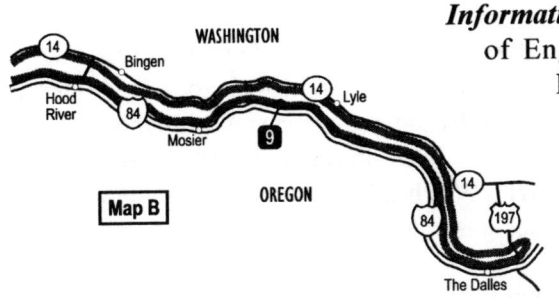

Map B

Information: U.S. Army Corps of Engineers, Bonneville Lock & Dam, Cascade Locks OR 97014 / 541-374-8442. Columbia River Gorge National Scenic Area, Hood River OR 97031 / 541-386-2333. Viento State Park, P.O. Box 472, Mosier OR 97040 / 541-374-8811. Memaloose State Park, P.O. Box 126, Hood River OR 97031 / 541-478-3008.

LAKE BONNEVILLE	▲	🚐	🚻	🪑	🚿	💧	🏪	📷	⛵	🏊	🚶	⚓	〰️
1 BRADFORD ISLAND					•	•			•				
2 WASHINGTON SHORE					•	•				•	•		
3 NAVIGATION LOCK							•						
4 FT. CASCADES					•	•			•				
5 BONNEVILLE FISH HATCHERY					•	•							
6 EAGLE CREEK CAMPGROUND	20				•	•			•	•			
7 WYETH CAMPGROUND	17					•	•						
8 VIENTO STATE PARK	75	58	•	•		•	•			•			
9 MEMALOOSE STATE PARK	110	43	•	•	•		•	•					

Lake Celilo

Lake Celilo is located in north-central Oregon 80 miles east of Portland and two miles east of The Dalles, Oregon. The Dalles Lock and Dam, constructed on the Columbia River, extends nearly two miles from the Oregon shore to the navigation lock on the Washington shore. A visitor center is located on the Oregon side of the lock and dam. It can be reached from I-84 by taking Exit 87.

Visitors may wish to catch the train ride at the visitor center in *Seufert Park*. The train takes visitors to the fish ladder and powerhouse for a

At A Glance
- ✓ Auto Touring
- ✓ Biking
- ✓ Boating
- ✓ Climbing
- ✓ Cultural or Historic Sites
- ✓ Camping
- ✓ Educational Programs
- ✓ Fishing
- ✓ Groceries / Supplies
- ✓ Hiking
- ✓ Horseback Riding
- ✓ Hunting
-   Lodging
-   Off Highway Vehicles
- ✓ Visitor Center

guided tour. Hours of operation vary depending on the time of year, contact the visitor center at 541-296-9778 for information.

Horsethief Lake State Park contains a large concentration of prehistoric rock art, both pictographs and petroglyphs. Within this National Historic Site is the petroglyph "Tsagaglalal - She Who Watches," one of the most famous rock art designs along the Columbia River.

Lake Celilo encompasses 24 miles of the Columbia River between the Dalles Lock and Dam and John Day Lock and Dam. Anglers will find good opportunities for catching walleye, trout, sturgeon, and bass. Fall and spring are the most productive times for steelhead and salmon fishing. General supplies are available from the concession service in *The Dalles Boat Basin* park.

Information: U.S. Army Corps of Engineers, The Dalles Lock & Dam - Lake Celilo, P.O. Box 564, The Dalles OR 97058 / 541-296-1181. Horsethief State Park, P.O. Box 426, Dalles Port WA 98617 / 509-767-1159. Maryhill State Park, 50 Highway 97, Goldendale WA 98620 / 509-773-5007. Deschutes State Park, 89600 Biggs-Rufus Hwy., Wasco OR 97065 / 541-739-2322. North Wasco County Parks and Recreation District, 541-296-9533.

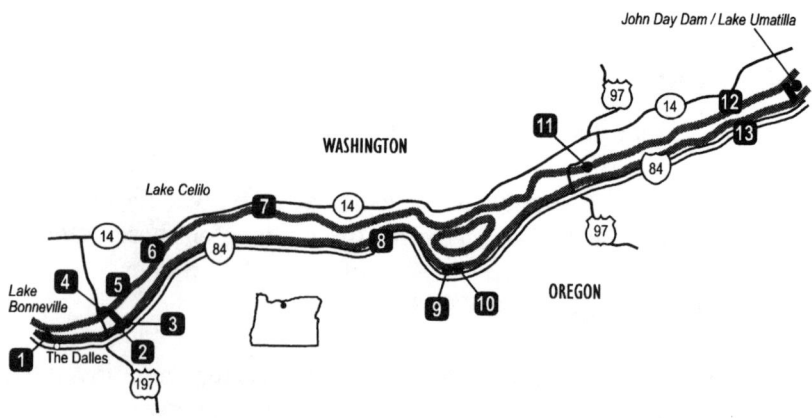

Oregon

Lake Celilo	⛺	🚐	🚽	💧	🪑	🎣	🏠	🚿	🏊	🚶	⚓	〰️
1 The Dalles Boat Basin				•	•		•				•	•
2 Seufert Park & Tour Train				•	•		•					•
3 The Dalles Dam				•	•		•					•
4 Hess Park					•							
5 Spearfish Park	•	•			•		•			•		•
6 Horsethief Lake State Park	12		•	•	•		•			•		•
7 Avery Boat Ramp	•	•			•		•					•
8 Celilo Park				•	•	•			•			•
9 Heritage Landing				•	•		•					•
10 Deschutes State Park	34	•		•	•		•			•		•
11 Maryhill State Park	70	50	•	•	•		•	•	•		•	•
12 The Cliffs	•				•		•					•
13 Giles French Park	•	•		•	•		•				•	•

Cottage Grove Lake

Cottage Grove Lake, on the Coast Fork of the Willamette River, is located about 20 miles south of Eugene in west-central Oregon. To reach the lake from Eugene, follow I-5 south to the London Road exit (Exit 172) and then go south about three miles. The project office is on Shortridge Hill Road near the west end of the dam.

At A Glance

Auto Touring
Biking
✓ Boating
Climbing
Cultural or Historic Sites
✓ Camping
✓ Educational Programs
✓ Fishing
Groceries / Supplies
Hiking
Horseback Riding
✓ Hunting
Lodging
Off Highway Vehicles
Visitor Center

Cottage Grove Lake is situated among the gently rolling hills of Oregon's Willamette Valley. The shoreline is managed to provide habitat for a wide variety of wildlife species including waterfowl, black-tailed deer, upland game birds, song birds, bald eagles, and osprey. Maps and information on hunting opportunities are available from the project office.

When Cottage Grove Lake is full, it covers 1,158 acres and stretches three miles. Anglers will find bass, rainbow trout, steelhead, walleye, crappie, and salmon in the river and lake. Fishing for trout and salmon is best in the fall and spring. In *Riverside Park* there is a paved path that has pull-outs suitable for wheelchairs and is close enough to the river for fishing.

Information: U.S. Army Corps of Engineers, Cottage Grove Lake, 75819 Shortridge Hill Road, Cottage Grove OR 97424 / 541-942-5631.

COTTAGE GROVE LAKE												
1 SHORTRIDGE				•	•		•					
2 WILSON CREEK				•	•	•	•		•			•
3 LAKESIDE				•	•		•		•			•
4 PINE MEADOWS	92		•	•			•	•	•	•	•	
5 PRIMITIVE CAMPGROUND	15			•			•					
6 RIVERSIDE PARK						•						

Cougar Lake

Cougar Lake lies within the Willamette National Forest in west-central Oregon about 42 miles east of Eugene. To reach the dam from Eugene travel east on SH 126 to FSR 19, which is about five miles east of the community of Blue River. Three miles south on FSR 19 takes you to the dam and two visitor viewpoints, one on each end of the dam. The two viewpoints offer spectacular views of the valley downstream and the vistas upstream around the lake.

AT A GLANCE
✓ AUTO TOURING
✓ BIKING
✓ BOATING
CLIMBING
CULTURAL OR HISTORIC SITES
✓ CAMPING
✓ EDUCATIONAL PROGRAMS
✓ FISHING
GROCERIES / SUPPLIES
✓ HIKING
HORSEBACK RIDING
✓ HUNTING
LODGING
OFF HIGHWAY VEHICLES
VISITOR CENTER

All of the lake's recreation areas are within the Willamette National Forest and are operated by U.S. Forest Service. All six have camping facilities for tents and recreational vehicles, however, none provide hookups.

Cougar Lake lies adjacent to the Robert Aufderheide Memorial Drive, a National Forest Scenic Byway. This scenic drive follows FSR 19 south for 65 miles to the town of Westfir. A free audio cassette of the tour is available from the ranger station in Blue River.

Cougar Lake is on the South Fork of the McKenzie River in Oregon's Willamette Valley region. A steep shoreline surrounds the scenic 1,280-acre lake with many miles of forested shoreline. The lake has a good reputation for trout fishing. Anglers will also find salmon, bass, catfish, crappie, walleye, steelhead, shad, and sockeye. Fishing for trout and salmon is best in the fall and spring. Boat ramps are located in three areas.

Information: U.S. Army Corps of Engineers, Cougar Lake Project Office, P.O. Box 429, Lowell OR 97452 / 541-533-3344. U.S. Forest Service, Willamette National Forest, Blue River Ranger District, Blue River OR 97413 / 541-822-3317.

COUGAR LAKE												
1 DELTA	38		•			•			•	•		
2 ECHO					•	•				•		•
3 SLIDE CREEK	16	•	•		•		•					•
4 SUNNYSIDE	13					•						
5 FRENCH PETE	17			•		•						
6 COUGAR CROSSING	12				•	•						•

Detroit Lake

Detroit Lake is located in the rugged mountain forests below Mount Jefferson in west-central Oregon. The project lies within the Willamette National Forest about 45 miles southeast of Salem along SH 22. The national forest has a ranger station just west of the town of Detroit where information is available.

The Detroit Lake project consists of two dams and two lakes: Detroit and Big Cliff. Big Cliff is a regulating dam and small reservoir located three miles downstream from Detroit Dam. There are no developed

> **AT A GLANCE**
> AUTO TOURING
> BIKING
> ✓ BOATING
> CLIMBING
> CULTURAL OR HISTORIC SITES
> ✓ CAMPING
> EDUCATIONAL PROGRAMS
> ✓ FISHING
> ✓ GROCERIES / SUPPLIES
> HIKING
> HORSEBACK RIDING
> HUNTING
> LODGING
> OFF HIGHWAY VEHICLES
> VISITOR CENTER

recreation areas on Big Cliff. The *Mongold* day use area and *Detroit Lake State Park* are operated by the Oregon Parks Department. The remaining recreation areas are managed by the U.S. Forest Service. There are 12 no-fee tent campsites on *Piety Island*. The amphitheater in the state park offers interpretive programs during the summer.

Both lakes were constructed in 1953 on the North Santiam River. Detroit Lake is the principal facility and provides 32 miles of wooded shoreline and 3,500 surface acres. Anglers will find good opportunities for chinook salmon, rainbow trout, and steelhead trout. Boat rentals, tackle, and general supplies are available from the marina and merchants in the community of Detroit. Please note that the water level at Detroit Lake varies according to downstream water and power requirements. During the recreation season, May to September, the lake is kept at the highest possible level.

Information: U.S. Army Corps of Engineers, Detroit Lake, P.O. Box 429, Lowell OR 97452 / 541-937-2131. U.S. Forest Service, Willamette National Forest, Detroit Ranger District, 48 N. Santiam Hwy., Detroit OR 97342 / 503-854-3366 or *mailing address* Willamette National Forest, HC 73 Box 320, Mill City OR 97360. Detroit Lake State Park, P.O. Box 549, Detroit OR 97342 / 503-854-3406. Campsite reservations, 800-452-5687.

DETROIT LAKE													
1 MONGOLD DAY USE AREA		•	•			•		•					•
2 DETROIT LAKE STATE PARK	311 179		•		•	•	•	•	•				•

continued next page

Oregon

DETROIT LAKE (continued)	▲	🚐	🚻	🍴	🏕	🏨	🚿	🎣	⬤	🚶	⚓	🌊
3 TOWN OF DETROIT		•	•		•				•			
4 HOOVER CAMPGROUND	37		•		•							•
5 PIETY ISLAND	12			•	•							
6 SOUTH SHORE CAMPGROUND	32		•	•	•							•
7 VIEWPOINT			•		•							
8 COVE CREEK CAMPGROUND	63				•			•	•			•

Dorena Lake

Dorena Lake is located in west-central Oregon in the foothills of the Cascade Mountains. The lake is nearly 20 miles south of Eugene and six miles east of Cottage Grove. To reach the lake from Cottage Grove, travel south on I-5 to the Row River Road exit (Exit 174). Head east on Row River Road to the dam and viewpoint area.

Dorena Lake was constructed on Row River and completed in 1949. The lake is set among the rolling and wooded hills of Oregon's Willamette Valley. The Corps of Engineers operates and maintains *Schwarz Park*, which offers camping facilities for tents and recreational vehicles. The two other recreation areas are operated by Lane County.

At A Glance
AUTO TOURING
✓ BIKING
✓ BOATING
CLIMBING
CULTURAL OR HISTORIC SITES
✓ CAMPING
✓ EDUCATIONAL PROGRAMS
✓ FISHING
✓ GROCERIES / SUPPLIES
✓ HIKING
HORSEBACK RIDING
✓ HUNTING
LODGING
OFF HIGHWAY VEHICLES
✓ VISITOR CENTER

The 1,749-acre Dorena Lake offers good year-round fishing opportunities below the dam for chinook salmon, rainbow and steelhead trout. Fishing for salmon and trout is best in the fall and spring. Other species in the lake include smallmouth bass, catfish, and crappie. Bait, tackle, and boat rentals are available at the *Baker Bay* concessionaire, phone 541-942-7669.

Information: U.S. Army Corps of Engineers, Dorena Lake Project Office, 75819 Shortridge Hill Road, Cottage Grove OR 97424 / 541-942-5631. Lane County Parks Department, 3040 N. Delta Hwy., Eugene OR 97408 / 541-682-6940.

Dorena Lake	▲	🚐	🚻	🚰	🍴	🎣	🏕	🚿	🧺	🥾	⚓	〰
1 Baker Bay	49	49	•	•	•		•	•	•		•	•
2 Harms Park				•	•							•
3 Schwarz Park	72	70	•	•		•	•	•		•		

Fall Creek Lake

Fall Creek Lake is in west-central Oregon about 25 miles southeast of Eugene. To reach the lake from Eugene, follow I-5 south to SH 58 (Exit 188). Travel southeast on SH 58 about 13 miles and head north through the town of Lowell to Big Fall Creek Road. Visitor viewpoints are located on each end of the dam.

> **At A Glance**
> Auto Touring
> Biking
> ✓ Boating
> Climbing
> Cultural or Historic Sites
> ✓ Camping
> Educational Programs
> ✓ Fishing
> Groceries / Supplies
> ✓ Hiking
> Horseback Riding
> ✓ Hunting
> Lodging
> Off Highway Vehicles
> Visitor Center

Visitors to the project will find seven recreation areas around the lake operated and maintained by Oregon State Parks. *North Shore Park* and *Winberry Creek* are day-use areas. *Cascara* is the primary campground on Fall Creek Lake. *Fisherman's Point* is a group camping area but may be used by individuals when not used by a group. The remaining recreation areas are minimally developed day-use parks.

Located a few miles east of the *Cascara* campground is the Fall Creek National Recreation Trail. This 14-mile trail meanders along Fall Creek into the Willamette National Forest. The trailhead is easily accessed from FSR

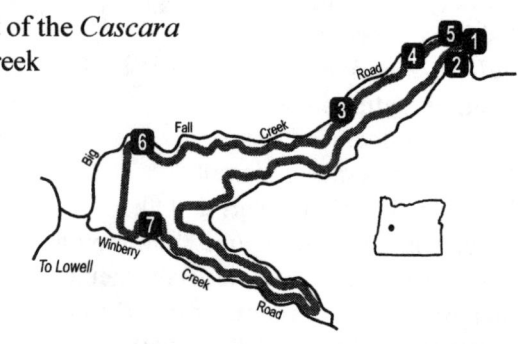

18 just south of Dolly Varden Campground.

The scenic 1,852-acre Fall Creek Lake offers 22 miles of forested shoreline for the fisherman. Downstream from the dam, anglers can fish year round for rainbow trout, chinook salmon and steelhead trout. Other species found in the lake include bass and crappie. Spring and fall are the best times of the year for catching trout and salmon.

Information: U.S. Army Corps of Engineers, Fall Creek Lake, P.O. Box 429, Lowell OR 97452 / 541-937-2131. Oregon State Parks, Fall Creek Lake, P.O. Box 511, Lowell OR 97452 / 541-937-1173.

Fall Creek Lake	🏕	🚐	🚻	🚰	⛱	👥	🏠	🚿	🏊	🥾	🎣	⚓	🛥
1 Cascara	55		•	•		•		•					•
2 Fisherman's Point	•			•	•		•						
3 Free Meadows					•		•						
4 Lakeside One					•		•						
5 Lakeside Two					•		•						
6 North Shore Park					•		•						•
7 Winberry Creek	•	•			•		•						•

Fern Ridge Lake

Fern Ridge Lake is located 12 miles west of Eugene off SH 126 in west-central Oregon. The dam forming the lake was constructed on the Long Tom River in 1941. It is reached from SH 126 by traveling north on Territorial Road to Clear Lake Road. The Corps project office is on the west end of the dam.

Fern Ridge Lake is a popular recreation area for sailing, boating, and water skiing. Visitors to the project will find five recreation areas on the lake. *Orchard Point, Richardson Park,* and *Zumwalt* are operated by Lane County. *Zumwalt* is an undeveloped area that can be reserved by large groups for picnicking and other activities. Camping facilities for tents and recreational vehicles is found in *Richardson Park.* The

At A Glance
Auto Touring
Biking
✓ Boating
Climbing
Cultural or Historic Sites
✓ Camping
Educational Programs
✓ Fishing
✓ Groceries / Supplies
✓ Hiking
Horseback Riding
✓ Hunting
Lodging
Off Highway Vehicles
✓ Visitor Center

remaining recreation areas are operated by the Corps of Engineers for day-use activities.

Fern Ridge Lake offers 9,000 acres for boating and fishing pursuits. For the angler, salmon and trout fishing can be very productive with fall and spring yielding the best results. The lake also offers bass, crappie, and walleye. A fishing dock is located in *Kirk Park*. Food and supplies are available from three concessionaires. Boat, sailboard, and jet ski rentals are available at *Orchard Point*; for more information call 541-689-4926.

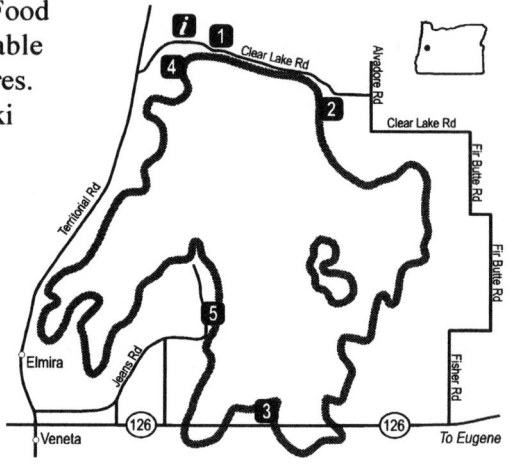

Information: U.S. Army Corps of Engineers, Fern Ridge Lake Project Office, P.O. Box 429, Lowell OR 97452 / 541-688-8147. Lane County Parks Department, 3040 N. Delta Hwy., Eugene OR 97408 / 541-682-6940.

Fern Ridge Lake	△												
1 Kirk Park					•	•			•				
2 Orchard Point					•	•	•		•			•	•
3 Perkins Peninsula					•	•	•		•		•		•
4 Richardson Park	50	50	•	•	•	•	•	•	•			•	•
5 Zumwalt						•							

Foster & Green Peter Lakes

Both of these lakes form one project with one lake regulating the output of the other. Both lakes are in west-central Oregon about 30 miles southeast of Albany near the town of Sweet Home. Foster Lake is four miles northeast from Sweet Home on US 20 and Green Peter Lake is ten miles northeast of Sweet Home along Quartzville Road. Information is

Oregon

available from the Willamette National Forest ranger station located just east of Sweet Home.

There are five developed recreation areas on Foster Lake and two on Green Peter Lake. The Corps of Engineers operates and maintains *Andrew S. Wiley* and *Shea Point* for day-use activities. All the remaining park areas are managed by Linn County. Visitors interested in camping will find one campground on each lake. Both accommodate tents and recreational vehicles; hookups are only available in *Sunnyside Park*.

At A Glance
Auto Touring
Biking
✓ Boating
Climbing
✓ Cultural or Historic Sites
✓ Camping
Educational Programs
✓ Fishing
Groceries / Supplies
✓ Hiking
Horseback Riding
✓ Hunting
Lodging
Off Highway Vehicles
Visitor Center

Foster Lake was constructed on the South Santiam River and is 1,220 acres. Green Peter Lake was constructed on the Middle Santiam River and covers 3,720 acres when full.

Anglers will find largemouth bass, smallmouth bass, bluegill, and crappie in both lakes. Rainbow and steelhead trout fishing are good in both rivers. Boat ramps are available in all but two of the recreation areas.

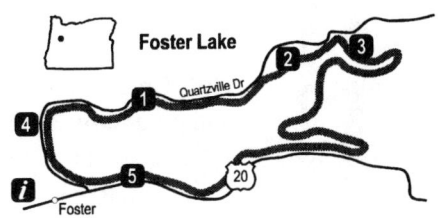

Information: U.S. Army Corps of Engineers, Foster & Green Peter Lakes, P.O. Box 429, Lowell OR 97452 / 541-937-2131. Linn County Parks Department, 3010 Ferry St. SW, Albany OR 97321 / 541-967-3917.

Foster Lake	⛺ 🚐 🚻 🚰 🪑 🔭 🏚 🥾 🛶 🚶 ⚓ 〰
1 Gedney Creek Park	• •
2 Lewis Creek Park	• • • • •
3 Sunnyside Park	• • • • • • • •
4 Andrew S. Wiley Park	• • •
5 Shea Point	• •

Green Peter Lake	⛺ 🚐 🚻 🚰 🪑 🔭 🏚 🥾 🛶 🚶 ⚓ 〰
1 Thistle Creek Park	• •
2 Whitcomb Creek Park	• • • • • •

Hills Creek Lake

Hills Creek Lake is in west-central Oregon 45 miles southeast of Eugene. The lake lies within the Willamette National Forest. Visitor viewpoints are located on either side of the dam and are reached from SH 58 by way of Kitson Springs Road and FSR 21. There is a national forest ranger station located just east of Oakridge. More information about the area is available here.

At A Glance
Auto Touring
Biking
✓ Boating
Climbing
Cultural or Historic Sites
✓ Camping
Educational Programs
✓ Fishing
Groceries / Supplies
✓ Hiking
Horseback Riding
✓ Hunting
Lodging
Off Highway Vehicles
Visitor Center

Hills Creek Lake is nestled among the forested hills and mountains of Oregon's scenic Willamette Valley. The Corps developed a 130-acre wildlife and wetland area below the dam. Visitors will find open fields, small ponds, and beaver dams in this area. The land surrounding the project is managed to provide habitat for a variety of wildlife including black-tailed deer, osprey, bald eagles, and numerous song birds.

Five recreation areas developed on the lake provide opportunities for camping and picnicking. All the areas are managed by the U.S. Forest Service. Camping is available in *Sand Prairie* and *Packard Creek*. Both campgrounds can accommodate tents and recreational vehicles but no hookups are provided.

Hills Creek Lake was constructed on the Middle Fork of the Willamette River and completed in 1961. The lake provides 44 miles of forested shoreline and 2,735 acres for boating and fishing. Inhabiting the lake and river are a variety of fish including trout, largemouth bass, and crappie. There are three boat ramps on the lake.

Information: U.S. Army Corps of Engineers, Hills Creek Lake, P.O. Box 429, Lowell OR 97452 / 541-937-2131. Willamette National Forest, Rigdon Ranger District, P.O. Box 1410, Oakridge OR 97463 / 541-782-2283.

HILLS CREEK LAKE	🏕	🚐	🚻	🗑	🛉	🥤	⛲	🚿	🏊	🧺	🚶	⚓	🎣
1 SAND PRAIRIE	21			•	•		•						
2 CLINE-CLARK					•		•						
3 C.T. BEACH					•		•						•
4 PACKARD CREEK	33			•	•		•		•		•		•
5 BINGHAM BOAT RAMP					•		•						•

Lookout Point & Dexter Lakes

Lookout Point and Dexter Lakes form a single project with one lake regulating the output of the other. The lakes are located in west-central Oregon about 22 miles southeast of Eugene. To reach the project from Eugene, travel south on I-5 to SH 58 (Exit 188) and then southeast on SH 58. The project office is located east of Lowell off North Shore Drive. Information about both lakes is available here. The U.S. Forest Service also has a ranger station in Lowell where information about the Willamette National Forest may be obtained.

AT A GLANCE
AUTO TOURING
✓ BIKING
✓ BOATING
CLIMBING
CULTURAL OR HISTORIC SITES
✓ CAMPING
✓ EDUCATIONAL PROGRAMS
✓ FISHING
✓ GROCERIES / SUPPLIES
✓ HIKING
✓ HORSEBACK RIDING
✓ HUNTING
LODGING
OFF HIGHWAY VEHICLES
✓ VISITOR CENTER

Lookout Point and Dexter Lakes are popular destinations for fishing, water skiing, sailing, swimming, picnicking, and hunting. A total of eight developed recreation areas surround the lakes. The southern portion of Lookout Point Lake lies within the Willamette National Forest. The forest manages two campgrounds here, *Black Canyon* and *Hampton*. The remaining recreation areas on both

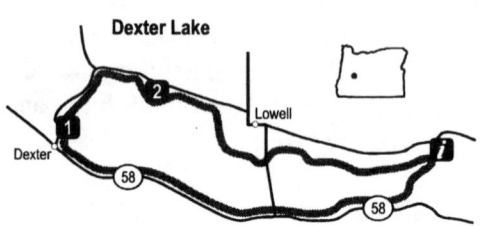

lakes are day-use areas. Oregon State Parks operates the recreation areas at Dexter Lake. Beginning in the year 2000, the Corps will be operating *Ivan Oaks* as a campground.

Lookout Point and Dexter Lakes are on the Middle Fork of the Willamette River. Lookout Point Lake, with 4,360 acres when full, is the principal facility. Dexter Lake covers 1,024 acres and is used to control water levels. Both lakes are popular for year-round fishing. Anglers can test their skills for salmon, steelhead, cutthroat and rainbow trout. Also inhabiting the lakes are crappie, largemouth bass, and catfish. Complete supplies and services are available in the community of Lowell.

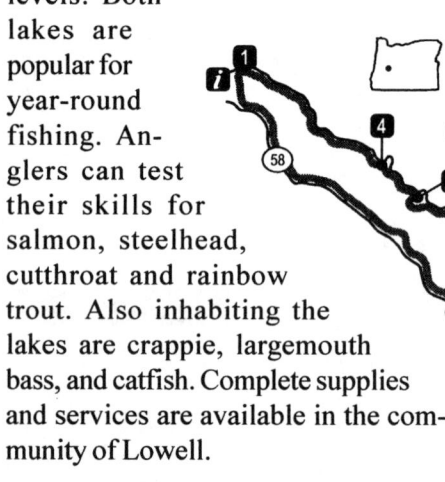

Information: U.S. Army Corps of Engineers, Lookout Point & Dexter Lakes, P.O. Box 429, Lowell OR 97452 / 541-937-2131. U.S. Forest Service, Willamette National Forest, Lowell Ranger District, 60 S. Pioneer, Lowell OR 97452 / 541-937-2129.

LOOKOUT POINT LAKE	🔺	🍽	🚻	🚮	⛱	🛖	🏠	🚿	🧺	🚶	⚓	〰
1 MERIDIAN PARK			•		•				•			•
2 IVAN OAKES PARK			•	•								

continued next page

Lookout Point *(continued)*	⛺	🚐	🚻	🚰	🍳	⛱	🏠	🏊	🎣	🚶	⚓	〰
3 Signal Point					•	•			•		•	
4 Landax					•	•		•				
5 Black Canyon Campground	72	59		•	•		•					•
6 Hampton Campground	•				•	•		•				•

Dexter Lake	⛺	🚐	🚻	🚰	🍳	⛱	🏠	🏊	🎣	🚶	⚓	〰
1 Dexter Park	•	•		•					•		•	
2 Lowell Park	•	•	•	•			•			•	•	

Lost Creek Lake

Lost Creek Lake is in southwest Oregon about 30 miles northeast of Medford and seven miles east of Trail. To reach the lake from Trail, follow SH 62 east to Takelma Drive. Information is available from the project office near the south end of the dam.

Lost Creek Lake was formed with the construction of William L. Jess Dam on the Rogue River. The lake lies in the scenic and mountainous Rogue River Valley. More than 30 miles of trails surround the lake and are part of the Rogue River National Scenic Trail system. The trails offer excellent opportunities for hiking and biking into the surrounding country.

> **At A Glance**
> Auto Touring
> ✓ Biking
> ✓ Boating
> Climbing
> Cultural or Historic Sites
> ✓ Camping
> ✓ Educational Programs
> ✓ Fishing
> ✓ Groceries / Supplies
> ✓ Hiking
> Horseback Riding
> ✓ Hunting
> Lodging
> Off Highway Vehicles
> ✓ Visitor Center

Eight recreation areas have been developed around Lost Creek Lake. *Stewart State Park* is the largest campground on the lake. Most of the campsites have hookups for recreational vehicles. Two small hike-in/boat-in primitive camping areas are managed by the Corps of Engineers. The remaining recreation areas provide day-use facilities.

The 3,430-acre lake is ten miles long and has 30 miles of shoreline. Anglers will find coho and chinook salmon, rainbow trout, crappie, bass, and catfish in the lake and river. A marina is located in *Stewart State Park*.

Information: U.S. Army Corps of Engineers, Lost Creek Lake Project Office, 100 Cole M. Rivers Dr., Trail OR 97541 / 541-878-2255. Stewart State Park, 35251 Highway 62, Trail OR 97541 / 541-560-3334. Casey State Park, Oregon Parks and Recreation Department, 1115 Commercial St. NE, Salem OR 97310 / 800-735-2900.

Lost Creek Lake		△	☐	🗃	🚻	♿	🛥	🏕	⛽	⚓	🚶	⚓	〰
1 Takelma			•	•		•					•		•
2 Stewart State Park	201 151	•	•	•	•	•	•	•			•	•	•
3 McGregor					•	•	•	•				•	•
4 Casey State Park						•		•				•	•
5 Four Corners	7				•		•				•		
6 Catfish Cove						•		•				•	
7 Fire Glen	4				•		•					•	
8 River's Edge			•	•		•		•				•	

Lake Umatilla

Lake Umatilla encompasses 76 miles of the Columbia River between the John Day Lock and Dam and McNary Lock and Dam. It is located about 110 miles east of Portland and 25 miles east of The Dalles. The dam crosses the river near Rufus and can be reached by taking Exit 109 on I-84.

Fifteen recreation areas have been developed along the lake. Nearly half of the parks have facilities for tent and RV campers. *Albert Philippi Park* is situated on the John Day River 3½ miles upriver from its confluence with the Columbia. Access to this campground is by boat and camping is free. Boaters are cautioned that one- to three-foot swells may be encountered along this stretch of the John Day River. Winds of

At A Glance
Auto Touring
Biking
✓ Boating
Climbing
Cultural or Historic Sites
✓ Camping
Educational Programs
✓ Fishing
Groceries / Supplies
✓ Hiking
Horseback Riding
✓ Hunting
Lodging
Off Highway Vehicles
✓ Visitor Center

Oregon

25 to 45 mph are not uncommon during the recreation season. *Crowe Butte State Park* is located 14 miles west of Paterson on the Washington side. Reservations are required to camp here.

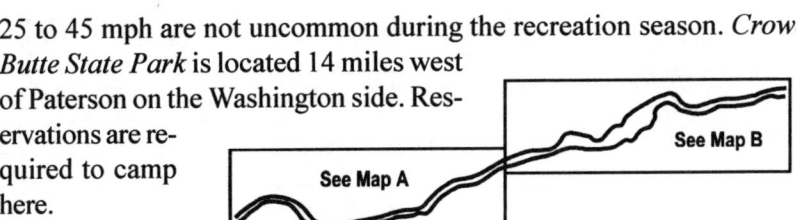

Lake Umatilla offers the angler rainbow and cutthroat trout, salmon, largemouth bass, bluegill, walleye, and numerous other species. Boat ramps may be found in all but two of the recreation areas. Boating and fishing supplies are available from the marinas in *Boardman*, *Irrigon*, and *Umatilla* parks.

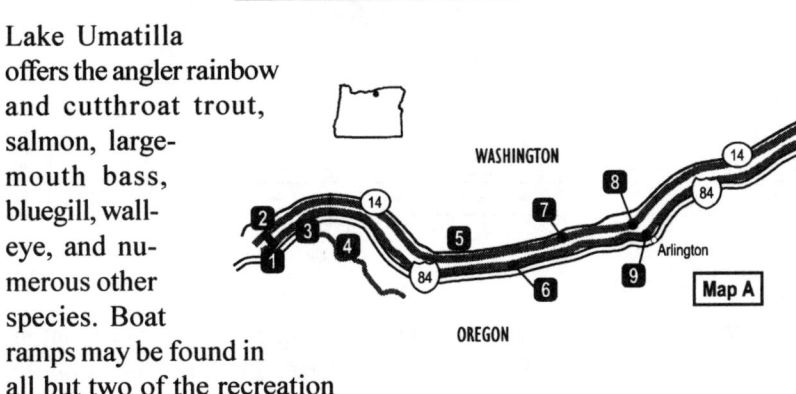

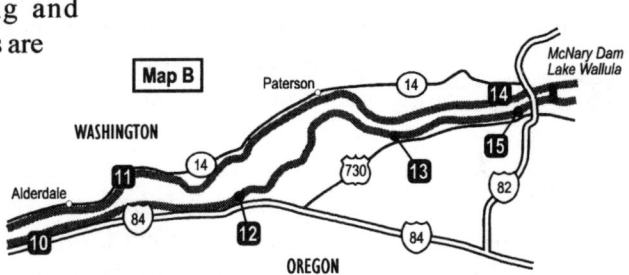

Information:
U.S. Army Corps of Engineers, John Day Lock &Dam - Lake Umatilla, P.O. Box 564, The Dalles OR 97058 / 541-296-1181. Crow Butte State Park, Paterson WA 99345 / 509-875-2643. Boardman Campground, Boardman Parks & Recreation Department., Boardman OR 97818 / 541-481-7217.

LAKE UMATILLA	△	⌂	🚻	🍽	⛺	☕	🏛	🏊	🛢	🚶	⚓	〰
1 JOHN DAY DAM					•	•	•					
2 RAILROAD ISLAND PARK							•					•
3 LEPAGE PARK	25	25	•	•	•		•	•	•	•	•	•

continued next page

Lake Umatilla (continued)	▲	🚐	🏠	🚽	🚰	🍴	🏕	🎣	🛶	🚶	⚓	🏊
4 Albert Philippi Park	•			•	•		•	•	•			
5 Rock Creek Park						•						•
6 Blalock Canyon												•
7 Sundale Park						•	•					•
8 Roosevelt Park	•				•	•	•	•	•			•
9 Arlington Park					•	•			•			•
10 Quesnel Park	•						•					
11 Crow Butte State Park	50	50	•	•			•	•	•	•		•
12 Boardman Campground	63	63	•	•	•	•	•	•	•		•	•
13 Irrigon Park				•	•	•	•		•		•	•
14 Plymouth Park	32	32	•	•			•	•				•
15 Umatilla Park	•	•		•	•		•	•			•	

Lake Wallula

Lake Wallula is located in northeast Oregon and southeast Washington. It was formed by the construction of McNary Lock and Dam on the Columbia River. Information is available from the Pacific Salmon Visitor Information Center and at several locations around the dam. Exhibits and displays depict the history and operation of the project.

At A Glance
- Auto Touring
- ✓ Biking
- ✓ Boating
- Climbing
- ✓ Cultural or Historic Sites
- ✓ Camping
- ✓ Educational Programs
- ✓ Fishing
- ✓ Groceries / Supplies
- ✓ Hiking
- Horseback Riding
- ✓ Hunting
- Lodging
- Off Highway Vehicles
- ✓ Visitor Center

Lake Wallula encompasses 62 miles of the Columbia River between McNary Lock and Dam and Ice Harbor Dam on the Snake River. Visitors to the project will find numerous recreation areas situated along the lake. Of the 29 parks, four have camping facilities for tents and recreational vehicles. The largest of these is *Columbia Park*, which is operated by the City of Kennewick. *McNary Beach* is a day-use waterside picnic area that overlooks a large swim beach and provides access to the Hat Rock Scenic Corridor. A trail passes through this secluded, scenic area that leads to *Hat Rock State Park*. The campground in this state park is privately owned, phone 541-567-4188 for information. Located at the confluence of the Snake and Columbia rivers is *Sacajawea State Park*, an area where Lewis and Clark once camped.

Oregon

Several Habitat Management Units are located around the lake. These areas offer unique opportunities for hiking, hunting, fishing, or watching wildlife. Among the species of wildlife inhabiting the region are waterfowl, mule deer, and golden eagles.

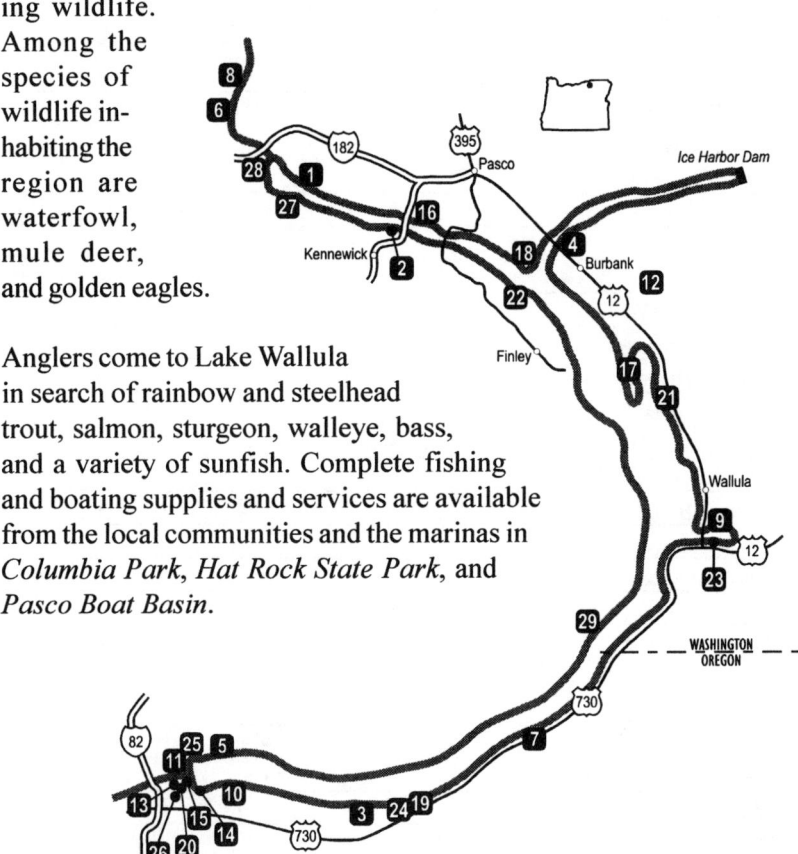

Anglers come to Lake Wallula in search of rainbow and steelhead trout, salmon, sturgeon, walleye, bass, and a variety of sunfish. Complete fishing and boating supplies and services are available from the local communities and the marinas in *Columbia Park*, *Hat Rock State Park*, and *Pasco Boat Basin*.

Information: U.S. Army Corps of Engineers, McNary Lock & Dam - Lake Wallula, RR 6 Box 693, Pasco WA 99301 / 509-543-3251. Hat Rock State Park, 541-567-5032. Sacajawea State Park, 509-545-2361. *Columbia Park* is operated by the city of Kennewick, 509-585-4200. *Leslie R. Groves, Howard Amon* and *Wye Parks* are operated by the city of Richland Parks Department, phone 509-943-9161. *Chiawana & Road 54 Parks* are operated by Franklin County, 509-545-3514. *Pasco Boat Basin* is operated by the city of Pasco, 509-545-3457. *Two Rivers Park* is operated by the Benton County Parks and Recreation Department, 509-783-3118.

Lake Wallula

		🏕	🚐	🚻	🚰	⛽	🍽	🏛	⛲	🎣	🚶	⚓	〰
1	Chiawana & Road 54 Parks				•	•	•	•				•		•
2	Columbia Park	318	18	•	•	•	•	•		•	•	•	•	•
3	Hat Rock State Park				•	•		•	•	•		•	•	
4	Hood Park	69	69	•	•	•	•	•	•	•	•	•		•
5	Horse Heaven HMU											•		
6	Howard Amon Park				•	•	•	•			•	•		•
7	Juniper Canyon HMU											•		
8	Leslie R. Groves Park				•	•	•	•			•	•		•
9	Madame Dorian	15		•	•	•		•						•
10	McNary Beach				•	•		•	•	•		•		
11	McNary L & D Vis. Ctr.				•	•		•						•
12	McNary NWR							•				•		
13	McNary Wildlife Nature Area					•		•				•		
14	Oregon Boat Ramp							•						•
15	Pacific Salmon Vis. Ctr.				•	•		•						
16	Pasco Boat Basin				•	•	•	•					•	•
17	Peninsula HMU											•		
18	Sacajawea State Park				•	•	•	•			•			•
19	Sand Station Park	10				•		•			•			
20	Spillway Park				•	•		•						
21	Two Rivers Habitat											•		
22	Two Rivers Park				•	•	•	•			•	•		•
23	Wallula HMU											•		
24	Warehouse Beach Park					•		•			•			
25	Washington Boat Ramp				•	•		•						•
26	West McNary Park				•	•		•						
27	Wye Park				•	•	•	•						•
28	Yakima River Delta Nature Area											•		
29	Yellepit HMU											•		

South Dakota

1. Cold Brook Lake
2. Cottonwood Springs Lake
3. Lake Francis Case
4. Lewis and Clark Lake
5. Lake Oahe
6. Lake Sharpe

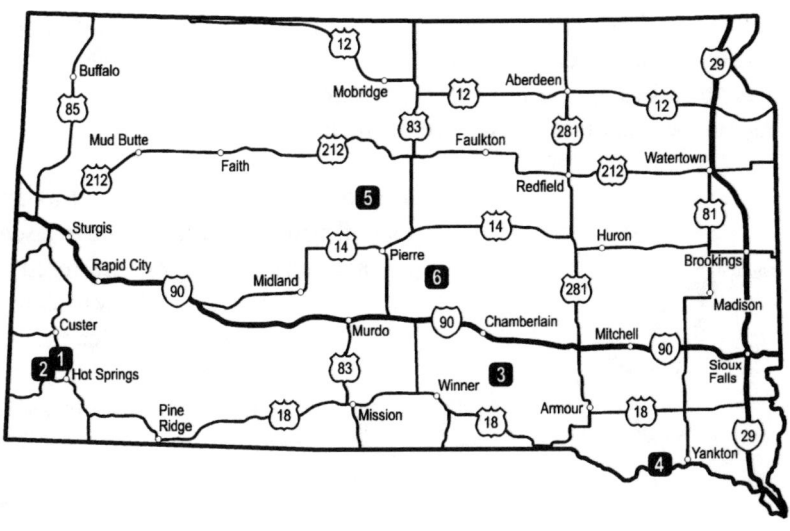

South Dakota Resources

- ***South Dakota Department of Tourism*** - 711 E. Wells Ave., Pierre SD 57501-3369 / (800) 732-5682 or (605) 773-3301
- ***South Dakota Dept. of Game, Fish, & Parks*** - (605) 773-3485 Hunting and Fishing; (605) 773-3391 Parks
- ***Road Condition Hotline*** - (605) 394-2255 or (605) 773-3536
- ***Road Construction Hotline*** - (605) 773-3571

Cold Brook Lake

Cold Brook Lake is located in southwest South Dakota on the fringe of the Black Hills. The small lake lies west of US 385 one mile north of Hot Springs. Information is available from the ranger station near the south end of the dam.

Ponderosa pines, crystal clear water and rugged canyon walls set the scene at Cold Brook Lake. Occasionally bald eagles can be spotted soaring overhead.

Camping and picnic areas on the north end of the lake are open year-round and provide easy access to a beach and boat ramp. An archery range is located on the east edge of the canyon.

At A Glance

- Auto Touring
- Biking
- ✓ Boating
- Climbing
- Cultural or Historic Sites
- ✓ Camping
- Educational Programs
- ✓ Fishing
- Groceries / Supplies
- ✓ Hiking
- Horseback Riding
- ✓ Hunting
- Lodging
- Off Highway Vehicles
- Visitor Center

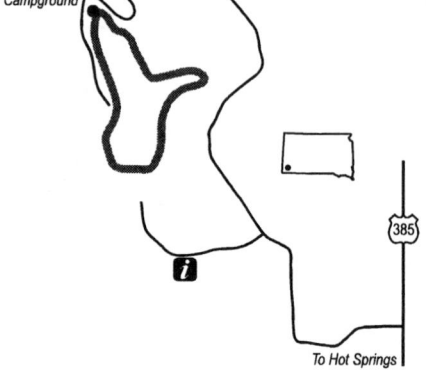

The one mile long Cold Brook Lake is a small 520-acre lake nestled in a scenic canyon. Anglers are lured to the lake for rainbow trout and largemouth bass. Ice fishing is also popular in the winter months. Boats are limited to electric motors only.

Hunting in the area is allowed with a bow only, no shotguns. For more information see the ranger station or contact the Corps project office.

Information: U.S. Army Corps of Engineers, Cold Brook Lake, P.O. Box 664, Hot Springs SD 57747 / 605-745-5476.

South Dakota

Cottonwood Springs Lake

Located on the fringe of the Black Hills in southwestern South Dakota. Cottonwood Springs Lake is located 4½ miles west of Hot Springs off US 18. The lake lies two miles north off US 18.

Ponderosa pine line the hills surrounding the lake and cottonwoods tower above the streams and bottomlands. Numerous hiking trails in the area offer scenic views of the Minnekahta Valley from a canyon rim.

At A Glance
Auto Touring
Biking
✓ Boating
Climbing
Cultural or Historic Sites
✓ Camping
Educational Programs
✓ Fishing
Groceries / Supplies
✓ Hiking
Horseback Riding
✓ Hunting
Lodging
Off Highway Vehicles
Visitor Center

A campground with 18 units is situated on the west side of the lake. A picnic area is located just north of the campground. The roads to both recreation areas are closed to vehicle traffic during the winter months. Visitors may, however, walk in to fish or camp.

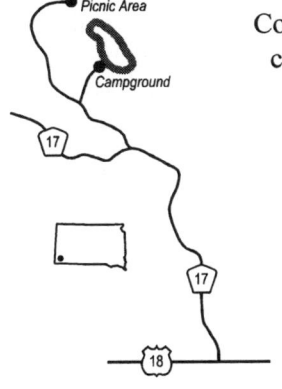

Cottonwood Springs Lake is a small dam and lake constructed to reduce flood damages in the Fall River basin. Although small, the lake provides good fishing opportunities for rainbow trout and largemouth bass. During the winter, ice fishing is a popular activity. Boaters should note that the lake is limited to boats with electric motors only.

Hunting is permitted outside the recreation areas only. More information on the areas open to the public for hunting is available from the Corps.

Information: U.S. Army Corps of Engineers, Cottonwood Springs Lake, P.O. Box 664, Hot Springs SD 57747 / 605-745-5476.

Cottonwood Springs Lake													
1 Cottonwood Springs Lake	18		•	•	•	•				•		•	

Lake Francis Case

The Fort Randall Dam and Lake Francis Case project is located along the Missouri River in south-central South Dakota. The lake extends 107 miles from Fort Randall Dam near Pickstown to Big Bend Dam near Fort Thompson.

At A Glance	
	Auto Touring
✓	Biking
✓	Boating
	Climbing
✓	Cultural or Historic Sites
✓	Camping
	Educational Programs
✓	Fishing
✓	Groceries / Supplies
✓	Hiking
	Horseback Riding
✓	Hunting
✓	Lodging
	Off Highway Vehicles
✓	Visitor Center

The lake's picturesque shoreline of grassy bluffs and ravines furnishes an ideal setting for the variety of recreational opportunities available. Water-skiers and boaters enjoy the large expanse of open water, while swimmers and sun-seekers head for the lake's sandy beaches. Walking or hiking along the lake gives visitors a chance to observe native plant and animal life. Tent campers and RVers will find camping facilities in all but three of the recreation areas around the lake. Camping cabins are available in the two state recreation areas.

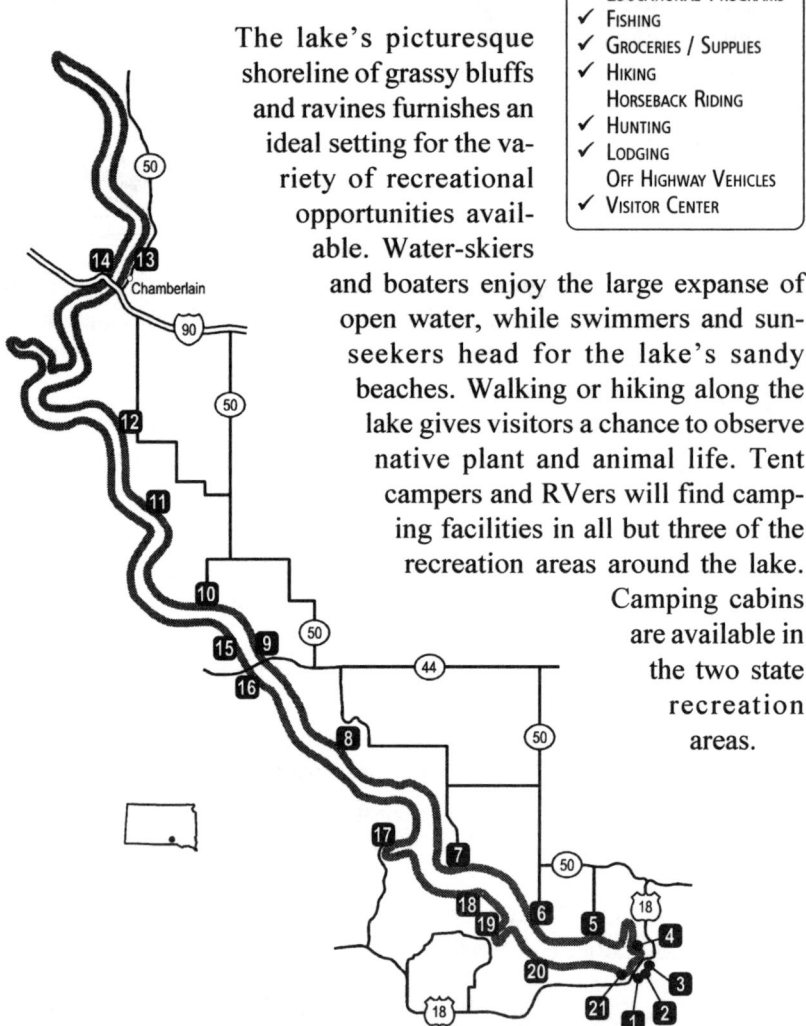

The 600-acre Karl Mundt National Wildlife Refuge, below the dam, is one of the first refuges maintained specifically for bald eagles. The area attracts one of America's largest wintering concentrations of bald and golden eagles. Other wildlife inhabiting the area includes rabbit, badger, red squirrel, red fox, muskrat, raccoon, beaver, and coyote. Mule and white-tailed deer may also be seen in the early morning and evening hours. Thousands of geese, ducks, wading birds and shore birds migrate through this area every year. Pheasants and sharp-tailed grouse also frequent the area. For information on the hunting opportunities and maps of open areas, contact the Corps project office.

Many historic and archeological sites can be found around the lake. From the explorations of Lewis and Clark in the early 1800s until the railroads steamed across the plains in the 1880s, trading posts, explorer camps, Indian agencies, military posts and steamboat landings dotted the basin. In 1882 Sitting Bull was held prisoner at Fort Randall, which was abandoned in 1892. Remains of the parade ground, excavations of building foundations, and ruins of the old chalkstone chapel are still visible.

At maximum pool, Lake Francis covers 102,000 acres and has 540 miles of shoreline. Anglers will find channel catfish, walleye, pike, sauger, white bass, white and black crappie, sheepshead, perch, sturgeon and bullheads. For the avid winter angler, ice fishing produces successful catches. Boat rentals are available in *American Creek* as well as the local communities around the lake.

Information: U.S. Army Corps of Engineers, Fort Randall Project, P.O. Box 199, Pickstown SD 57367 / 605-487-7845. Snake Creek SRA *and* Platte Creek SRA, 35316 SD Hwy 44, Platte SD 57369 / 605-337-2587.

Lake Francis Case	△	⌂	🚻	🚰	⚡	🎣	⛺	🏞	🎯	🍽	🚶	⚓	〰
1 Randall Creek	134	134	•	•	•	•	•	•					•
2 Tailrace	N	O		F	A	C	I	L	I	T	I	E	S
3 Spillway	•			•		•							•
4 North Point	75	75	•	•	•	•	•	•	•				•
5 White Swan	6			•		•							•

continued next page

Lake Francis Case (continued)

		▲	⊟	🚰	⛲	⛺	♨	⛰	⚓	🏊	⚓	🚻
6	Pease Creek	14		•	•		•						•
7	North Wheeler	20		•			•						•
8	Platte Creek SRA	54	34	•	•	•		•	•	•		•	•
9	Snake Creek SRA	90	87	•	•	•	•	•	•	•	•	•	•
10	Turgeon Wells	N	O	F	A	C	I	L	I	T	I	E	S
11	Elm Creek	6			•	•							•
12	Boyer						•						
13	American Creek	60	60	•	•	•	•	•	•			•	•
14	Dude Ranch	4					•						•
15	Buryanek	•			•		•	•					•
16	West Bridge						•						•
17	Whetstone Bay	19		•	•		•						•
18	South Wheeler				•		•						•
19	South Scalp Creek	15		•	•		•						•
20	Joe Day Bay						•						•
21	South Shore	9			•		•						•

Lewis and Clark Lake

Gavins Point Dam, which formed Lewis and Clark Lake, straddles the Nebraska/South Dakota state line. The lake was constructed on the Missouri River in southeast South Dakota near Yankton. To reach the north end of the dam from Yankton, follow SH 52 west four miles. The south end of the dam is reached from Yankton by following US 81 south to Nebraska SH 121 and then west four miles. Project information is available from the Lewis and Clark Regional Visitor Center located on the south end of the dam. The visitor center is located on the site of a historic meeting between Lewis and Clark and the Sioux Indians in 1804. Tours of the power plant are given daily during summer months.

> **At A Glance**
> ✓ Auto Touring
> ✓ Biking
> ✓ Boating
>   Climbing
> ✓ Cultural or Historic Sites
> ✓ Camping
> ✓ Educational Programs
> ✓ Fishing
> ✓ Groceries / Supplies
> ✓ Hiking
> ✓ Horseback Riding
> ✓ Hunting
> ✓ Lodging
>   Off Highway Vehicles
> ✓ Visitor Center

Visitors to Lewis and Clark Lake will find 26 recreation areas surrounding the lake. Fourteen of these have camping facilities for tents and recreational vehicles. Three trails can be found in the dam area, including a paved trail that extends from the north end of the dam to Yankton. Trails may also be found in the *Lewis and Clark SRA* and *Niobrara State Park*. These state-operated areas also have cabins available for rent.

Lewis and Clark Lake attracts anglers from across the nation for its largemouth and smallmouth bass. The 31,400-acre lake, at maximum pool level, encompasses 25 miles of the Missouri River and offers the

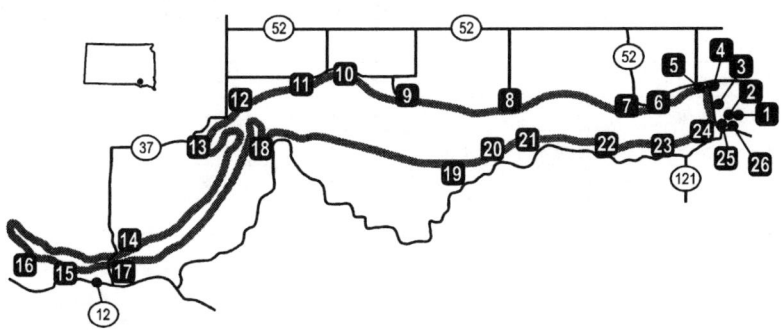

angler 90 miles of shoreline. Year-round fishing opportunities include channel catfish, walleye, sauger, white bass, crappie and perch. The *Nebraska Tailwaters* and *Training Dike* areas are popular with anglers. Fishing piers for the physically challenged are located on the south shore of Lake Yankton, located below the dam, and in the *Nebraska Tailwaters* area. Complete boating supplies and rentals are available from the Lewis and Clark marina, phone 605-665-3111.

Over 17,800 acres of land surrounding the lake is managed by the Corps and wildlife agencies from Nebraska and South Dakota. Mule and white-tailed deer are common big game in the area. Other wildlife inhabiting the area includes beaver, coyote, rabbit, badger, red squirrel, red fox, muskrat, raccoon, pheasants, geese and ducks. For information on the hunting opportunities and maps of public hunting areas, contact the Corps project office.

Information: U.S. Army Corps of Engineers, Gavins Point Project Office, P.O. Box 710, Yankton SD 57078 / 402-667-7873. Lewis and Clark SRA *and* Springfield SRA, 43349 SD Hwy 52, Yankton SD 57078 / 605-668-2985. Information on the recreation areas in Nebraska, except the state park, is available from: Nebraska Game and Parks Commission, Lewis & Clark SRA, 54731 897 Road, Crofton NE 68730 / 402-388-4169. Niobrara State Park, P.O. Box 226, Niobrara NE 68760 / 402-857-3373.

Lewis & Clark Lake			1	2	3	4	5	6	7	8	9	10	11	12
1 Chief White Crane	116	104	•	•	•	•	•	•						
2 Training Dike				•	•	•	•		•					•
3 Cottonwood	78	63		•	•	•	•							•
4 Pierson Ranch Campground	74	68	•	•	•	•	•	•				•		
5 Resort / Marina Area				•	•		•	•						•
6 Lewis & Clark SRA (SD)	374	307	•	•	•	•	•	•	•			•		•
7 Trails Area	•			•	•	•	•		•			•		•
8 Tabor	•			•	•		•							•
9 Charley Creek	N	O	F	A	C	I	L	I	T	I	E	S		
10 Snatch Creek	N	O	F	A	C	I	L	I	T	I	E	S		
11 Sand Creek	•			•	•	•	•							•
12 Springfield State Rec. Area	12	6	•	•	•	•	•	•						•
13 Emanuel Creek	N	O	F	A	C	I	L	I	T	I	E	S		
14 Running Water						•								•
15 Niobrara Ramp						•								•
16 Niobrara State Park	150	69	•	•	•	•	•	•	•			•		•
17 Bazille Creek														•
18 Santee														•
19 Devils Nest	N	O	F	A	C	I	L	I	T	I	E	S		
20 Miller Creek	•			•	•		•							•
21 Bloomfield	36	30		•	•	•								•
22 Weigand / Burbach	150	100	•	•	•	•	•	•				•	•	•
23 Deep Water						•	•							
24 South Shore						•	•							•
25 Visitors Center					•	•	•					•	•	
26 Nebraska Tailwaters	44	32	•	•	•	•	•							•

Lake Oahe

Lake Oahe extends from Pierre, South Dakota to Bismarck, North Dakota. Construction of the dam on the Missouri River began in 1948 and was completed in 1962. The lake is the fourth largest man-made reservoir in the United States. It is 231 miles long, has 2,250 miles of shoreline, and a maximum depth of 205 feet. The dam can be reached from Pierre by traveling seven miles north on SH 1804. A visitor center is located in the *East Shore* recreation area north of the dam.

At A Glance
✓ Auto Touring
✓ Biking
✓ Boating
Climbing
✓ Cultural or Historic Sites
✓ Camping
✓ Educational Programs
✓ Fishing
✓ Groceries / Supplies
✓ Hiking
✓ Horseback Riding
✓ Hunting
✓ Lodging
✓ Off Highway Vehicles
✓ Visitor Center

The crystal-clear waters of Lake Oahe are surrounded by chalky bluffs, grassy knolls and sandy shores. Several hiking and biking trails can be found all along the Missouri River. Some of the ranches surrounding the project offer horseback riding. The Triple U Buffalo Ranch, located northwest of Pierre, was the site of many scenes from the movie "Dances With Wolves." The 60,000-acre ranch is home to nearly 4,000 bison and is open to the public for touring.

Those interested in camping will find many developed and primitive sites up and down the river. The developed recreation areas offer campsites with hookups, shower facilities, and drinking water. Camping is free in many of the primitive areas. Privately owned campgrounds and resorts, offering everything from cabin rentals to casino gambling, may also be found in the area.

History buffs will be interested in the many historical sites. West of Mobridge, South Dakota, is the Sitting Bull Monument. The famous Sioux Chief lies buried on a bluff overlooking the lake. The monument marking his grave is a seven-ton granite bust carved by the late Korczak Ziolkowski. Other points of interest include Fort

Manuel Trading Post where Sacajawea, the Shoshone Indian woman guide for Lewis and Clark, is said to be buried; the military outpost of Fort Sully; Indian missions and "ghost towns" of the old steamboat days.

Anglers come to Lake Oahe in search of a variety of sport fish. Species include walleye, channel catfish, chinook salmon, northern pike, white bass, sauger, trout, blue gill and crappie. Fishing supplies and boat rentals are available along the lake at concession services and local communities.

Wildlife most common to the area includes mink, weasel, coyote, beaver, fox, muskrat, rabbit, squirrel, skunk, and raccoon. Thousands of geese, ducks, wading birds and shore birds migrate through the area. Pheasant and sharp-tailed grouse are also common to the region. Public hunting grounds offer excellent waterfowl, upland game and big game hunting opportunities. Big game hunters will find antelope, mule deer and white-tailed deer. White-tailed deer prefer the woods and meadow areas while mule deer inhabit rough breaks adjacent to the lake. Other hunting opportunities include pheasants, grouse, prairie chickens, turkeys, geese and ducks.

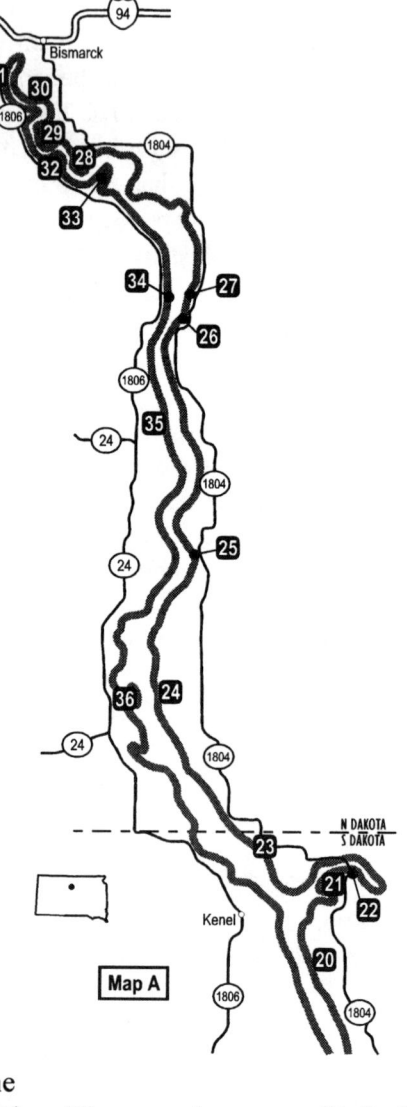

South Dakota

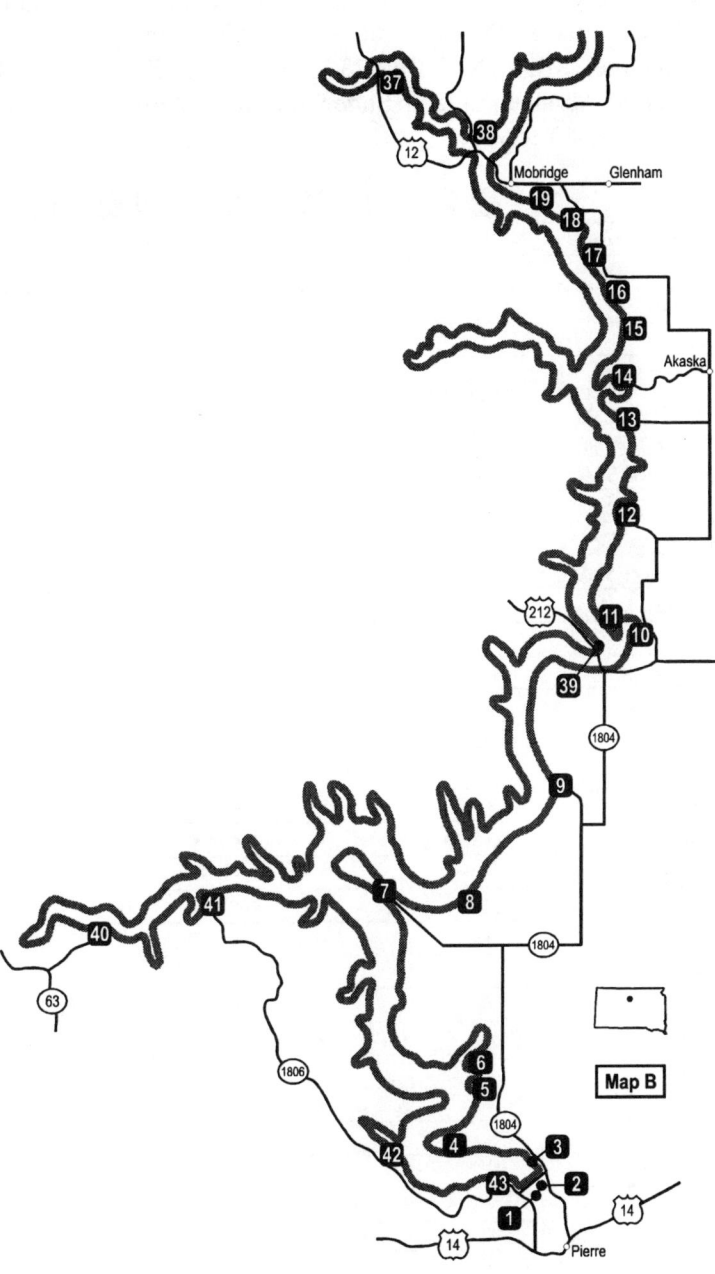

Information: U.S. Army Corps of Engineers, Lake Oahe, 28563 Powerhouse Road, Pierre SD 57501 / 605-224-5862. West Whitlock SRA *and* Swan Creek SRA, HC 3 Box 73A, Gettysburg SD 57442 / 605-765-9410. Fort Abraham Lincoln State Park, Route 2 Box 139, Mandan ND 58554 / 701-63-9571.

Lake Oahe	△	🚐	🚻	🚰	🍴	😊	🏕	⛺	🎣	🛥	🚶	⚓	〰
1 Oahe Downstream	206	•	•	•	•	•	•	•	•	•	•	•	•
2 Tailrace						•							•
3 East Shore					•	•							•
4 Peoria Flats						•							•
5 Cow Spring Creek	51			•	•		•					•	•
6 Okobojo Point	19				•		•						•
7 Little Bend SRA	13						•						•
8 Bush's Landing SRA	•						•						•
9 Sutton Bay SRA	•				•		•						•
10 East Whitlock Bay SRA	•				•		•						•
11 West Whitlock SRA	103	•	•	•	•	•	•	•				•	•
12 Dodge Draw SRA	•						•						•
13 Le Beau	•						•						•
14 Swan Creek SRA	22	•	•	•	•	•	•					•	•
15 Bowdle Beach	•						•						
16 Walth Bay	•						•						•
17 Thomas Bay	•						•						•
18 Blue Blanket	•						•						
19 Indian Creek	113	•	•	•	•	•	•	•	•			•	•
20 Shaw Creek	•						•						•
21 West Pollock	20						•		•				•
22 Pollock	•					•	•						•
23 Vander Vorste Bay	•						•						
24 Winona	•						•						•
25 Beaver Creek	•		•			•	•	•	•				•
26 Badger Bay	•						•						
27 Hazelton	•				•		•						•
28 Kimball	•						•						•
29 Sibley Nature Park							•				•		
30 General Sibley Park	•	•	•		•	•	•	•					•
31 Fort Abraham Lincoln SP	95	38	•	•	•		•	•			•		
32 Little Heart	•						•						

continued next page

Lake Oahe (continued)	⛺	🏠	🚻	🍴	🛏️	🎣	🏕️	🏊	🚿	🚶	⚓	〰️
33 Sugarloaf	•			•		•						•
34 Fort Rice	•					•						•
35 Cannonball	•					•						
36 Fort Yates	•					•						•
37 Grand River	•				•							•
38 Indian Memorial	81	•	•	•	•	•	•	•			•	•
39 Forest City	•					•						•
40 Foster Bay	19					•						•
41 Minneconjou	•					•						•
42 Chantier Creek	•					•						•
43 West Shore	•					•						•

Lake Sharpe

Located in central South Dakota, Lake Sharpe stretches from the Big Bend Dam, near Fort Thompson, to Pierre. The dam can be reached from Fort Thompson by traveling two miles south on SH 47. A visitor center is located a quarter-mile west of the spillway bridge and contains exhibits and displays of the Lewis and Clark Expedition and early Indian habitation. A visitor center is also located in the *Farm Island* recreation area.

AT A GLANCE
- ✓ Auto Touring
- ✓ Biking
- ✓ Boating
-    Climbing
- ✓ Cultural or Historic Sites
- ✓ Camping
-    Educational Programs
- ✓ Fishing
- ✓ Groceries / Supplies
- ✓ Hiking
-    Horseback Riding
- ✓ Hunting
- ✓ Lodging
- ✓ Off Highway Vehicles
- ✓ Visitor Center

Lake Sharpe is one of six large lakes constructed on the Missouri River. The lake is surrounded by prairie grasslands with ash, oak, and cedar trees lining the ravines. Numerous village sites of early Indian culture dot the area. Great numbers of waterfowl, wading birds, and shore birds use the protected bays of Lake Sharpe during migration.

Lake Sharpe offers 61,000 surface acres at maximum pool level. The lake encompasses 80 miles of the Missouri River and entices anglers with over 200 miles of shoreline. Fishing is popular year-round in the lake and tailwaters of the dam. Opportunities for the angler include walleye, sauger, sturgeon, perch, bullhead, crappie, catfish, salmon, pike, white bass and, occasionally, paddlefish. Supplies and boat

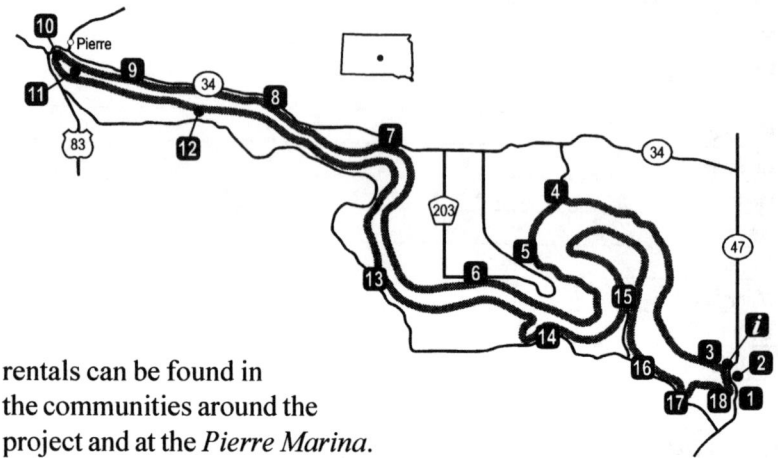

rentals can be found in the communities around the project and at the *Pierre Marina*.

Hunters enjoy excellent upland game hunting around the project. Regulations are enforced by the state of South Dakota, the Lower Brule and Crow Creek Tribal Councils. For information and maps of open hunting areas, contact the project office.

Information: U.S. Army Corps of Engineers, Big Bend Project Office, HC 69 Box 74, Chamberlain SD 57325 / 605-245-2255. West Bend SRA *and* Farm Island SRA, 1301 Farm Island Rd., Pierre SD 57501 / 605-224-5605.

Lake Sharpe													
1 Tailrace	72	72	•	•	•	•	•	•					•
2 Fort Thompson	•				•	•	•	•					
3 North Shore	•			•	•	•	•		•				•
4 North Bend	•						•						•
5 West Bend SRA	126	68	•	•	•	•	•	•					•
6 Joe Creek	•				•	•		•					•
7 De Grey	•					•		•					•
8 Rousseau	N	O	F	A	C	I	L	I	T	I	E	S	
9 Farm Island SRA	90	36	•	•	•	•	•	•	•		•		•
10 Pierre Marina					•	•	•	•				•	•
11 La Framboise Island					•	•		•				•	•
12 Antelope Creek	N	O	F	A	C	I	L	I	T	I	E	S	

continued next page

South Dakota

LAKE SHARPE (continued)	⛺	🚐	🚻	🥤	🎪	🛶	🏠	🛣	🏊	📻	🚶	⚓	〰
13 CEDAR CREEK	•												•
14 IRON NATION	84	72		•	•	•	•						•
15 NARROWS	N	O		F	A	C	I	L	I	T	I	E	S
16 LOWER BRULE	N	O		F	A	C	I	L	I	T	I	E	S
17 COUNSELOR CREEK													•
18 GOOD SOLDIER CREEK	•			•	•		•						•

Texas

1. Aquilla Lake
2. Bardwell Lake
3. Belton Lake
4. Benbrook Lake
5. Canyon Lake
6. Lake Georgetown
7. Granger Lake
8. Grapevine Lake
9. Hords Creek Lake
10. Jim Chapman Lake
11. Joe Pool Lake
12. Lake O' The Pines
13. Lavon Lake
14. Lewisville Lake
15. Navarro Mills Lake
16. O.C. Fisher Lake
17. Pat Mayse Lake
18. Proctor Lake
19. Ray Roberts Lake
20. Sam Rayburn Reservoir
21. Somerville Lake
22. Steinhagen Lake
23. Stillhouse Hollow Lake
24. Waco Lake
25. Whitney Lake
26. Wright Patman Lake

Texas Resources

- **_Texas Dept. of Commerce Tourism Division_** - PO Box 12728, Austin TX 78711 / (800) 888-8839 or (512) 462-9191
- **_Texas Parks & Wildlife Dept._** - (800) 792-1112 or (512) 389-4800
- **_Road Condition Hotline_** - (800) 452-9292

Aquilla Lake

Aquilla Lake is in east-central Texas about 72 miles south of Dallas and 36 miles north of Waco. To reach the dam from Waco, follow I-5 north for 30 miles to FM 310 (Exit 364A) and then west on FM 310 for six miles. Information about the project is available from the project office on the east end of the dam.

At A Glance
Auto Touring
Biking
✓ Boating
Climbing
Cultural or Historic Sites
Camping
Educational Programs
✓ Fishing
Groceries / Supplies
Hiking
Horseback Riding
✓ Hunting
Lodging
Off Highway Vehicles
Visitor Center

Visitors to Aquilla Lake will find five developed recreation areas. All are day-use areas and do not provide facilities for overnight camping. Located about ten miles west of this lake is Lake Whitney, a Corps of Engineers project with camping facilities.

Aquilla Lake was constructed on Aquilla Creek and was completed in 1983. The lake offers 3,280 acres for boating and fishing. A fishing platform is located in the outlet channel below the dam. Among the species of fish in Aquilla Lake are crappie, catfish, largemouth bass, and a variety of sunfish.

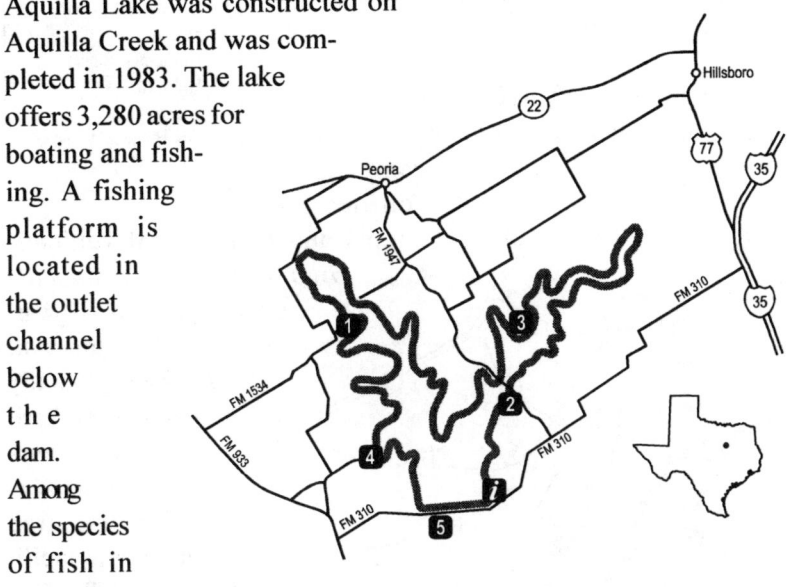

Information: U.S. Army Corps of Engineers, Aquilla Dam & Lake,

P.O. Box 5038 LPS, Clifton TX 76634 / 254-694-3189.

Aquilla Lake			
1 Aquilla Creek Park		•	
2 Dairy Hill Ramp		•	•
3 Hackberry Creek		•	
4 Old School Ramp		•	•
5 Outlet Area		•	

Bardwell Lake

Bardwell Lake is in northeast Texas about 40 miles south of Dallas and five miles west of Ennis. To reach the dam from Ennis, follow SH 34 west to Lakeview Drive. Turn south on Lakeview Drive and travel about three miles. Information about the project is available from the office located just north of the dam. An overlook near the project office provides a view of the lake and dam.

At A Glance
Auto Touring
Biking
✓ Boating
Climbing
Cultural or Historic Sites
✓ Camping
Educational Programs
✓ Fishing
✓ Groceries / Supplies
✓ Hiking
Horseback Riding
✓ Hunting
Lodging
Off Highway Vehicles
✓ Visitor Center

Five recreation areas have been developed around Bardwell Lake. Three of these have camping facilities for tents and recreational vehicles. *High View* and *Waxahachie Creek* are open all year; *Love Park* and *Mott Park* are generally open from April through September. *Love Park* is a day-use area with picnic facilities, sand volley ball court, and horseshoe pits. A ½-mile nature trail is available in *Waxahachie*

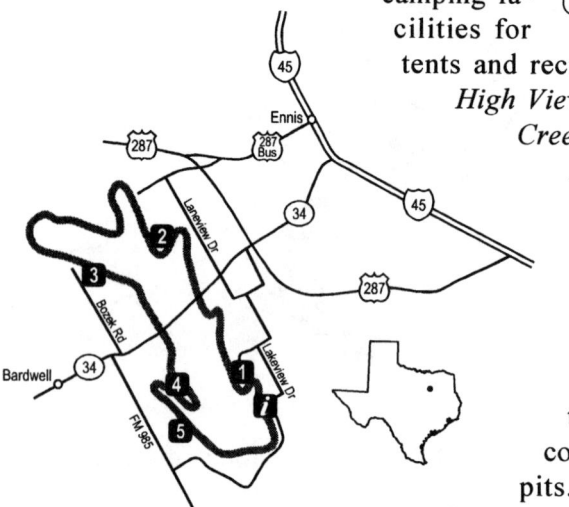

Creek. Another trail, a ¾-mile nature trail, is located on the south side of the dam.

Bardwell Lake was constructed on Waxahachie Creek and offers 3,570 acres for boating and fishing. Boat storage and rentals, fishing bait and supplies are available at the marina in *High View*. Largemouth bass, crappie, catfish, and various sunfish inhabit the lake. Four-lane concrete boat ramps are located in all of the parks. Two designated fishing areas with easy access to the lake are in *Mott Park*. Complete camping and fishing supplies are available in Ennis.

Information: U.S. Army Corps of Engineers, Bardwell Lake, 4000 Observation Drive, Ennis TX 75119 / 972-875-5711.

Bardwell Lake												
1 Love Park						•	•		•	•		•
2 Little Mustang Creek												•
3 Waxahachie Creek	72	65	•	•	•			•	•			•
4 High View	39	39	•	•	•			•	•		•	•
5 Mott Park	40	36	•	•	•			•	•			•

Belton Lake

Belton Lake is located in central Texas between Temple and Killeen. To reach the dam from Belton, travel about three miles north on SH 317, then northwest on FM 439 for one mile. Information is available from the project office on the south end of the dam.

Located below the dam is the Miller Springs Nature Center. The 266-acre nature area is open daily from dawn to dusk. Sixteen recreation areas have been developed around the lake. Camping is permitted in all but three parks. Campsites with water and electric hookups are available in *Live Oak Ridge*, *Cedar Ridge*, and *Westcliff*. These three campgrounds are open all year. Wildlife inhabiting the region includes mourning dove, rabbit, squirrel, and quail.

At A Glance
Auto Touring
✓ Biking
✓ Boating
Climbing
✓ Cultural or Historic Sites
✓ Camping
✓ Educational Programs
✓ Fishing
✓ Groceries / Supplies
✓ Hiking
Horseback Riding
✓ Hunting
✓ Lodging
Off Highway Vehicles
✓ Visitor Center

Hunting is permitted in certain areas; maps are available from the project office.

This scenic 12,300-acre lake has numerous arms and coves along its 110 miles of shoreline. The brushy areas are prime locations for largemouth and smallmouth bass, crappie, catfish, and sunfish. Other catches in the lake include walleye, white bass, and striped bass. A fishing dock is located in *Cedar Ridge*. The Pier 36 Marina in *Cedar Ridge* offers snacks, bait, gas, and a restaurant, phone 254-986-2466. Frank's Marina in *Belton Lakeview* has boat rentals, jet ski rentals, a snack bar, gas, and a covered fishing dock, phone 254-939-7443. Fishing docks are also in *Temple's Lake* and *Leona* parks.

Information: U.S. Army Corps of Engineers, Belton Lake, 3740 FM 1670, Belton TX 76513 / 254-939-2461.

Belton Lake	▲	⌂	🚻	🚰	🛏	🏊	🏠	🍴	⛵	👣	⚓	〜
1 Belton Lakeview				•	•	•	•			•	•	•
2 Miller Springs	•				•		•					
3 Miller Spgs. Nature Area									•			
4 Live Oak Ridge	48	48	•	•	•			•	•	•		•
5 Temple's Lake				•	•	•	•	•	•			•
6 Rogers			•		•		•					•

continued next page

Texas

Belton Lake (continued)	△	⌂	🚻	🚰	⛺	🏕	🏠	🚿	🏊	🍴	🚶	⚓	〰
7 Cedar Ridge	80	68	•	•	•	•	•	•	•			•	•
8 McGregor	•				•	•						•	
9 Leona	•				•	•						•	
10 Mother Neff State Park	21		•		•	•	•	•		•		•	
11 Iron Bridge	•				•							•	
12 Winkler	15			•	•		•	•					
13 White Flint	•				•		•						•
14 Owl Creek	•			•	•		•						•
15 Sparta Valley	•				•		•						•
16 Westcliff	38	27	•	•		•	•	•	•				•

Benbrook Lake

At A Glance
- Auto Touring
- Biking
- ✓ Boating
- Climbing
- Cultural or Historic Sites
- ✓ Camping
- Educational Programs
- ✓ Fishing
- ✓ Groceries / Supplies
- ✓ Hiking
- ✓ Horseback Riding
- ✓ Hunting
- Lodging
- Off Highway Vehicles
- ✓ Visitor Center

Benbrook Lake is in northeast Texas just outside Fort Worth. To reach the dam from Benbrook, follow US 377 south for one mile and then east for two miles on CR 1042. The project office is on the east end of the dam off Dirks Road.

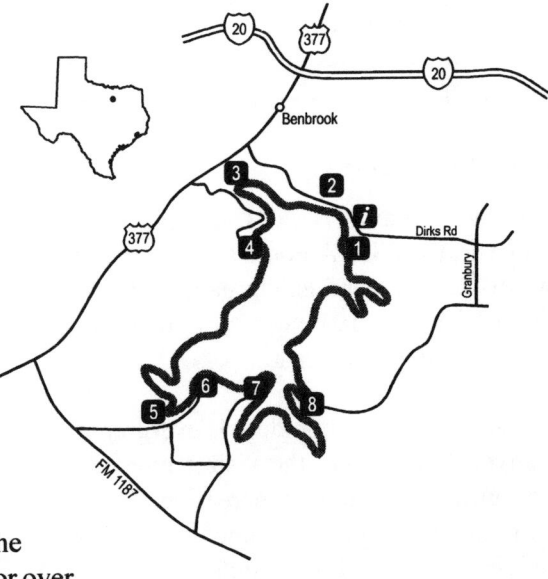

The city of Forth Worth manages *Pecan Valley* park below the dam; there is a golf course here. A hiking and horseback riding trail follows the lake's western shore for over seven miles. The terrain encountered is of open spaces, rolling hills, dense wooded areas, and challenging slopes. Excellent views of the lake and surrounding countryside reward the hiker or horseback rider. Rental horses are available through local stables. Five campgrounds on the lake provide sites for tent campers and RVers. Water and electric hookups are also available at many sites.

Benbrook Lake is a 3,770-acre impoundment constructed on the Clear Fork of the Trinity River. Among the species of fish inhabiting the lake are largemouth bass, smallmouth bass, striped bass, catfish, crappie, and various sunfish. Boat rentals, fishing supplies and snacks are available at the marina.

Information: U.S. Army Corps of Engineers, Benbrook Lake, P.O. Box 26619, Fort Worth TX 76126 / 817-292-2400.

Benbrook Lake			⛺	🚐	🚻	🚰	🔥	🛥	🍴	⛽	🎣	🏊	🚶	⚓	🏕
1 Longhorn					•	•		•							•
2 Pecan Valley					•	•		•								
3 Dutch Branch					•	•	•	•			•				•
4 Holiday Park	105	70	•	•	•			•	•			•			
5 Westcreek Circle	4							•							•
6 Bear Creek Campground	46	46	•	•	•			•	•						•
7 Mustang Point	11			•	•	•		•	•						
8 Rocky Creek	17		•	•	•			•						•	•

Canyon Lake

Located in central Texas, Canyon Lake lies 40 miles north of San Antonio and 20 miles northwest of New Braunfels. The dam can be reached from I-35 Exit 191 near New Braunfels by following FM 306 north.

Set among steep-shouldered, evergreen hills, Canyon Lake offers the visitor plenty of opportunities for outdoor recreation. Two yacht clubs and fishing groups schedule a host of activities. *North Park* is a popular area with scuba divers. *North Park, Canyon Park, Potters*

At A Glance

    Auto Touring
✓ Biking
✓ Boating
    Climbing
    Cultural or Historic Sites
✓ Camping
    Educational Programs
✓ Fishing
✓ Groceries / Supplies
✓ Hiking
✓ Horseback Riding
✓ Hunting
✓ Lodging
    Off Highway Vehicles
✓ Visitor Center

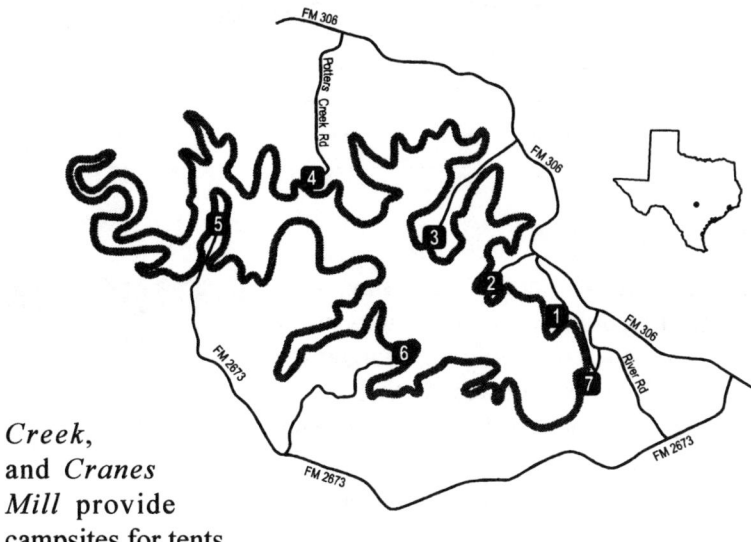

Creek, and *Cranes Mill* provide campsites for tents and recreational vehicles. Electrical hookups are available in *Potters Creek*. *Cranes Mill* and *Potters Creek* campgrounds are open all year. *Canyon Park* is open from April through September and *North Park* from March through October.

Constructed on Guadalupe River, Canyon Lake offers 8,240 acres for boating and fishing. Largemouth bass, flathead catfish, striped bass, smallmouth bass, and various sunfish are among the species found in the lake. Anglers have taken rainbow and brown trout from the river below the dam. Boat rentals, supplies, and a restaurant are available from the marina in *Canyon Park*. The marina in *Cranes Mill* has bait and boat rentals. A fishing pier is located in *Cranes Mill* and a fishing jetty is in *Potters Creek*.

Information: U.S. Army Corps of Engineers, Canyon Lake, 601 C.O.E. Road, Canyon Lake TX 78133 / 830-964-3341. Guadalupe River Information, 830-964-3342.

Canyon Lake		▲	🚐	🚻	🍴	⛱	🚿	🏠	🎣	🏊	🍽	🚶	⚓	▦
1	North Park	20			•	•		•						
2	Jacobs Creek			•	•			•	•					•
3	Canyon Park	150	•	•	•		•		•		•	•	•	

continued next page

Canyon Lake (continued)	⛺	🚐	🚻	🚰	🪑	⛵	🏕️	🚿	🏊	🎣	🚶	⚓	〰️
4 Potters Creek	125	61	•	•	•		•	•	•			•
5 Cranes Mill	49			•	•		•	•	•		•	•
6 Comal Park				•	•	•	•		•			•
7 Overlook				•		•				•		•

Lake Georgetown

Lake Georgetown is in central Texas about four miles west of Georgetown and 30 miles north of Austin. The lake is reached from Georgetown by following FM 2338 northwest for three miles to Cedar Breaks Road. Follow Cedar Breaks Road to the dam. The project office is located along Cedar Breaks Road near the northeast end of the dam.

At A Glance
Auto Touring
✓ Biking
✓ Boating
Climbing
Cultural or Historic Sites
✓ Camping
Educational Programs
✓ Fishing
Groceries / Supplies
✓ Hiking
Horseback Riding
✓ Hunting
Lodging
Off Highway Vehicles
Visitor Center

Lake Georgetown was constructed on the North Fork of the San Gabriel River. It lies in the scenic hill country of central Texas. Seven recreation areas are situated along the lake; three provide developed facilities. *Jim Hogg Park* is the largest campground with nearly 150 sites. All campsites have water and electric hookups. *Cedar Breaks Park* has 64 campsites with water and electric hookups. Both are open all year.

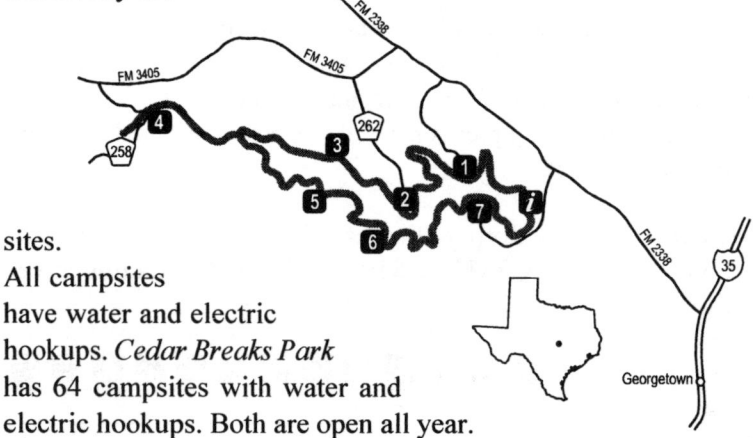

The Good Water Hiking Trail is a rugged 16½-mile trail that connects

Cedar Breaks and *Russell* parks. Four primitive camping areas are located along the trail. *Tejas Camp* is the only primitive campground that is also accessible by car. Drinking water is only available in *Tejas Camp*; hikers are encouraged to carry their own. Hikers are advised to make transportation arrangements prior to walking the entire trail as it does not form a complete loop.

Lake Georgetown offers 1,310 acres for fishing and boating. The lake is well-stocked with smallmouth bass, largemouth bass, and channel catfish. Other species in the lake include walleye, flathead catfish, white crappie, white bass, and various sunfish. Boat ramps are located in the three developed recreation areas.

Information: U.S. Army Corps of Engineers, Lake Georgetown Project Office, 500 Cedar Breaks Road, Georgetown TX 78628 / 512-819-9046. Lake information line: 512-930-5253.

Lake Georgetown												
1 Jim Hogg Park	148	148	•	•			•	•				•
2 Russell Park			•	•			•	•		•		•
3 Walnut Springs Camp	•						•			•		
4 Tejas Camp	12			•			•			•		
5 Sawyer Camp	•						•			•		
6 Cedar Hollow Camp	•						•			•		
7 Cedar Breaks Park	64	64	•	•	•		•	•		•		•

Granger Lake

Granger Lake is in central Texas about 35 miles northeast of Austin near Granger, Texas. The dam is reached from Granger by traveling seven miles east on FM 971. Information about the lake is available from the project office on the north end of the dam.

Granger Lake offers four developed recreation areas for camping and picnicking. Campgrounds are located in *Willis Creek*, *Taylor*, and *Wilson H. Fox* parks. All of the campsites have water and electric hookups. The campground

At A Glance
Auto Touring
✓ Biking
✓ Boating
Climbing
Cultural or Historic Sites
✓ Camping
Educational Programs
✓ Fishing
Groceries / Supplies
✓ Hiking
Horseback Riding
✓ Hunting
Lodging
Off Highway Vehicles
Visitor Center

in *Taylor Park* is open March through September; the others are open year-round. *Friendship Park* is a day-use area with swimming beach.

Both the sportsman and naturalist enjoy the four wildlife management areas surrounding the lake. These areas offer such activities as bird watching, mountain biking, hunting, or hiking. Wildife inhabiting the region includes white-tailed deer, mourning dove, bobwhite quail, and various waterfowl.

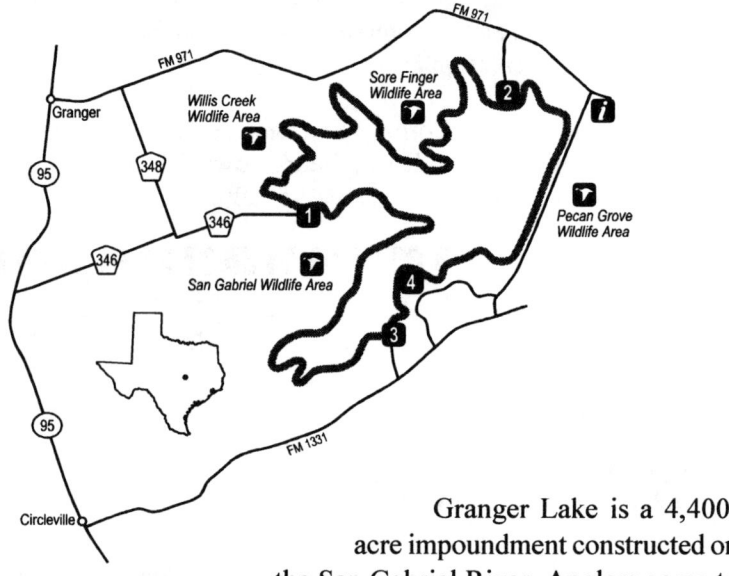

Granger Lake is a 4,400-acre impoundment constructed on the San Gabriel River. Anglers come to the lake in search of largemouth bass, crappie, channel and flathead catfish, and a variety of sunfish. A fishing dock is in *Wilson H. Fox*. Boat ramps are in all the parks.

Information: U.S. Army Corps of Engineers, Granger Lake, 3100 Granger Dam Road, Granger TX 76530 / 512-859-2668.

Granger Lake	▲	🚐	🚻	🥤	🪑	🛥	🏕	🥾	🎣	🗑	🚶	⚓	〰
1 Willis Creek	27	27	•	•	•			•	•				•
2 Friendship				•			•			•			•
3 Taylor	48	48	•	•	•			•	•			•	•
4 Wilson H. Fox	58	58	•	•	•			•	•	•			•

Grapevine Lake

Grapevine Lake lies north of the Dallas/Fort Worth area in northeast Texas. The project office is on the south end of the dam. It can be reached from Grapevine by following SH 26 east to Fairway Drive and traveling north.

Grapevine Lake was constructed on Denton Creek and placed in operation in 1952. It is the home of the Dallas Water Ski Club. Many shows and competitions are staged throughout spring and summer. Those interested in an afternoon of golf will find a public course located below the dam. An off-road vehicle area is in *Marshall Creek*. The area offers about 250 acres of challenging terrain. Wildlife inhabiting the area includes deer, waterfowl, squirrel, fox, and numerous song birds.

At A Glance	
	Auto Touring
✓	Biking
✓	Boating
	Climbing
	Cultural or Historic Sites
✓	Camping
	Educational Programs
✓	Fishing
✓	Groceries / Supplies
✓	Hiking
✓	Horseback Riding
✓	Hunting
	Lodging
✓	Off Highway Vehicles
✓	Visitor Center

Over 30 miles of trails exist within the project. All are open to horseback riders, bicyclists, and hikers. The Northshore Trail has trailheads in *Rockledge*, *Murrell*, and *Twin Coves*. The trail winds along the lake's shore for about nine miles. Knob Hills Trail is on the west end of the lake and is four miles long. Nature trails of less than one mile are in *Silverlake* and *Twin Coves*. Three trails used primarily by horseback riders are Walnut Grove, Cross Timbers, and Rocky Point. Walnut Grove is in the southwest portion of the lake and can vary in length from short distances to more than ten miles. Cross Timber is in the lake's northwest portion and is approximately five miles long. Rocky Point offers scenic views of the lake and is about three miles in length.

Four recreation areas have facilities for tent campers and RVers. Tent camping is available in *Murrell* and *Oak Grove* parks. Campsites with water and electric hookups are in *Twin Coves* and *Silverlake*. The *Twin Coves* campground is open March through September. The campground in *Silverlake* is open year-round.

Grapevine Lake is a 7,380-acre reservoir with 60 miles of shoreline. Opportunities for the angler include largemouth and smallmouth bass,

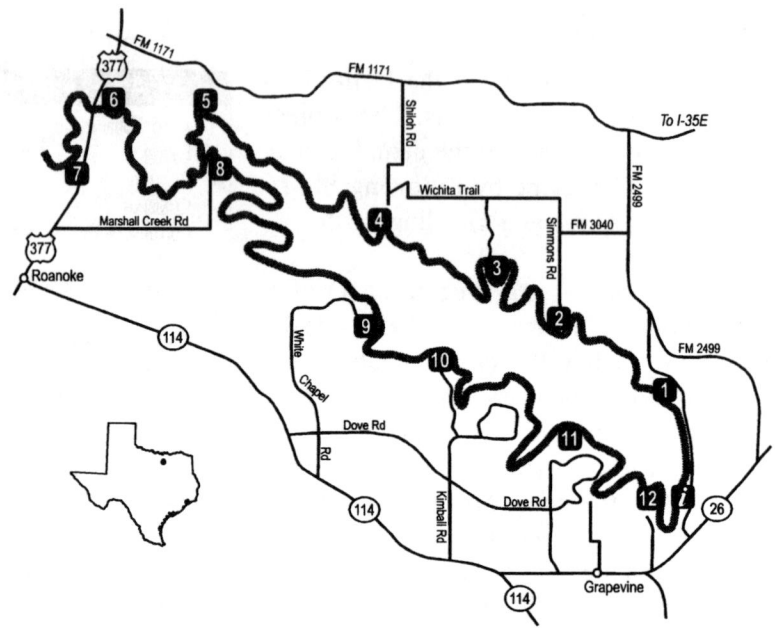

crappie, flathead catfish, and various types of sunfish. Boat ramps are found in all the parks but *Rockledge* and *Rocky Point*. Complete boating and fishing supplies are available in the communities surrounding the lake.

Information: U.S. Army Corps of Engineers, Grapevine Lake, 110 Fairway Dr., Grapevine TX 76051 / 817-481-4541.

Grapevine Lake													
1 Rockledge				•	•	•	•				•		
2 Murrell	•			•	•		•				•	•	•
3 Twin Coves	44	42	•	•	•	•	•	•	•		•		•
4 Rocky Point											•		
5 Knob Hills	N	O	F	A	C	I	L	I	T	I	E	S	
6 North Shore	N	O	F	A	C	I	L	I	T	I	E	S	
7 Roanoke	N	O	F	A	C	I	L	I	T	I	E	S	
8 Marshall Creek				•	•		•				•		•
9 Walnut Grove	N	O	F	A	C	I	L	I	T	I	E	S	
10 Meadowmere				•	•		•	•	•				•
11 Oak Grove	18			•	•	•	•				•	•	
12 Silverlake	61	53	•	•	•	•	•	•	•		•		•

Hords Creek Lake

Hords Creek Dam and Lake is in central Texas about 55 miles south of Abilene and eight miles west of Coleman. To reach the dam from Coleman, follow SH 153 west for eight miles. An information center is located adjacent to the project office on the north end of the dam. The information center contains a topographical map of the entire lake and a cutaway section of the dam and outlet works. The center also periodically features special displays on topics such as water safety, wildlife, and plants.

At A Glance
Auto Touring
Biking
✓ Boating
Climbing
Cultural or Historic Sites
✓ Camping
Educational Programs
✓ Fishing
Groceries / Supplies
✓ Hiking
Horseback Riding
✓ Hunting
Lodging
Off Highway Vehicles
✓ Visitor Center

Hords Creek Lake was the first Corps of Engineers project in the Colorado River Basin to be placed in operation. The lake offers a variety of outdoor recreation in addition to an abundance of fish and wildlife. Two parks have camping areas suitable for tents and recreational vehicles. Campsites with water and electric hookups are in *Lakeside* and *Flatrock*. Several sites in *Flatrock* and *Lakeside* also have electric, water, and sewer hookups. *Friendship Park* is strictly a day-use area with picnic facilities. *Lakeside* and *Friendship* are open all year; *Flatrock* is open mid-May to mid-October. Camp Colorado, a military outpost replica, may be seen in nearby Coleman.

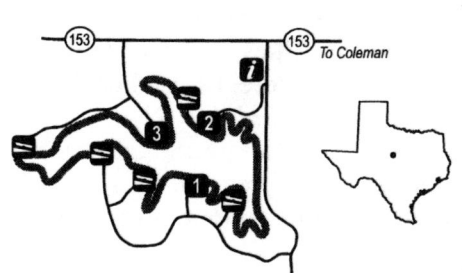

This 510-acre conservation reservoir is located in the Colorado River Basin on Hords Creek. Fishing Piers are located in *Flat Rock* and *Lakeside*. Anglers will find largemouth bass, catfish, crappie, and sunfish in the small lake. Several boat ramps are located around the lake as well as in all three park areas.

Information: U.S. Army Corps of Engineers, Hords Creek Lake, HC

75 Box 33, Coleman TX 76834 / 915-625-2322.

Hords Creek Lake	△	🚗	🏠	🚽	🎣	⛵	🏕	🚿	🏊	🍽	🚶	⚓	〰
1 Flatrock	122	61	•	•	•		•	•	•				•
2 Friendship				•	•	•		•		•			•
3 Lakeside	62	62	•	•	•		•	•	•				•

Jim Chapman Lake

Cooper Dam and Jim Chapman Lake (also known as Cooper Lake) lies in northeast Texas about 80 miles northeast of Dallas and 15 miles north of Sulphur Springs. To reach the dam from Sulphur Springs, follow SH 19/154 north to CR 4795 and turn west. The project office is off CR 4795 on the south end of the dam.

At A Glance
Auto Touring
✓ Biking
✓ Boating
Climbing
Cultural or Historic Sites
✓ Camping
✓ Educational Programs
✓ Fishing
Groceries / Supplies
✓ Hiking
✓ Horseback Riding
✓ Hunting
✓ Lodging
Off Highway Vehicles
Visitor Center

Two developed recreation areas on the lake are operated as units of Cooper Lake State Park. The *Doctor's Creek Unit* is on the lake's northern shore. It has a campground, swimming beach, picnic facilities, a nature trail, and a Texas State Parks Store. Located on the south shore is the *South Sulphur Unit*. This unit offers the same facilities plus an equestrian trail and camping area, 15 rental cabins, and a hiking trail that leads to a primitive camping area.

On the lake's western portion is the Cooper Wildlife Management Area. Hunting is permitted in this area. Wildlife inhabiting the region includes white-tailed deer, quail, mourning dove, waterfowl, squirrel, and rabbit. Inquire at the wildlife office for more information, phone 903-945-3132.

Jim Chapman Lake is a 19,280-acre impoundment created on the South Sulphur River. Among the fish found in the lake are largemouth bass, white and hybrid bass, striped bass, channel and flathead catfish, blue catfish, black and white crappie, and various sunfish. Two lighted fishing piers are located in *South Sulphur Unit*. Besides the boat ramps in both units of the state park, two boat ramps are located in the Cooper Wildlife Management Area.

Texas

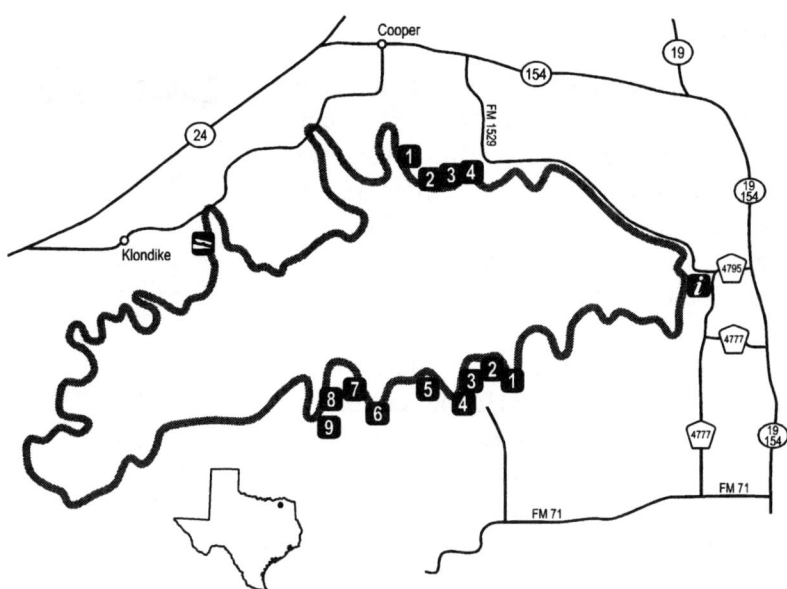

Information: U.S. Army Corps of Engineers, Cooper Project Office, P.O. Box 461, Cooper TX 75432 / 903-945-2108. Cooper Lake State Park, Doctor's Creek Unit, Route 1 Box 231-A15, Cooper TX 75432 / 903-395-3100. Cooper Lake State Park, South Sulphur Unit, Route 3 Box 741, Sulphur Springs TX 75482 / 903-945-5256.

Jim Chapman Lake													
Doctors Creek Unit													
1 Liberty Grove	42	42			•		•	•		•	•		
2 Pelican Point				•	•	•	•	•	•	•		•	
3 Bluebonnet						•	•						
4 Lone Pine Boat Ramp								•					•
South Sulphur Unit													
1 Heron Harbor					•	•	•	•	•	•		•	
2 Gulls Bluff					•	•		•					•
3 Eagle Point					•			•	•				
4 Sunset Cove							•		•				
5 Bright Star	46	46	•		•			•	•				
6 Honey Creek								•					•
7 Oak Grove	15				•			•	•				
8 Deer Haven	41	41			•			•	•				
9 Buggy Whip Equestrian	15							•	•		•		

Joe Pool Lake

Joe Pool Lake lies south of the Dallas/Forth Worth area in northeast Texas. The dam is reached by following FM 1382 north from the intersection with US 67 near Cedar Hill. It can also be reached from I-20 Exit 457 by following FM 1382 south. The project office and an overlook are on the east end of the dam.

Joe Pool Lake offers a variety of activities for the outdoor enthusiast. Hiking and bicycling trails can be found in *Cedar Hill State Park*. Maps of the trail system are available from the park's headquarters. For the sun-seeker and swimmer, beaches are located in the state park, *Lynn Creek Park*, and *Loyd Park*. Camping facilities for tents and recreational vehicles are in *Loyd Park* and *Cedar Hill State Park*. Most of the campsites in both parks have water and electric hookups. *Lynn Creek* is a day-use only park with picnic facilities, beach, and children's playground.

Joe Pool Lake is a 7,470-acre impoundment on Mountain Creek. Fishing is good for largemouth bass, flathead and channel catfish, crappie, and various sunfish. Several fishing piers and jetties, two of which are lighted, are located in *Cedar Hill State Park*. The state park also has a perch fishing pond for youngsters.

At A Glance

Auto Touring
✓ Biking
✓ Boating
Climbing
✓ Cultural or Historic Sites
✓ Camping
✓ Educational Programs
✓ Fishing
✓ Groceries / Supplies
✓ Hiking
✓ Horseback Riding
Hunting
Lodging
Off Highway Vehicles
✓ Visitor Center

Boat ramps can be found in three of the four recreation areas. Boating and fishing supplies are available from the marinas in *Lynn Creek* and the state park.

Information: U.S. Army Corps of Engineers, Joe Pool Lake, P.O. Box 872, Cedar Hill TX 75106 / 972-299-2227. Cedar Hill State Park, Box 2649, Cedar Hill TX 75106 / 972-291-3900

Joe Pool Lake													
1 Lynn Creek				•	•	•		•	•		•		
2 Loyd Park	221	•	•	•	•	•	•	•		•		•	
3 Britton Park	N	O		F	A	C	I	L	I	T	I	E	S
4 Cedar Hill State Park	375	355	•	•	•	•	•	•	•		•	•	•

Lake O' The Pines

Lake O' The Pines is in eastern Texas about ten miles west of Jefferson and 30 miles northeast of Longview. To reach the dam from Longview, follow US 259 north to FM 726 and turn east. Follow FM 726 for approximately 15 miles to the dam. Information about the lake and its recreation areas is available from the project office on the east end of the dam.

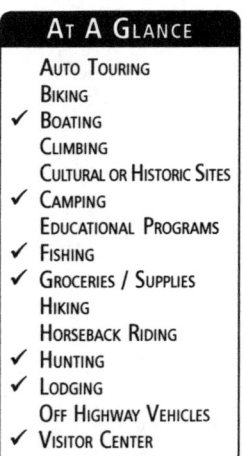

At A Glance
Auto Touring
Biking
✓ Boating
Climbing
Cultural or Historic Sites
✓ Camping
Educational Programs
✓ Fishing
✓ Groceries / Supplies
Hiking
Horseback Riding
✓ Hunting
✓ Lodging
Off Highway Vehicles
✓ Visitor Center

Lake O' The Pines offers varied outdoor recreation among the natural scenic beauty of east Texas. Seven campgrounds operated by the Corps of Engineers provide campsites for tents and recreational vehicles. There are seven more campgrounds that are operated by commercial concession. Nearly all of the campgrounds have sites with hookups for RVs. Many of the parks also provide day-use areas with picnic facilities and swimming beaches.

Constructed on Big Cypress Creek, Lake O' The Pines offers 18,700 acres for boating and fishing. A variety of fish species inhabit the lake including largemouth and smallmouth bass, flathead and channel catfish, crappie, and sunfish. Some record-size fish are: smallmouth

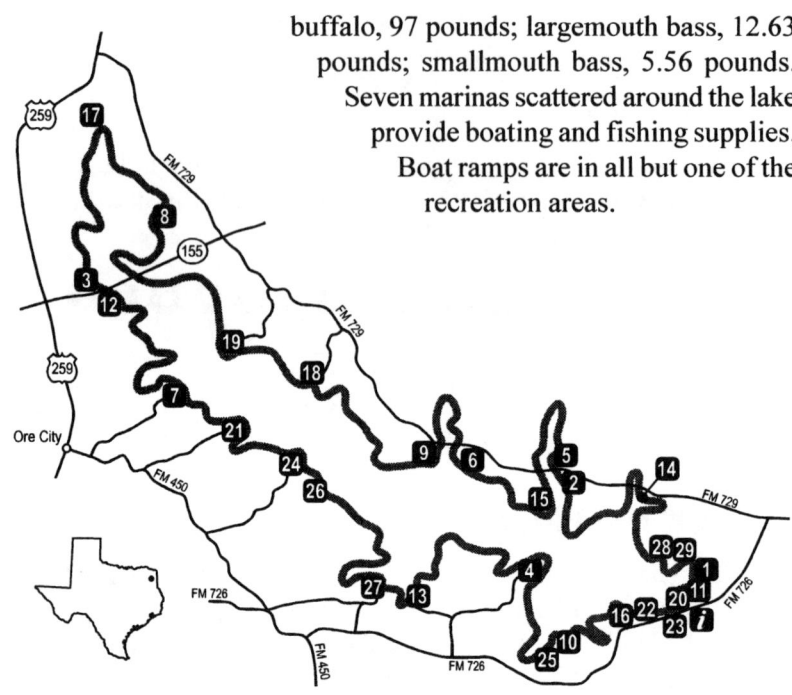

buffalo, 97 pounds; largemouth bass, 12.63 pounds; smallmouth bass, 5.56 pounds. Seven marinas scattered around the lake provide boating and fishing supplies. Boat ramps are in all but one of the recreation areas.

Information: U.S. Army Corps of Engineers, Lake O' The Pines, P.O. Drawer W, Jefferson TX 75657 / 903-665-2336.

LAKE O' THE PINES	⛺	🚐	🚻	🥤	🪑	🍴	🏪	🚿	🏊	🛥	🚶	⚓	🏕
1 BIG CYPRESS MARINA	•	•			•		•	•				•	•
2 JOHNSON CREEK MARINA	•	•					•					•	•
3 HIGHWAY 155 MARINA	•	•	•		•		•	•				•	•
4 ISLAND VIEW MARINA	•				•							•	•
5 BULLFROG MARINA	•	•	•		•	•						•	•
6 LAKESIDE MOTEL & MARINA					•							•	
7 SUNRISE COVE	•	•			•		•	•				•	•
8 WILLOW POINT	•	•			•		•						•
9 ALLEY CREEK	75	49	•	•	•		•	•	•				•
10 BRUSHY CREEK	111	83	•	•	•	•	•	•	•				•
11 BUCKHORN CREEK	100	62	•	•	•		•	•	•				•
12 CEDAR SPRINGS	15		•		•		•		•				•
13 COPELAND CREEK													•

continued next page

Lake O' The Pines (continued)												
14 Hurricane Creek	20				•		•					•
15 Johnson Creek	85	73	•	•	•	•	•	•	•	•		•
16 Lakeside						•		•		•		•
17 Lone Star												•
18 Mims Chapel												•
19 Oak Valley	10				•		•					•
20 Overlook					•		•					•
21 Pine Hill												•
22 Shady Grove					•		•		•			•
23 Outlet						•						•
24 Pop's Landing												•
25 Tejas												•
26 Oak Ridge												•
27 Woodie's Ramp												•
28 Pine Harbor												•
29 Holiday Harbor												•

Lavon Lake

Lavon Lake is in northeastern Texas about 15 miles northeast of Garland. To reach the dam from Garland, follow SH 78 north. The dam may also be reached from I-30 Exit 68 east of Dallas by following SH 205 north to SH 78. The project office is on the west end of the dam, about one mile north of SH 78.

Sixteen recreation areas have been developed on Lavon Lake. Of the six parks that offer camping, only *East Fork, Tickey Creek* and *Collin Park* are open year-round. The other three parks are open from March through September. Water and electric hookups are available at campsites in *Clearlake, Collin, East Fork,* and *Lavonia* parks. *Caddo Park* was specially designed for easy accessibility to the handicapped.

Numerous trails can be found within the project. An off-road vehicle area is below the dam and has several motorcycle and four-wheeler

At A Glance
- Auto Touring
- ✓ Biking
- ✓ Boating
- Climbing
- Cultural or Historic Sites
- ✓ Camping
- Educational Programs
- ✓ Fishing
- ✓ Groceries / Supplies
- ✓ Hiking
- ✓ Horseback Riding
- ✓ Hunting
- Lodging
- ✓ Off Highway Vehicles
- ✓ Visitor Center

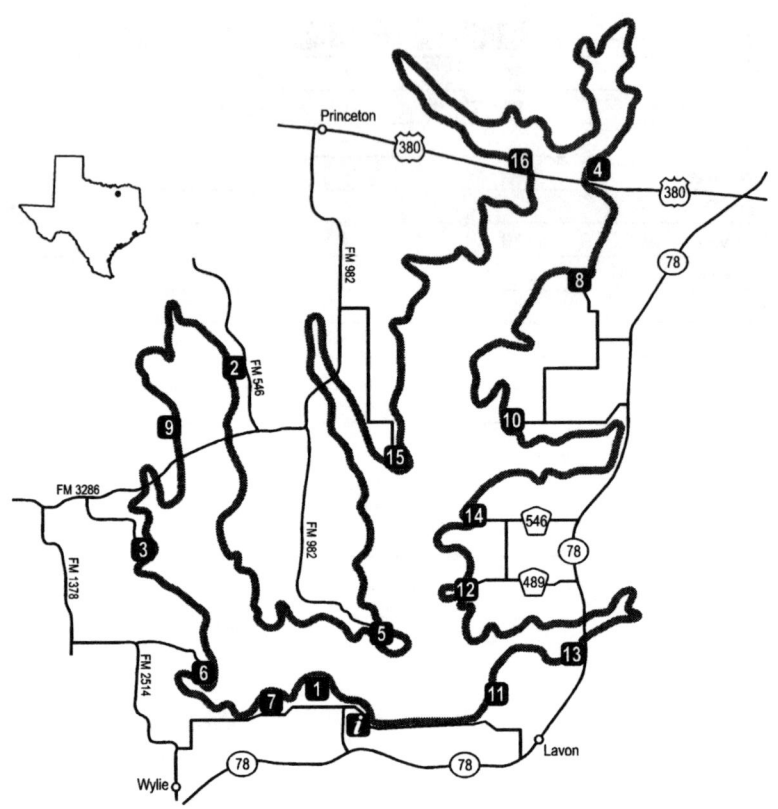

trails. The Trinity Trail offers ten miles of equestrian and hiking trails; trail heads are in *Brockdale* and *East Fork* parks. Sister Grove Bike Trail is six miles long and is used for hiking as well as off-road bicycles.

The 21,400-acre reservoir was constructed on the East Fork of the Trinity River. Anglers will find good fishing for striped bass and white crappie. Other species include largemouth bass, catfish, and various sunfish. Bait, tackle, and boat rentals are available from the East Fork Harbor Marina in *East Fork*. The fishing area below the dam offers a universally accessible fishing pier on the west wing wall. Boat ramps are located in all recreation areas.

Information: U.S. Army Corps of Engineers, Lavon Lake, 3375 Skyview Drive, Wylie TX 75098 / 972-442-3141.

Lavon Lake	⛺	🚐	🚮	🚻	🍽	🏖	🏠	🚿	🛥	🏪	🥾	⚓	🏊
1 Avalon				•	•		•						•
2 Bratonia							•						•
3 Brockdale					•		•				•		•
4 Caddo Park					•		•						•
5 Clearlake	23	23	•	•	•		•	•					•
6 Collin Park	44	32	•	•	•		•	•	•			•	•
7 East Fork	62	50	•	•	•	•	•	•	•		•	•	•
8 Elm Creek							•						•
9 Highland							•						•
10 Lakeland	32			•	•		•						•
11 Lavonia Park	53	38	•	•	•	•	•	•	•		•	•	•
12 Little Ridge				•	•		•						•
13 Mallard Park				•			•		•				•
14 Pebble Beach				•	•		•		•				•
15 Tickey Creek	17			•	•		•						•
16 Twin Groves							•						•

Lewisville Lake

Lewisville Lake is in northeast Texas nearly 30 miles northwest of downtown Dallas. The project office is on the west end of the dam. It can be reached from Dallas by follow I-35E north to Exit 454 (Lake Park Road).

The visitor to Lewisville Lake will find 22 recreation areas for camping, picnicking, and swimming. Eleven parks provide camping facilities for tents and recreational vehicles. Campsites with water and electric hookups are available in *Hidden Cove, Oakland, Hickory Creek, Pilot Knoll,* and *Lewisville Lake* parks. The campgrounds in these parks are open all year. *Lewisville Lake Park* also has an 18-hole golf course, fishing barge, softball diamonds, and soccer fields.

At A Glance
Auto Touring
Biking
✓ Boating
Climbing
Cultural or Historic Sites
✓ Camping
✓ Educational Programs
✓ Fishing
✓ Groceries / Supplies
✓ Hiking
✓ Horseback Riding
✓ Hunting
Lodging
Off Highway Vehicles
✓ Visitor Center

Lewisville Lake is a 23,280-acre impoundment on the Elm Fork Trinity River. Among the species inhabiting the lake are largemouth bass,

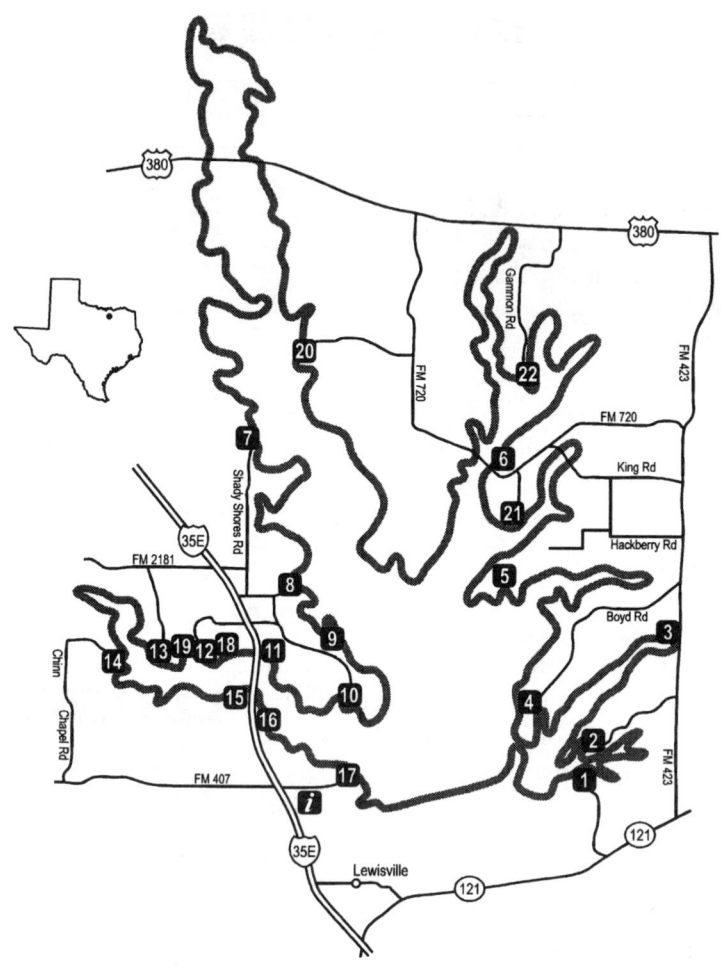

striped bass, crappie, catfish, and sunfish. Boat ramps are located in nearly all the recreation areas. A marina is located in *Lewisville Lake Park*.

Information: U.S. Army Corps of Engineers, Lewisville Lake, 1801 N. Mill St., Lewisville TX 75057 / 972-434-1666.

Lewisville Lake	▲	⌂	🚻	🚰	⛱	☕	🏠	🍴	🏊	🛢	🚶	⚓	〰
1 East Hill Park				•	•			•	•				•

continued next page

Lewisville Lake (continued)	⛺	🚐	🚻	🚽	🧺	🍽	🚿	🏊	⛽	🥾	⚓	🚤
2 Stewart Creek	•		•	•	•		•		•			•
3 Eastvale Park	•				•	•						•
4 Wynnewood	N	O		F	A	C	I	L	I	T	I	E	S
5 Hidden Cove Park	50	50	•	•	•	•	•	•	•			•
6 Little Elm	•			•	•	•	•		•			•
7 Big Sandy Access												•
8 Willow Grove	•				•		•					
9 Westlake Park				•	•			•				•
10 Oakland Park	101	65	•	•		•	•	•				•
11 Arrowhead Access					•		•					
12 Hickory Creek	114	104	•	•	•	•	•	•	•	•	•	•
13 Sycamore Bend	15			•	•		•					•
14 Pilot Knoll	54	54	•	•	•	•	•	•	•	•		•
15 Copperas Branch					•		•		•			
16 Tower Bay Access							•					•
17 Lewisville Lake Park	113	91	•	•	•		•	•	•		•	•
18 Point Vista Access												•
19 Harbor Lane						•						
20 Crescent Oaks												•
21 Cottonwood Park	•				•		•					
22 Doe Branch Access												•

Navarro Mills Lake

Located in northeast Texas, Navarro Mills Lake lies about 75 miles south of Dallas and 18 miles southwest of Corsicana. To reach the dam from Corsicana, follow SH 31 to FM 667 and turn north. The project office is on the east end of the dam about one mile north of SH 31 along FM 667. An overlook is located adjacent to the project office.

There are five recreation areas on Navarro Mills Lake. Camping facilities are available in all the parks. Campsites with water and electric hookups are in *Oak Park, Wolf Creek Park,* and *Liberty Hill Park*. All of the campgrounds are

At A Glance

Auto Touring
Biking
✓ Boating
Climbing
Cultural or Historic Sites
✓ Camping
Educational Programs
✓ Fishing
✓ Groceries / Supplies
✓ Hiking
Horseback Riding
✓ Hunting
Lodging
Off Highway Vehicles
Visitor Center

open year-round except *Pecan Point*, which is closed from November through February.

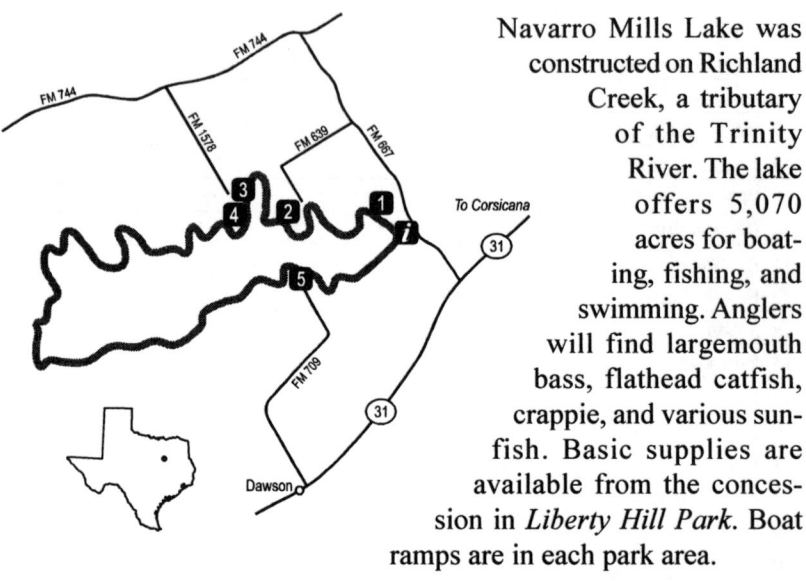

Navarro Mills Lake was constructed on Richland Creek, a tributary of the Trinity River. The lake offers 5,070 acres for boating, fishing, and swimming. Anglers will find largemouth bass, flathead catfish, crappie, and various sunfish. Basic supplies are available from the concession in *Liberty Hill Park*. Boat ramps are in each park area.

Information: U.S. Army Corps of Engineers, Navarro Mills Lake, Route 1 Box 33D, Purdon TX 76679 / 254-578-1431.

Navarro Mills Lake														
1 Oak Park	48	48	•	•	•		•	•	•		•		•	
2 Wolf Creek Park	73	50	•	•	•		•	•	•				•	
3 Brushie Prairie	10			•	•		•		•				•	
4 Pecan Point	45			•	•		•		•				•	
5 Liberty Hill Park	102	96	•	•	•		•	•	•			•	•	

O.C. Fisher Lake

O.C. Fisher Lake is in west-central Texas just west of San Angelo. The lake's headquarters is near the south end of the dam. It can be reached from San Angelo by following US 67 south to FM 853. Follow FM 853 west about one mile to Mercedes Street and turn north. The project office is on the north side of Mercedes Street.

O.C. Fisher Lake is also known as North Concho Lake or Lake San

Angelo. There are seven recreation areas managed by the Texas Parks and Wildlife Department as units of the San Angelo State Park. Camping facilities for tents and recreational vehicles are provided in all the parks. A total of 82 campsites have water and electric hookups. Primitive walk-in campsites can also be found. San Angelo State Park is open year-round. An extensive trail system between *Red Arroyo* and *North Concho* parks is available for those interested in hiking, horseback riding, or mountain biking. There are six cabins available for rent in *Red Arroyo*.

At A Glance
Auto Touring
✓ Biking
✓ Boating
Climbing
Cultural or Historic Sites
✓ Camping
✓ Educational Programs
✓ Fishing
✓ Groceries / Supplies
✓ Hiking
✓ Horseback Riding
✓ Hunting
✓ Lodging
✓ Off Highway Vehicles
Visitor Center

O.C. Fisher Lake is a 5,440-acre reservoir on the North Concho River. Anglers will find channel and flathead catfish, largemouth bass, walleye, crappie, and sunfish in the lake. Boat ramps are in *Lakeview* and *Red Arroyo* parks. Camping, fishing, and boating supplies can be found in San Angelo.

Information: San Angelo State Park, 3900 Mercedes St., San Angelo TX 76901 / 915-949-4757.

O.C. Fisher Lake											
1 Lakeview Park		•		•	•		•			•	

continued next page

O.C. Fisher Lake (continued)	△	▭	🚻	🚰	🎣	🚤	🏠	🌲	⛵	🔋	🚶	⚓	〜
2 Red Arroyo Park	•	•	•		•	•	•	•		•	•		•
3 Isabel Harte Park	•			•	•		•			•			
4 Potts Creek Park	•			•	•					•			
5 River Bend Park	•			•	•		•			•			
6 North Concho Park	•		•	•	•		•			•			
7 Bald Eagle Park	•	•	•	•	•	•	•	•					

Pat Mayse Lake

Pat Mayse Lake is located about 12 miles north of Paris in northeast Texas. The dam is reached from Paris by traveling ten miles north on US 271 and two miles west on FM 906. Information is available from the project office located on the east end of the dam.

Visitors to Pat Mayse Lake will find four recreation areas. All four parks provide camping facilities for tents and recreational vehicles. Water and electric hookups are available in *Pat Mayse East*, *Pat Mayse West*, and *Sanders Cove*. All four camping areas are open year-round.

At A Glance
Auto Touring
Biking
✓ Boating
Climbing
Cultural or Historic Sites
✓ Camping
Educational Programs
✓ Fishing
Groceries / Supplies
Hiking
Horseback Riding
✓ Hunting
✓ Lodging
Off Highway Vehicles
Visitor Center

Land surrounding the lake is managed for wildlife and is open to the public for hunting. Wildlife inhabiting the area includes white-tailed deer, bobwhite quail, fox and grey squirrel, mourning dove, cottontail

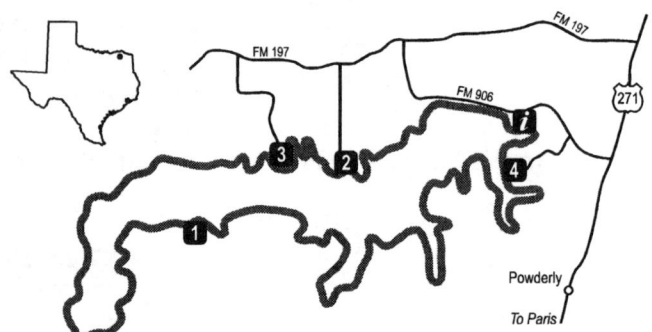

rabbit, raccoon, and fox. A few miles north of the project is the famed Red River Bottoms where waterfowl congregate in great numbers.

The nearly 6,000-acre lake, with 62 miles of shoreline, was constructed on Sanders Creek in the Red River Basin. Anglers will find largemouth bass, white crappie, white bass, channel and flathead catfish, and sunfish in the lake. There are boat ramps in four parks. Boating and fishing supplies are available nearby.

Information: U.S. Army Corps of Engineers, Pat Mayse Lake, P.O. Box 129, Powderly TX 75473 / 903-732-3020.

Pat Mayse Lake	⛺	🏠	🏢	🚻	🪑	🛥	🏕	🚿	🎣	🚶	⚓	〰
1 Lamar Point	8		•	•	•		•	•				•
2 Pat Mayse East	26	26	•	•	•		•		•			•
3 Pat Mayse West	88	78	•	•	•		•	•				•
4 Sanders Cove	89	88	•	•	•		•	•	•			•

Proctor Lake

Proctor Lake is in central Texas about 97 miles southwest of Fort Worth and eight miles northeast of Comanche. The dam can be reached from Comanche by following US 67/377 northeast for six miles and FM 2861 two miles. The project office is on the west end of the dam. An overlook is located adjacent to the project office.

Visitors to Proctor Lake will find four developed recreation areas. All four provide camping facilities for tents and recreational vehicles. *Sowell Creek, Promontory,* and *Copperas Creek* have campsites with water and electric hookups. *High Point Park* is currently closed for renovation work but is expected to be open by summer 1999.

Proctor Lake is a 4,610-acre impoundment on the Leon River. Species of fish inhabiting the lake include bass, crappie, catfish, and various

At A Glance
Auto Touring
Biking
✓ Boating
Climbing
Cultural or Historic Sites
✓ Camping
✓ Educational Programs
✓ Fishing
✓ Groceries / Supplies
Hiking
Horseback Riding
✓ Hunting
Lodging
Off Highway Vehicles
✓ Visitor Center

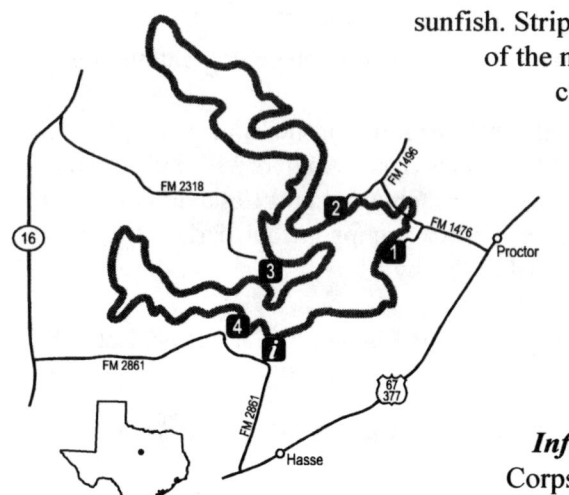

sunfish. Striped hybrid bass is one of the most sought after species. Fishing docks are in *Sowell Creek*, *Promontory*, and *Copperas Creek* parks. There are boat ramps in each park. Fishing supplies may be found nearby.

Information: U.S. Army Corps of Engineers, Proctor Lake, Route 1, Box 71A, Comanche TX 76442 / 254-879-2424.

Proctor Lake	⛺	🚐	🚻	🍽	🏕	♿	👥	🔥	🏞	🚶	⚓	🎣
1 Sowell Creek	60	60	•	•	•		•	•	•	•		•
2 High Point	20		•	•	•		•					•
3 Promontory	100	50	•	•	•		•	•	•		•	•
4 Copperas Creek	66	66	•	•	•		•	•	•			•

Ray Roberts Lake

Ray Roberts Lake is in northeast Texas about 12 miles north of Denton and 50 miles north of Dallas. To reach the dam from Denton, follow I-35 north for approximately ten miles to FM 455 (Exit 478). Follow FM 455 east to the dam. Information about the lake is available from the Ray Roberts Lake State Park office just east of the dam.

The recreation areas surrounding Ray Roberts Lake are managed by the state of Texas as units of Ray Roberts Lake State Park. There are two primary parks and four satellite parks. Camping

At A Glance
Auto Touring
✓ Biking
✓ Boating
Climbing
Cultural or Historic Sites
✓ Camping
Educational Programs
✓ Fishing
✓ Groceries / Supplies
✓ Hiking
✓ Horseback Riding
✓ Hunting
Lodging
Off Highway Vehicles
✓ Visitor Center

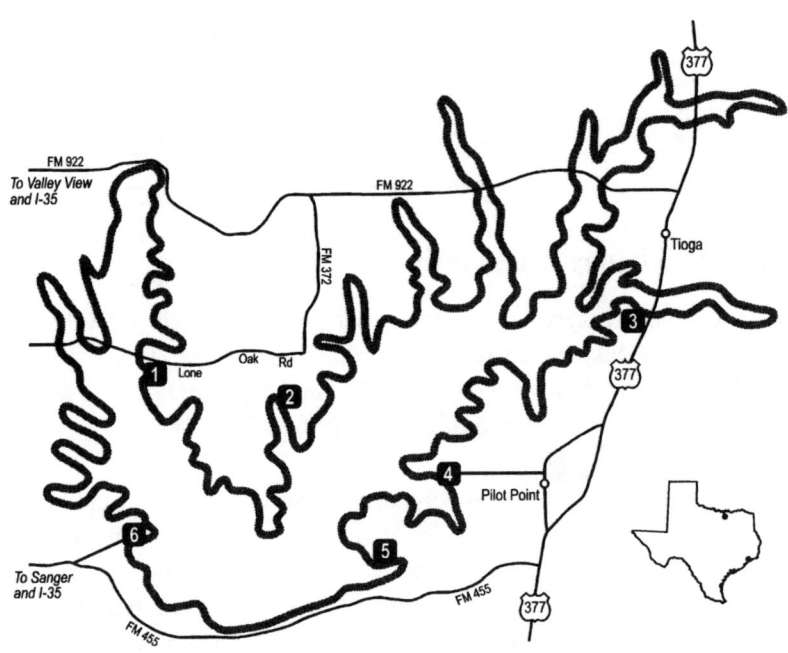

facilities for tents and recreational vehicles are provided in *Isle du Bois* and *Johnson Branch*. Most of the campsites have water and electric hookups. *Isle de Bois* offers nearly 17 miles of dirt trail for hiking, horseback riding, and mountain biking. A 4½ mile paved trail accessible to the disabled is also in the park. There is a total of nine miles of dirt and paved trail in *Johnson Branch*.

Ray Roberts is a 29,350-acre lake on the Elm Fork of the Trinity River. Species of fish in the lake include bass, crappie, catfish, and sunfish. A lighted fishing pier is located in *Isle du Bois*. Boating and fishing supplies are available from the marina in *Sanger Park*.

Information: U.S. Army Corps of Engineers, Ray Roberts Lake, 1801 N. Mill St., Lewisville TX 75067 / 972-434-1667. Ray Roberts Lake State Park, 100 PW 4137, Pilot Point TX 76258 / 940-686-2148.

Ray Roberts Lake													
1 Pecan Creek			•			•							•
2 Johnson Branch	187	184	•	•	•	•	•	•	•	•		•	•

continued next page

Ray Roberts Lake (continued)	⛺												
3 Buck Creek								•					•
4 Jordan Park								•			•		•
5 Isle du Bois	184 115	•	•	•	•	•	•	•	•	•	•		•
6 Sanger								•			•		•

Sam Rayburn Reservoir

Sam Rayburn Reservoir is in southeast Texas approximately 15 miles northwest of Jasper. To reach the lake from Jasper, travel 10 miles north on US 96, then west on FM 255. The project office is at the west end of dam on FM 255.

At A Glance
Auto Touring
Biking
✓ Boating
Climbing
Cultural or Historic Sites
✓ Camping
Educational Programs
✓ Fishing
✓ Groceries / Supplies
✓ Hiking
Horseback Riding
✓ Hunting
✓ Lodging
Off Highway Vehicles
✓ Visitor Center

Sam Rayburn Reservoir is the largest body of water in Texas. The lake is on most fishing tournament trails, including professional tournaments. There are 21 recreation areas, most with facilities for tent campers and RVers. In addition to camping, *Twin Dikes* offers 17 rental cabins, a bath house and laundry facilities. The *Shirley Creek* concessionaire offers camping facilities, 14 rental cabins, a restaurant, propane, and groceries. The concessionaire in *Powell Park* offers camping facilities, ten cabin rentals, a lodge, groceries, restaurant, game room, and bath house. Four recreation areas are managed by the Angelina National Forest: *Letney, Sandy Creek, Bayou,* and *Caney Creek*. The *Letney* recreation area is open by reservation only (409-639-8620) and is popular with horseback riders. *Harvey Creek* and *Townsend Park* are managed by the county of San Augustine.

Sam Rayburn Reservoir is one of the healthiest fisheries in Texas and one of the most popular fishing destinations in the country. The 114,500-acre reservoir with 750 miles of shoreline is on the Angelina River. It runs through the heart of the Angelina National Forest. Anglers come to the lake in search of largemouth bass, flathead and bullhead catfish, white and black crappie, and various sunfish. During the summer, white

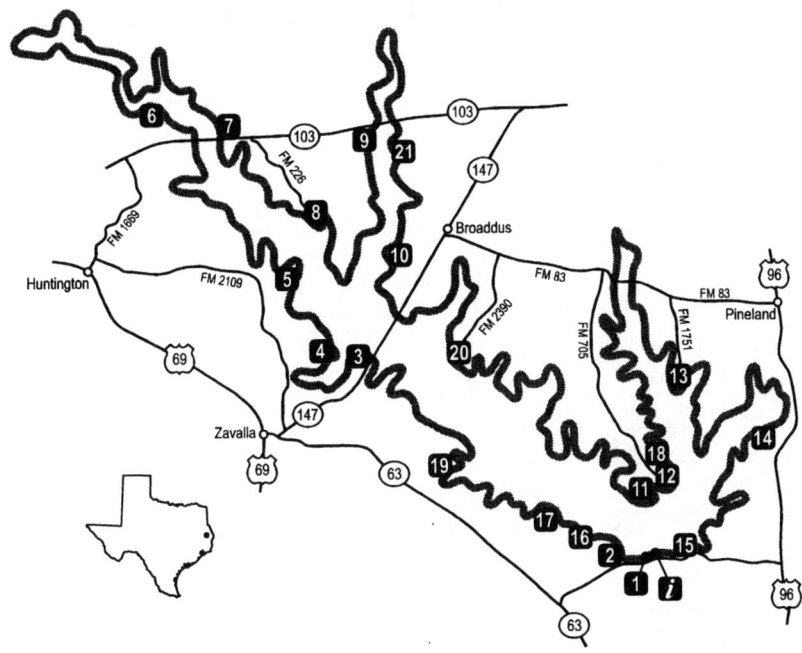

bass, stripers, and hybrids may be found on the southern end of the lake and near the outlet works.

A fishing pier, bait, tackle, groceries and gas are available from the marina in *Twin Dikes*, phone 409-698-2696. Boat rentals, bait and motor repair service are available from the marina in *Shirley Creek*, phone 409-854-2233. The *Powell Park* marina offers bait and tackle, boat rental, and a fishing pier, phone 409-584-2624. *Jackson Hill* marina offers boat rentals and fuel, 409-872-3551.

Information: U.S. Army Corps of Engineers, Sam Rayburn Reservoir, Route 3 Box 486, Jasper TX 75951 / 409-384-5716. Angelina National Forest, 1907 Atkinson Dr., Lufkin TX 75901 / 409-639-8620.

Sam Rayburn Reservoir	△	🚐	🍴	🍺	🏕	👁	🏨	⛽	🎣	🚮	🚶	⚓	≋
1 Overlook Park				•	•		•						
2 Ebenezer Park	30		•	•	•		•		•				
3 Cassells-Boykin	27		•	•	•		•						•

continued next page

228 Texas

SAM RAYBURN (continued)	⛺	🍽	🚻	🚰	⛽	♿	🏫	📡	🏊	🛒	🚶	⚓	🌊
4 Monterey Park								•					•
5 Hanks Creek	44	44	•	•	•	•	•	•			•		•
6 Marion Ferry							•						•
7 Etoile Park	9			•	•		•						•
8 Shirley Creek	89	89	•	•	•		•	•				•	•
9 Ralph McAlister Park							•						•
10 Jackson Hill	40		•	•	•		•		•			•	•
11 Rayburn Park	74	24	•	•	•	•	•	•					•
12 Powell Park	123	53	•	•	•		•	•				•	•
13 San Augustine	100	100	•	•	•	•	•	•	•		•		•
14 Mill Creek	110	110	•	•	•	•	•	•	•				•
15 Twin Dikes	136	93	•	•	•		•	•				•	•
16 Letney Recreation Site	N	O	F	A	C	I	L	I	T	I	E		S
17 Sandy Creek	15			•	•		•	•					•
18 Bayou Recreation Site													•
19 Caney Creek	123			•	•		•	•		•			•
20 Harvey Creek	19			•	•		•						•
21 Townsend Park	14			•	•		•						•

Somerville Lake

Somerville Lake is located in southeast Texas near Somerville and about 26 miles southwest of College Station. The lake's headquarters is near the north end of the dam. It is reached from Somerville by following Eighth Street west to Thornberry Drive.

Seven developed recreation areas surround Somerville Lake. Camping is permitted in all the parks. Two parks, *Birch Creek* and *Nails Creek*, are operated by the state of Texas as units of the Lake Somerville State Park. Campsites with water and electric hookups are available in both units. A 21-mile trail connects the two units and is used by hikers, bikers, and equestrians. Primitive camping areas are located along the trail for backpackers. A nature trail is in *Yegua Creek* and an all-terrain vehicle area is nearby. *Welch Park* is

AT A GLANCE

Auto Touring
✓ Biking
✓ Boating
  Climbing
  Cultural or Historic Sites
✓ Camping
  Educational Programs
✓ Fishing
✓ Groceries / Supplies
✓ Hiking
✓ Horseback Riding
✓ Hunting
  Lodging
✓ Off Highway Vehicles
✓ Visitor Center

leased to the city of Somerville (409-596-1122) and *Big Creek* is operated by private concession, Big Creek Marina (409-596-1616).

The Texas Parks and Wildlife Department manages over 3,000 acres of land for wildlife which can be enjoyed by nature observers and hunters. Wildlife common to the region includes white-tailed deer, fox, coyote, armadillo, raccoon, rabbit, bobwhite quail, and various waterfowl. Wildflowers abound in spring and summer. Nearly 200 species of birds inhabit the area. Bald eagles can sometimes be seen during the winter.

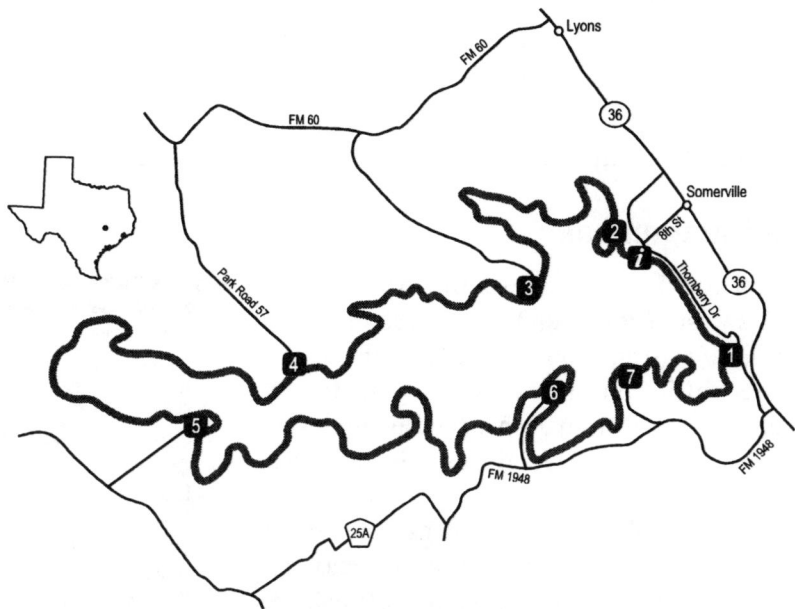

Somerville Lake is on Yegua Creek, a principal tributary of the Brazos River. The lake has 85 miles of shoreline and 11,460 acres for fishing and boating. Found in the lake are largemouth bass, white bass, crappie, catfish, and sunfish. Somerville Lake has enjoyed a reputation of being an excellent catfish lake for many years. Two marinas provide boating and fishing supplies. Boat ramps are located in each of the parks.

Information: U.S. Army Corps of Engineers, Somerville Lake, P.O. Box 549, Somerville TX 77879 / 409-596-1622. Lake Somerville State

Park, Birch Creek Unit, Route 1 Box 499, Somerville TX 77879 / 409-535-7763. Lake Somerville State Park, Nails Creek Unit, Route 1 Box 61-C, Ledbetter TX 78946 / 409-289-2392. Welch Park, City of Somerville, P.O. Box 159, Somerville TX 77879 / 409-596-1122. Big Creek Park, Big Creek Marina, P.O. Box 418, Lyons TX 77863 / 409-596-1616.

Somerville Lake	⛺	🚐	🚻	🚽	⛱	🚿	🍴	☂	🎣	⚓	🚶	⚓	🏊
1 Overlook Park	65	25	•	•	•	•	•	•	•			•	•
2 Welch Park	40			•	•			•	•				•
3 Big Creek	59	21	•	•	•		•	•	•			•	•
4 Birch Creek (State Park)	173	103	•	•	•		•	•	•				•
5 Nails Creek (State Park)	110	40	•	•	•		•	•	•				•
6 Rocky Creek	195	74	•	•	•	•	•	•	•	•			•
7 Yegua Creek	82	47	•	•			•	•	•	•			•

Steinhagen Lake

Steinhagen Lake lies in eastern Texas about 15 miles west of Jasper and 60 miles southeast of Lufkin. Information is available from the project office on the west end of the dam. It can be reached from Jasper by traveling west 15 miles on US 190 and then south on FM 92.

Steinhagen Lake is also known as Town Bluff Reservoir. There are nine recreation areas that provide opportunities for camping, picnicking, hiking, and fishing. Three parks are operated by Texas Parks and Wildlife as units of the Martin Dies Jr. State Park. *Hen House Ridge* and *Walnut Ridge* units have nearly 200 campsites, many with water and electric hookups. The *Cherokee Park* unit (divided into north and south units) offers camping only when the other two units are full. Camping is available in the remaining parks except *Bluff View*. All are open year-round.

At A Glance
Auto Touring
✓ Biking
✓ Boating
Climbing
Cultural or Historic Sites
✓ Camping
Educational Programs
✓ Fishing
✓ Groceries / Supplies
✓ Hiking
Horseback Riding
✓ Hunting
Lodging
Off Highway Vehicles
Visitor Center

Steinhagen Lake is a 13,700-acre impoundment on the Neches River. Anglers will find largemouth bass, crappie, catfish, and sunfish in the lake. Boat rentals are available from all three units of the state park. There are boat ramps in all the parks except *Bluff View*. A marina in *Beech Grove Park* offers the angler all the necessary fishing supplies.

Information: U.S. Army Corps of Engineers, Steinhagen Lake, 890 FM 92, Woodville TX 75979 / 409-429-3491. Martin Dies Jr. State Park, Route 4 Box 274, Jasper TX 75951 / 409-384-5231.

Steinhagen Lake													
1 East End Park	6			•		•							•
2 Bluff View				•	•		•						
3 Campers Cove	25			•	•		•						•
4 Magnolia Ridge	41	35	•	•	•	•	•	•			•		•
5 Beech Grove	•	•		•			•					•	•
6 Sandy Creek	72	66	•	•	•		•						•
7 Cherokee Units (SP)	•	•		•	•	•	•			•		•	•
8 Hen House Ridge (SP)	100	56	•	•	•	•	•			•		•	•
9 Walnut Ridge (SP)	82	59		•	•	•	•			•		•	•

Stillhouse Hollow Lake

Stillhouse Hollow Lake lies south of US 190 in central Texas between Temple and Killeen. The dam is reached from Belton by following US 190 about three miles miles west to FM 1670. Follow FM 1670 south for two miles. The project office is near the north end of the dam.

At A Glance

- Auto Touring
- ✓ Biking
- ✓ Boating
- Climbing
- Cultural or Historic Sites
- ✓ Camping
- ✓ Educational Programs
- ✓ Fishing
- ✓ Groceries / Supplies
- ✓ Hiking
- ✓ Horseback Riding
- ✓ Hunting
- Lodging
- Off Highway Vehicles
- ✓ Visitor Center

Visitors to the project will find seven developed recreation areas on the lake. Two of the parks have camping facilities for tents and recreational vehicles. All of the campsites have water and electric hookups. Both campgrounds are open year-round. A hiking, biking, and equestrian trail is located at the entrance to *Dana Peak Park*. Another trail of about five miles in length is located below the dam in *Chalk Ridge Falls*. Wildlife found in the area includes deer, mourning dove, quail, and various waterfowl.

Stillhouse Hollow Lake is a 6,430-acre impoundment of the Lampasas River. Among the fish in the lake are largemouth and smallmouth bass, catfish, crappie, and various sun-

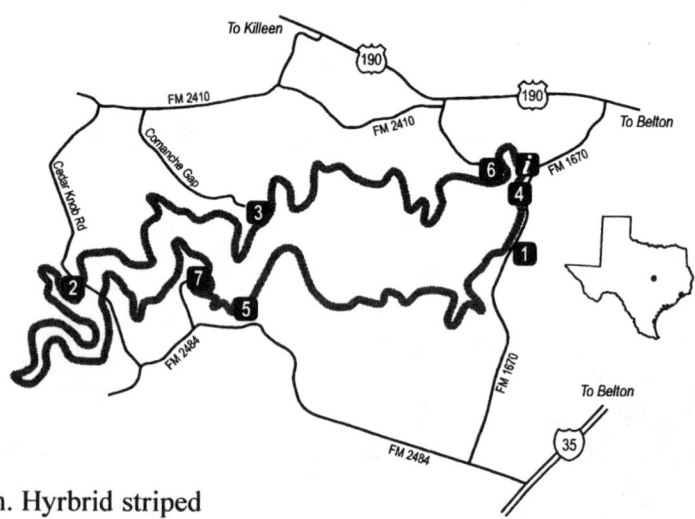

fish. Hyrbrid striped bass and walleye can also be taken from the lake. A fishing dock is in *Union Grove*. Fishing supplies are available from the marina in *Stillhouse Park*.

Information: U.S. Army Corps of Engineers, Stillhouse Hollow Reservoir, Route 3 Box 340, Belton TX 76513 / 254-939-2461.

Stillhouse Hollow	⛺	🚐	🚻	🚽	⛽	🎣	🍴	🏊	🛥	🚶	⚓	🌊
1 Chalk Ridge Falls						•			•			
2 Cedar Gap						•						•
3 Dana Peak	25	25	•	•		•	•	•		•		•
4 Overlook			•	•	•							
5 River's Bend			•	•	•							•
6 Stillhouse Park			•	•		•	•				•	•
7 Union Grove	37	37	•	•	•	•	•	•	•			•

Waco Lake

Waco Lake is in central Texas just west of Waco. The lake's headquarters is on the west end of the dam. It can be reached from I-35 Exit 339 near Waco by following FM 3051 southwest for six miles.

At A Glance

Auto Touring
Biking
✓ Boating
Climbing
Cultural or Historic Sites
✓ Camping
Educational Programs
✓ Fishing
✓ Groceries / Supplies
✓ Hiking
Horseback Riding
✓ Hunting
Lodging
✓ Off Highway Vehicles
Visitor Center

Waco Lake offers the visitor a variety of outdoor recreation activities. Eight parks have been constructed around the lake; camping facilities are in four. Water and electric hookups are available at most of the campsites. All of the parks are open year-round. An off-road vehicle area is on the lake's western shore just off SH 6 near *Speegleville III Park*. It consists of nearly 600 acres of trails. An extensive system of hiking and bicycling trails can be found in *Speegleville II Park*. Educational programs are presented on weekends during the summer at the amphitheater in *Speegleville I Park*.

Constructed on the Bosque River, Waco Lake provides 60 miles of shoreline and 7,270 acres for boating and fishing. More than 50 species of fish inhabit the lake including largemouth bass, white bass, crappie, channel and flathead catfish, and various sunfish. The lake's record fish is a 19.6 pound striped bass. Marinas are located in *Airport Park* and *Speegleville III Park*.

Information: U.S. Army Corps of Engineers, Waco Lake, Route 10 Box 173G, Waco TX 76708 / 254-756-5359.

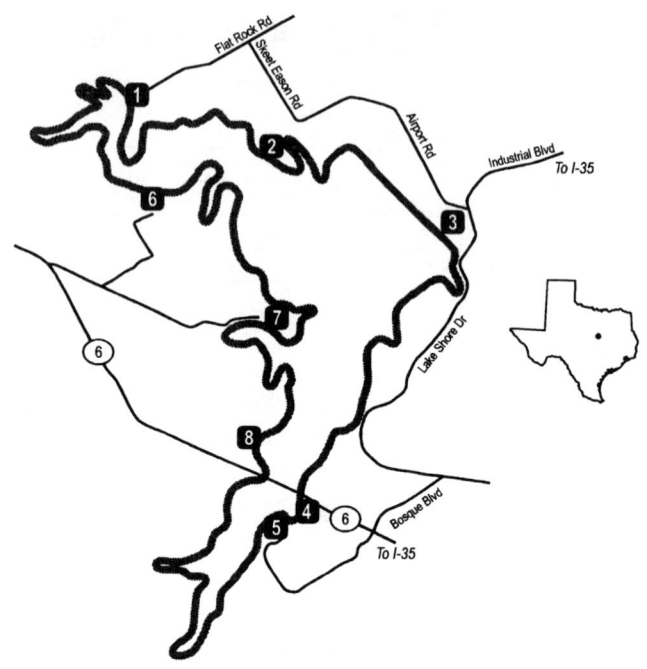

Waco Lake			⛺	🚐	🚻	🚾	🎪	🚣	🍴	🚿	🏊	🏇	⚓	〰
1 Flat Rock Park						•								•
2 Airport Park	63	20	•	•	•			•	•	•			•	•
3 Bosque Park								•						
4 Midway Park	37	37			•	•	•	•	•					•
5 Woodway Park					•	•	•	•				•		
6 Speegleville I	100	94	•	•	•			•	•		•	•	•	•
7 Speegleville II						•			•				•	•
8 Speegleville III	10	10	•	•	•			•	•				•	•

Whitney Lake

Whitney Lake lies in central Texas about five miles west of Whitney and 40 miles northwest of Waco. To reach the dam from Whitney, follow SH 22 south about seven miles. The project office is on the south end of the dam.

Rocky cliffs often come up to the water's edge of this scenic lake.

Scuba divers enjoy exploring the depths of the lake, reaching 100 feet in some places. Fifteen recreation areas have been developed on Whitney Lake. Campgrounds are located in each park; many have sites with water and electric hookups. Some of the camping areas have limited facilities during the winter. Canoes can be launched on the east side of the Brazos River in *Riverside Park*. The first take-out point is 8.4 miles down river at FM 2114. A nature trail of one mile in length is located in *Lake Whitney State Park*. Swimming areas are provided in seven of the parks.

At A Glance
Auto Touring
Biking
✓ Boating
Climbing
Cultural or Historic Sites
✓ Camping
Educational Programs
✓ Fishing
✓ Groceries / Supplies
✓ Hiking
Horseback Riding
✓ Hunting
Lodging
Off Highway Vehicles
✓ Visitor Center

Whitney Lake is a 23,560-acre impoundment of the Brazos River. The lake stretches some 45 miles up the Brazos River Valley. Anglers will find a large variety of fish in the lake. Species include largemouth and smallmouth bass, white and black crappie, flathead and channel catfish, and various sunfish. There are three marinas on the lake that provide a full range of supplies and services. Boat ramps can be found in all but two of the parks.

Information: U.S. Army Corps of Engineers, Whitney Lake, P.O. Box 5038, Clifton TX 76634 / 254-694-3189. Lake Whitney State Park, Box 1175, Whitney TX 76692 / 254-694-3793.

Whitney Lake	🏕	🚐	🚻	🚿	♿	🎣	🍽	🏪	🥾	🏊	⚓	🛥
1 Lofers Bend	134	128	•	•	•	•	•	•	•	•	•	•
2 McCown Valley	54	51	•		•	•	•	•	•			•
3 Cedron Creek	57	57	•	•		•	•	•	•			•
4 Riverside	5				•	•		•				
5 Cedar Creek	20				•	•		•		•		•
6 Kimball Bend	11					•		•		•		•
7 Plowman Creek	34	34	•	•				•	•	•		•
8 Steele Creek	21				•			•				•
9 Walling Bend	10					•		•				•
10 Soldiers Bluff	14				•	•		•				
11 Lake Whitney State Park	137	66	•	•	•	•	•	•	•	•	•	•
12 Juniper Cove	115	95	•	•		•	•	•	•			•
13 Chisholm Trail	•				•			•				•
14 Morgan - Lakeside	•	•	•	•			•	•			•	•
15 Old Fort	5				•			•				•

Wright Patman Lake

Wright Patman Lake is located in northeast Texas about eight miles southwest of Texarkana. Lake information is available from the project office on the south end of the dam. To reach the office from Texarkana, follow US 59 south about eight miles.

Twenty developed recreation areas are scattered along the shore. On the lake's southern shore is *Atlanta State Park*. The park offers camping facilities, nature and hiking trails, a volleyball area, playground, and amphitheater. There are 59 campsites with hookups. Ice, snacks, and soft drinks are available from the concession service. The state park is open all year. Other parks that have campsites with hookups include *Big Creek, Clear Springs, Kelly Creek,*

At A Glance

Auto Touring
Biking
✓ Boating
Climbing
Cultural or Historic Sites
✓ Camping
Educational Programs
✓ Fishing
✓ Groceries / Supplies
✓ Hiking
Horseback Riding
✓ Hunting
Lodging
Off Highway Vehicles
✓ Visitor Center

Moores Landing, *Piney Point*, and *Rocky Point*. *Moores Landing* is a county-operated park with 46 sites and a two-acre tent camping area.

Wright Patman Lake is a 20,300-acre reservoir constructed on the Sulphur River. Fishing is consistently good. Among the species found in the lake are bass, crappie, catfish, and sunfish. A fishing dock is in *Kelly Creek* and *Sulphur Point*.

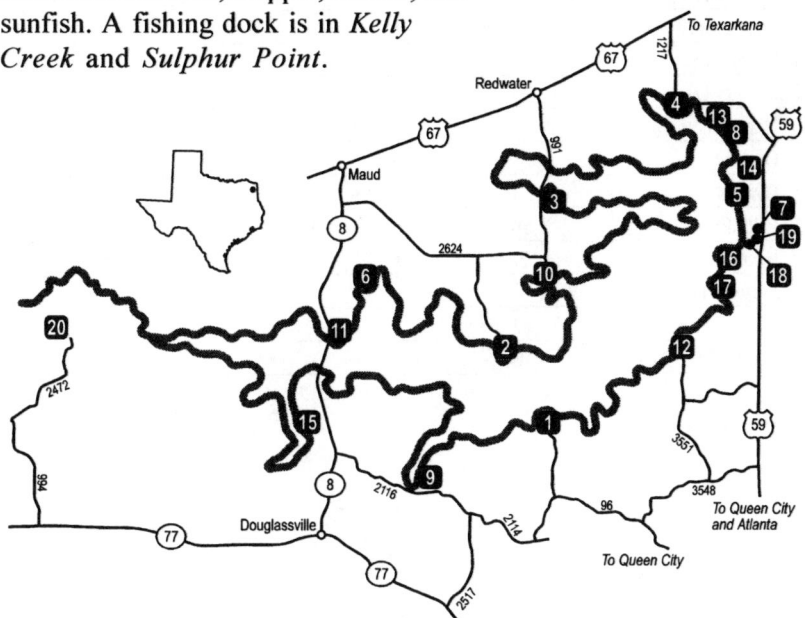

The marina in *Kelly Creek* offers bait, tackle, boat rentals and groceries; phone 903-585-5453. Two additional marinas are located in other parks. Boat ramps can be found in all but three of the parks.

Information: U.S. Army Corps of Engineers, Wright Patman Lake, P.O. Box 1817, Texarkana TX 75504 / 903-838-8781. Atlanta State Park, Route 1 Box 116, Atlanta TX 75551 / 903-796-6476.

Wright Patman														
1 Atlanta State Park	59	59	•	•	•	•	•	•	•	•	•	•	•	•
2 Berry Farm Park	18				•		•							•
3 Big Creek	29	29	•	•		•								•
4 Clear Springs	101	88	•	•		•	•	•	•		•			•

continued next page

Wright Patman (continued)	1	2	3	4	5	6	7	8	9	10	11	12
5 Elliott Bluff												•
6 Herron Creek	14			•	•		•					•
7 Highway 59 Park												•
8 Intake Hill	24		•	•	•		•			•	•	•
9 Jackson Creek	10			•	•		•					•
10 Kelly Creek	80	80	•	•	•		•	•			•	•
11 Malden Lake	14				•		•					•
12 Moores Landing	45	45	•	•	•	•	•	•				•
13 North Shore				•	•	•	•	•	•		•	•
14 Oak Park				•	•	•		•				
15 Overcup	14				•		•					•
16 Piney Point	68	48	•	•	•	•	•	•			•	•
17 Rocky Point	124	124	•	•		•	•	•	•	•	•	•
18 Spillway Park						•						
19 Sulphur Point	12	•		•			•				•	
20 Thomas Lake Park	10				•		•					•

WASHINGTON

1. Lake Bryan
2. Lake Herbert G. West
3. Lower Granite Lake
4. Mill Creek & Bennington Lake
5. Rufus Woods Lake
6. Lake Sacajawea
7. Wynoochee Lake

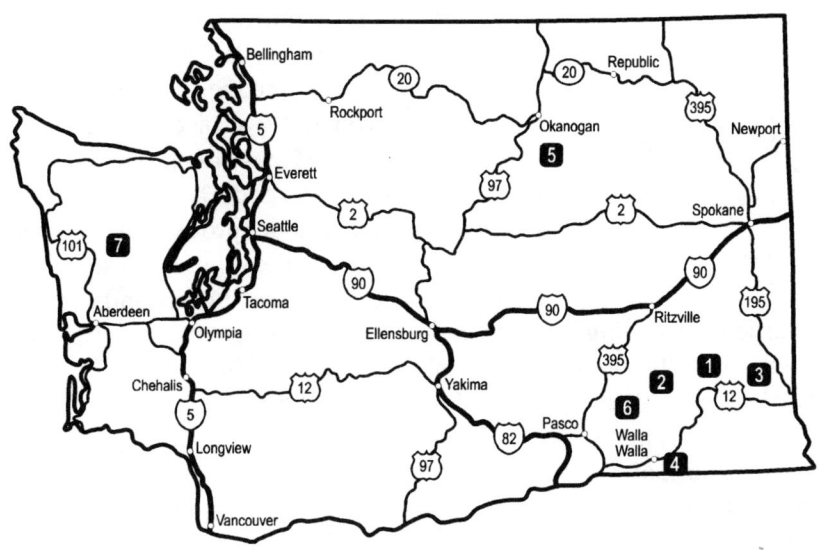

Washington Resources

- ***Washington State Tourism*** - P.O. Box 42500, Olympia WA 98504 / (800) 544-1800 or (360) 586-2088
- ***Washington State Dept. of Fish & Wildlife*** - (360) 902-2200
- ***Road Condition Hotline*** - Mountain Pass Report, October 15 through April 15 (206) 368-4499 or (888) 766-4636.
- ***Road Construction Hotline*** - (360) 705-7075 weekdays

Lake Bryan

Lake Bryan is in southeast Washington about 45 miles north of Walla Walla and eight miles northeast of Starbuck. To reach the visitor center on the south end of the dam, follow the Little Goose Dam access road east out of Starbuck. The visitor center is open year-round during daylight hours.

At A Glance
Auto Touring
Biking
✓ Boating
Climbing
Cultural or Historic Sites
✓ Camping
Educational Programs
✓ Fishing
✓ Groceries / Supplies
Hiking
Horseback Riding
✓ Hunting
✓ Lodging
Off Highway Vehicles
✓ Visitor Center

The Corps' Lower Snake River Project consists of four major locks and dams along the Snake River, the waterway of the Gold Rush days. The Snake River is a major tributary of the Columbia River and is, in itself, one of the largest rivers in the United States. Lake Bryan, the third reservoir in the project, stretches 37 miles between Little Goose Lock and Dam and Lower Granite Lock and Dam. The visitor facilities at the fish ladder provide an excellent opportunity to see Pacific salmon and steelhead trout en route from rearing grounds in the Pacific to spawning grounds in the Snake River headwaters. Wildlife common to the area includes pheasant, quail, chukar, hawks, geese, ducks, owls, and cottontail rabbits. Eagles, pelicans, herons, swans, deer and otter also visit the area.

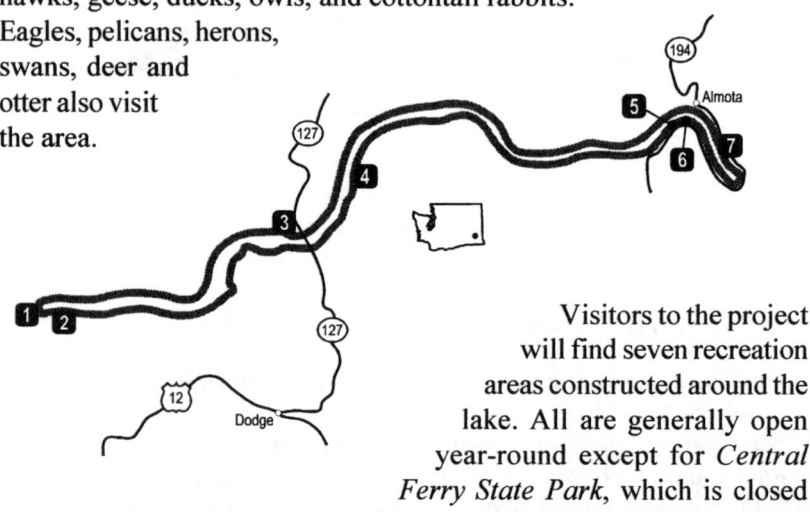

Visitors to the project will find seven recreation areas constructed around the lake. All are generally open year-round except for *Central Ferry State Park*, which is closed between mid-November and mid-March. The state park has nearly 70 campsites for tents and recreational vehicles with most having hookups.

Lake Bryan has a surface area of 10,025 acres. The river is well known for its salmon and steelhead fishing. Bass, crappie, perch, catfish, and sturgeon are also popular Snake River species. The *Boyer Park* marina has boating supplies and services, a one-room motel, restaurant and grocery store. For more information, call 509-397-3791.

Information: U.S. Army Corps of Engineers, Lake Bryan-Eastern Project Office, 100 Fair Street, Clarkston WA 99403 / 509-751-0244. Central Ferry State Park, 10152 SR 127, Pomeroy WA 99347 / 509-549-3551 or 800-233-0321 park information; 800-452-5687 camping reservations.

Lake Bryan												
1 Little Goose Dam				•	•		•					
2 Little Goose Landing		•				•		•				•
3 Central Ferry State Park	68	60	•	•	•		•	•	•			•
4 Willow Landing		•				•		•				•
5 Illia Dunes								•				
6 Illia Landing		•				•		•				•
7 Boyer Park & Marina	28	28	•	•	•		•	•	•		•	•

Lake Herbert G. West

Lake Herbert G. West is situated in the sunny and dry desert of southeastern Washington about 45 miles northeast of Kennewick and six miles south of Kahlotus. To reach the dam from Kahlotus, travel six miles south on Devil's Canyon Road (SH 263). The visitor center, open 9:00 a.m. to 5:00 p.m. April through October, is located on the northwest end of the dam.

The Corps' Lower Snake River Project consists of four major locks and dams along the Snake River, the waterway of the Gold Rush days. The Snake River is a major tributary of the Columbia River and is one of the largest rivers in the United States. Lake Herbert G. West, the second reservoir in the project, stretches 28 miles upstream from the Lower Monumental Lock and

At A Glance

Auto Touring
Biking
✓ Boating
Climbing
✓ Cultural or Historic Sites
✓ Camping
Educational Programs
✓ Fishing
✓ Groceries / Supplies
✓ Hiking
Horseback Riding
Hunting
✓ Lodging
Off Highway Vehicles
✓ Visitor Center

Dam to the Little Goose Lock and Dam. Excellent facilities for viewing Pacific salmon and steelhead trout en route to their spawning grounds on the Snake River are located at the dam. Wildlife common to the area includes pheasant, quail, chukar, hawks, geese, ducks, owls, and cottontail rabbits. Eagles, pelicans, herons, swans, deer and otter also visit the area.

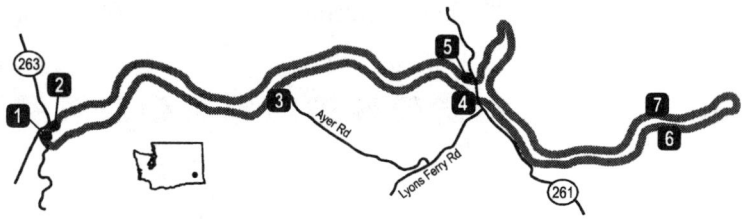

Seven recreation areas have been constructed along Lake Herbert G. West. *Devils Bench*, *Ayer Boat Basin* and *Riparia* are primitive camping areas open all year. The 1,177-acre *Lyons Ferry State Park* is open from April through September.

The 6,590-acre reservoir is well known for its salmon and steelhead fishing. Bass, crappie, perch, catfish, and sturgeon are also popular Snake River species. The *Lyons Ferry Marina*, closed on Tuesdays, offers basic supplies and services as well as a restaurant. The marina can be reached at 509-399-2001.

Information: U.S. Army Corps of Engineers, Lake Herbert G. West, RR 6 Box 693, Pasco WA 99301 / 509-543-3251. Lyons Ferry State Park, Park Manager, Box 157, Starbuck WA 99359 / 509-646-3252.

Lake Herbert G. West	⛺	🚐	🚻	🚰	⛲	🍴	🏚	⚠	🏞	🛢	🚶	⚓	🌊
1 Lower Monumental Dam					•		•						
2 Devils Bench	•					•							•
3 Ayer Boat Basin	20				•	•							•

continued next page

Lake Herbert G. West (cont.)	▲	🚐	🚻	🚽	🎪	🚿	🏚	🎣	🍽	🚶	⚓	〰
4 Lyons Ferry Marina	58	18	•	•	•		•	•			•	•
5 Lyons Ferry State Park	52		•	•	•		•	•	•	•	•	•
6 Texas Rapids				•	•		•					•
7 Riparia				•			•	•				

Lower Granite Lake

Lower Granite Dam is about 35 miles northeast of Pomeroy in southeast Washington. To reach the dam from Pomeroy, travel west on US 12 to SH 127. Follow SH 127 north to Lower Deadman Road and then travel east to the dam. The visitor center, open year-round, is located on the south side of the dam.

The Corps' Lower Snake River Project consists of four major locks and dams along the Snake River, the waterway of the Gold Rush days. The Snake River is a major tributary of the Columbia River and is, in itself, one of the largest rivers in the United States. Lower Granite Lake is the last reservoir in the Lower Snake River Project and extends 33 miles from the Lower Granite Lock and Dam to Lewiston, Idaho. Wildlife common to the area includes pheasant, quail, chukar, hawks, geese, ducks, owls, and cottontail rabbits. Eagles, pelicans, herons, swans, deer and otter also visit the area.

At A Glance
- Auto Touring
- ✓ Biking
- ✓ Boating
- Climbing
- Cultural or Historic Sites
- ✓ Camping
- ✓ Educational Programs
- ✓ Fishing
- ✓ Groceries / Supplies
- ✓ Hiking
- ✓ Horseback Riding
- ✓ Hunting
- Lodging
- Off Highway Vehicles
- ✓ Visitor Center

Running through the center of the Lewis & Clark Valley, Lower Granite Lake provides numerous opportunities for outdoor recreation. Hiking, biking, and nature trails can be found throughout the area. The *Chief Timothy Habitat Management Unit*, located west of Colton off Rimrock Road, provides little more than shade for those seeking some solitude. *Chief Timothy State Park* is located on the site of the Alpowia encampment of the Nez Perce Indian Tribe. An interpretive center is located near the original site of the village, which existed during the mid-1800s. *Hells Gate State Park*, located south of Lewiston, is operated by the Idaho Department of Parks and Recreation. Among the 200 acres bordering the Snake River is a large swimming beach and plenty of grassy areas for picnicking. The park also connects with the Lewiston Clearwater and Snake River National Recreation Trail.

Lower Granite Lake encompasses nearly 9,000 acres of the Snake River. Anglers come from all around to enjoy the famous steelhead runs of the Snake, Salmon, and Clearwater rivers. Bass, crappie, perch, catfish, and sturgeon are also popular Snake River species. A fishing pond for persons with disabilities and children 14 years old and under is located in

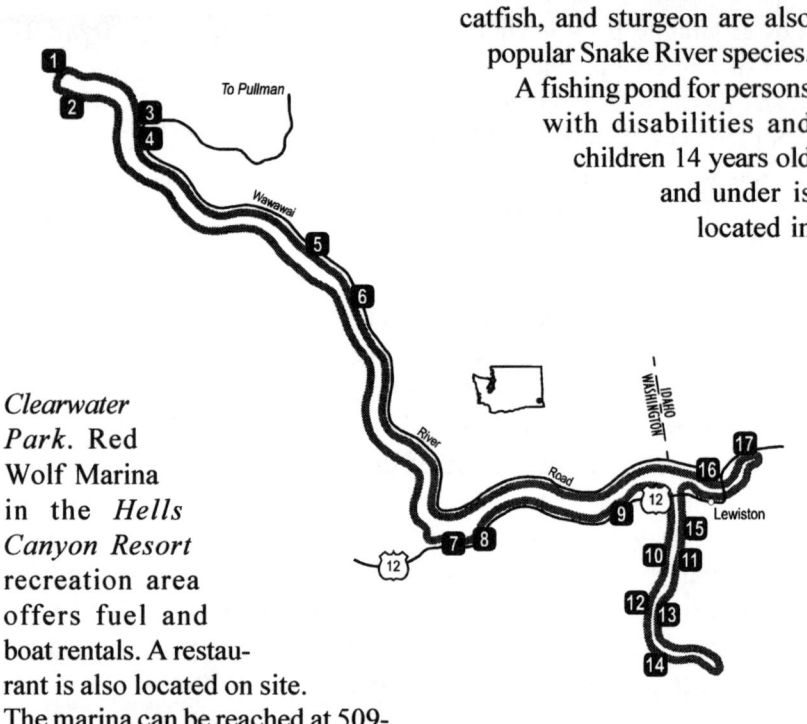

Clearwater Park. Red Wolf Marina in the *Hells Canyon Resort* recreation area offers fuel and boat rentals. A restaurant is also located on site. The marina can be reached at 509-758-6963. The marina in *Hells Gate State Park* offers boat rentals, fuel, and basic supplies, phone 208-799-5016. The marina in *Chief Looking Glass Park*, phone 509-243-4412, offers boating supplies and services. A grocery store is also located here.

Information: U.S. Army Corps of Engineers, Lower Granite Lake, 100 Fair Street, Clarkston WA 99403 / 509-751-0244. Chief Timothy State Park, 13766 Hwy 12, Clarkston WA 99403 / 509-758-9580. Hells Gate State Park, 3620 Snake River Ave., Lewiston ID 83501 / 208-799-5015.

LOWER GRANITE LAKE	🏕	🚐	🚻	🚰	🧺	🎠	🏠	🎣	🚤	🏪	🚶	⚓	🏊
1 LOWER GRANITE DAM				•		•							
2 OFFIELD LANDING					•	•							•
3 WAWAWAI COUNTY PARK	9			•	•	•	•				•		
4 WAWAWAI LANDING	•				•		•						•
5 BLYTON LANDING	•				•		•						•
6 NISQUALLY JOHN LANDING	•				•		•						•
7 CHIEF TIMOTHY STATE PARK	66	33	•	•	•	•	•	•	•	•	•	•	•
8 CHIEF TIMOTHY HMU	N	O	F	A	C	I	L	I	T	I	E	S	
9 HELLS CANYON RESORT				•			•	•				•	•
10 GREENBELT RAMP				•			•				•		•
11 SOUTHWAY RAMP											•		•
12 SWALLOWS PARK				•	•	•	•				•		•
13 HELLS GATE STATE PARK	93	64	•	•	•	•	•	•	•	•	•	•	•
14 CHIEF LOOKING GLASS PARK				•	•	•	•	•				•	•
15 LEWISTON LEVEE PARKWAY				•	•		•				•		
16 CLEARWATER PARK				•	•		•						
17 NORTH LEWISTON RAMP							•				•		•

Mill Creek & Bennington Lake

Mill Creek and Virgil B. Bennington Lake are about three miles east of Walla Walla in southeast Washington. To reach the lake from Walla Walla, travel east on US 12 and head south ½ mile on Tausick Way to Reservoir Road. (Follow the Bennington Lake or Rooks Park signs from US 12.) The Corps project office is located off Reservoir Road.

This small, scenic lake lies on the western edge of the Blue Mountains. The project covers 612 acres and is open year-round except for *Rooks Park*, which is open seasonally from late March through mid-October. The area provides day-use facilities for picnicking, trail use, and fishing. Approximately 13 miles of trails are available year-round for walkers, joggers, bicyclists, horseback riders, and cross-country skiers. An abundance of fish and wildlife, including various species of ducks, quail, pheasants, rabbits,

AT A GLANCE
AUTO TOURING
✓ BIKING
✓ BOATING
CLIMBING
CULTURAL OR HISTORIC SITES
CAMPING
EDUCATIONAL PROGRAMS
✓ FISHING
GROCERIES / SUPPLIES
✓ HIKING
✓ HORSEBACK RIDING
✓ HUNTING
LODGING
OFF HIGHWAY VEHICLES
VISITOR CENTER

mink, deer, beaver, and coyotes are common in the area. In the spring and fall, migratory birds can be seen resting and feeding along Mill Creek and Bennington Lake.

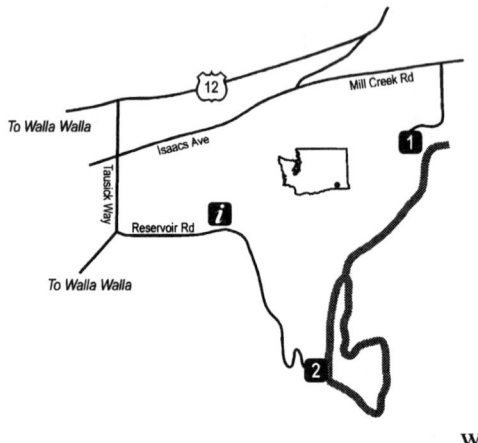

Bennington Lake is filled with clean mountain runoff water each spring. When the lake is full, there is approximately 53 surface acres of water. The lake is stocked with rainbow trout by the Washington Department of Fish and Wildlife. Due to the lake's small size, those wishing to boat on the lake are limited to row boats or electric motors. Substantial water loss is experienced throughout the summer and early fall seasons.

Information: U.S. Army Corps of Engineers, Bennington Lake, 3200 Reservoir Rd., Walla Walla WA 99362 / 509-527-7161.

Bennington Lake												
1 Rooks Park	•	•	•	•					•			
2 Bennington Lake	•	•		•						•		•

Rufus Woods Lake

Rufus Woods Lake is located on the Columbia River in north-central Washington just east of Bridgeport. Both sides of the dam can be accessed from SH 17. An orientation area just off SH 17 on the north side of the river offers a commanding view of the dam, exhibits, and a trail to a riverside overlook. A visitor center is located within the project's powerhouse. Tours of the dam are offered. Information is also available from the project office on the south side of the river.

Chief Joseph Dam stretches over one mile across the Columbia River and is the Corps' largest power-producing dam. There is only one developed recreation area on the lake. *Bridgeport State Park*, located two miles upstream of the dam, offers a sandy swimming beach, boat launching facilities, picnic areas, campground, and campfire programs every Saturday evening during the summer. The state park is generally open from April through October. Adjacent to the park is Lake Woods Golf Course, a nine-hole public course. Rufus Woods Lake is popular with boaters, water-skiers and jet skiers. It is also a great area for viewing wildlife and bird watching. Wildlife in the area includes mule deer, white-tailed deer, black bear, coyote, beaver and a variety of waterfowl, raptors and upland game birds.

At A Glance
Auto Touring
Biking
✓ Boating
Climbing
Cultural or Historic Sites
✓ Camping
✓ Educational Programs
✓ Fishing
✓ Groceries / Supplies
Hiking
Horseback Riding
Hunting
Lodging
Off Highway Vehicles
✓ Visitor Center

The 8,400-acre lake extends 51 miles upstream from Chief Joseph Dam to the Grand Coulee Dam. For the angler, the lake provides excellent kokanee and walleye fishing. Whitefish and trout fishing is also considered good. In addition to the boat ramp in *Bridgeport State Park*, a boat ramp is also located near the dam.

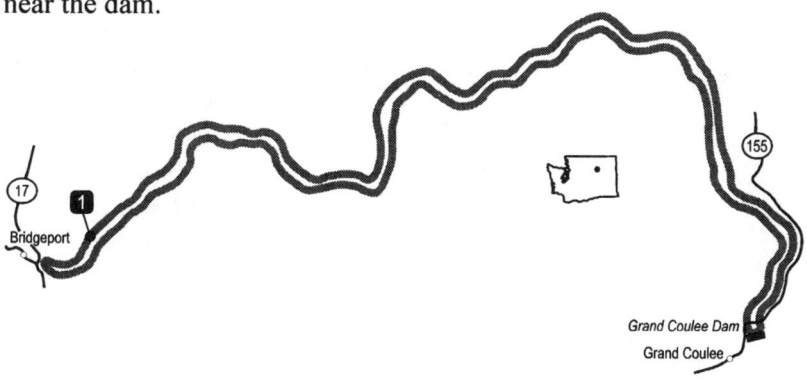

Information: U.S. Army Corps of Engineers, Rufus Woods Lake, P.O. Box 1120, Bridgeport WA 98813 / 509-686-5501. Bridgeport State Park, Box 846, Bridgeport WA 98813 / 509-686-7231.

Rufus Woods Lake	🔺 🏠 🚻 🚽 🧺 ⛽ 🚿 🏕 🥾 ⚓ 🏊
1 Bridgeport State Park	34 20 • • • • • • •

Lake Sacajawea

Lake Sacajawea, formed by the construction of Ice Harbor Lock and Dam on the Snake River, is in southeast Washington eight miles east of Burbank. To reach the dam from Burbank, travel 5½ miles east on SH 124 and then 2½ miles north on Ice Harbor Dam Road. The visitor center on the south end of the dam

At A Glance
- Auto Touring
- Biking
- ✓ Boating
- Climbing
- Cultural or Historic Sites
- ✓ Camping
- Educational Programs
- ✓ Fishing
- ✓ Groceries / Supplies
- ✓ Hiking
- Horseback Riding
- ✓ Hunting
- Lodging
- Off Highway Vehicles
- ✓ Visitor Center

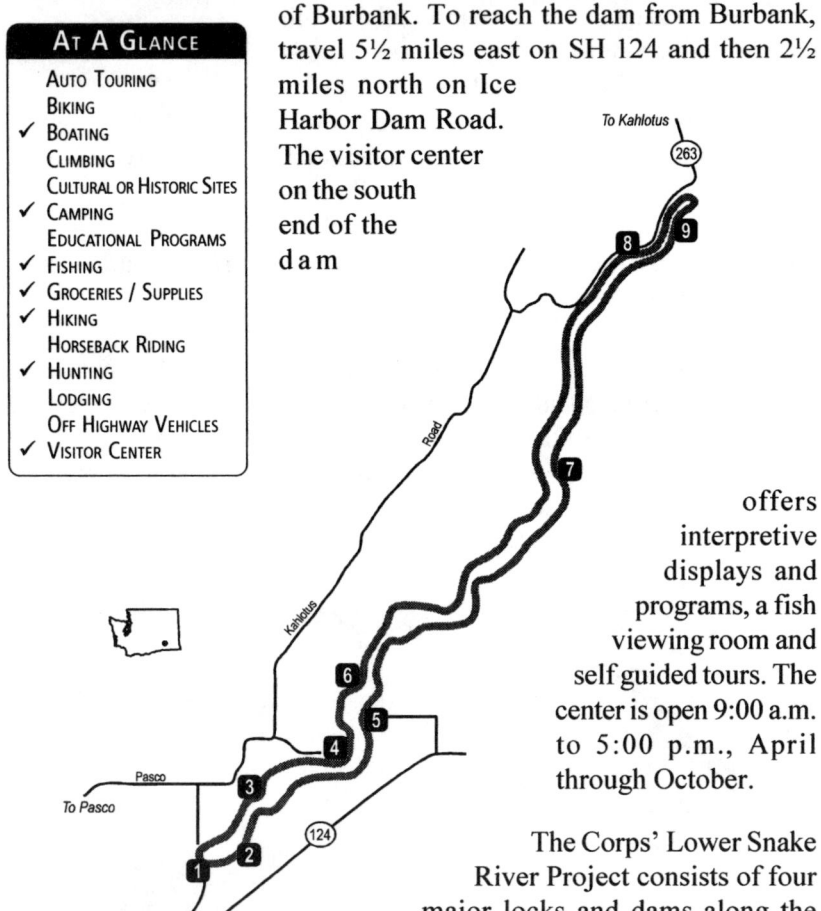

offers interpretive displays and programs, a fish viewing room and self guided tours. The center is open 9:00 a.m. to 5:00 p.m., April through October.

The Corps' Lower Snake River Project consists of four major locks and dams along the Snake River, the waterway of the Gold Rush days. The Snake River is a major tributary of the Columbia River and is one of the largest rivers in the United States. Sacajawea Lake is the first reservoir in the project and stretches 32 miles between Ice Harbor Lock and Dam and Lower

Monumental Lock and Dam. The reservoir offers miles of scenic shoreline and white sandy beaches. The area provides outstanding opportunities for boating, hiking, hunting, and fishing. Wildlife common to the area includes pheasant, quail, chukar, hawks, geese, ducks, owls, and cottontail rabbits. Eagles, pelicans, herons, swans, deer and otter also visit the area.

Lake Sacajawea offers 9,200 acres of clear blue waters for the boating and fishing enthusiast. The river is known for its salmon and steelhead fishing. Bass, crappie, perch, catfish, and sturgeon are also popular Snake River species. The marina in *Charbonneau Park* offers boat rentals, fuel, and a small store. The marina can be reached at 509-545-1573.

Information: U.S. Army Corps of Engineers, Lake Sacajawea, RR 6 Box 693, Pasco WA 99301 / 509-547-7781.

Lake Sacajawea	🛖	🚐	🚻	🚽	🎣	🛥	🍴	🚿	🏊	🍽	🚶	⚓	♿
1 Ice Harbor Dam			•	•		•				•			•
2 Charbonneau Park	54	54	•	•	•	•	•	•	•			•	•
3 Levey Park				•	•	•	•	•	•	•			•
4 Big Flat	•												•
5 Fishhook Park	61	41	•	•	•	•	•	•	•				•
6 Lake Emma	•												
7 Walker	•												
8 Windust	24		•	•	•	•	•		•				•
9 Matthews	•					•							•

Wynoochee Lake

Wynoochee Lake is located in a narrow canyon of the Wynoochee River in northwest Washington. To reach the dam from Montesano, travel one mile west on US 12 and turn north on Wynoochee Valley Road; head north for approximately 35 miles. Wynoochee Valley Road becomes FSR 22 once it enters the Olympic National Forest. From FSR 22 turn right onto FSR 2294. The visitor center, operated by Tacoma Power, is located just off FSR 2294. Note that the last 19 miles of road leading to the project are unpaved. Also, no commercial

At A Glance

- Auto Touring
- Biking
- ✓ Boating
- Climbing
- Cultural or Historic Sites
- ✓ Camping
- Educational Programs
- ✓ Fishing
- Groceries / Supplies
- ✓ Hiking
- Horseback Riding
- ✓ Hunting
- Lodging
- Off Highway Vehicles
- ✓ Visitor Center

services are available at the lake; motorists should have sufficient fuel for return trips.

From its source in the Olympic Mountains, the Wynoochee River meanders through lush forests and fertile farmlands before merging with the Chehalis River. Wynoochee Lake lies entirely within the Olympic National Forest and is set among the scenic Olympic Mountains. From the visitor area on the west bank of the dam, visitors can enjoy a dramatic view of the structure and the river gorge. Interpretive exhibits tell the story of the project. Wildlife common to the area includes elk, deer, bear, beaver, blue grouse, and mountain lion. Goldeneyes, wood ducks, and hooded mergansers are among the waterfowl nesting nearby. The project was originally constructed by the Corps of Engineers but is managed by Tacoma Power.

Recreation facilities on the lake are operated by the U.S. Forest Service. *Coho Campground* has 56 sites and is open mid-April through mid-October. A 16-mile hiking trail begins in the campground and winds through the forest around the lake. *Chetwoot* is a primitive hike-in / boat-in only campground.

When full, Wynoochee Lake is 4½ miles long, 164 feet deep, and covers 1,140 acres. Between October and March the lake level is lowered to provide storage for winter flood waters. Anglers will find good salmon and trout fishing in the river and lake. Lake and rivers open for fishing on June 1.

Information: Wynoochee Lake, Olympic National Forest, Hood Canal Ranger District, P.O. Box 68, Hoodsport WA 98548 / 360-877-5254. Tacoma Power Wynoochee Dam/River information, 888-502-8690.

Wynoochee Lake	△	▭	🚻	🚰	⊼		⛲		≈		🚶	⚓	≋
1 Coho Campground	56	•	•	•			•					•	•
2 Chetwoot	•												

Appendix A

Alphabetical List of Lakes

Name	District	Page
Abiquiu Reservoir	Albuquerque	96
Alamo Lake	Los Angeles	19
Albeni Falls Dam / Lake Pend Oreille	Seattle	48
Applegate Lake	Portland	157
Aquilla Lake	Fort Worth	197
Arcadia Lake	Tulsa	111
Ashtabula, Lake	St. Paul	102
Bardwell Lake	Fort Worth	198
Bear Creek Lake	Omaha	41
Belton Lake	Fort Worth	199
Benbrook Lake	Fort Worth	201
Big Hill Lake	Tulsa	54
Birch Lake	Tulsa	112
Black Butte Lake	Sacramento	21
Blue River Lake	Portland	158
Bluestem SRA	Omaha	90
Bonneville, Lake	Portland	159
Bowman-Haley Lake	Omaha	103
Branched Oak SRA	Omaha	90
Broken Bow Lake	Tulsa	113
Bryan, Lake	Walla Walla	240
Canton Lake	Tulsa	114
Canyon Lake	Fort Worth	202
Celilo, Lake	Portland	161
Chatfield Lake	Omaha	42
Chena River Lakes	Alaska	16
Cherry Creek Lake	Omaha	43
Chouteau Lock and Dam	Tulsa	115
Clinton Lake	Kansas City	55
Cochiti Lake	Albuquerque	97
Cold Brook Lake	Omaha	182

Corps of Engineers

Name	District	Page
Conchas Lake	Albuquerque	98
Conestoga SRA	Omaha	91
Copan Lake	Tulsa	117
Cottage Grove Lake	Portland	163
Cottonwood Springs Lake	Omaha	183
Cougar Lake	Portland	164
Council Grove Lake	Tulsa	56
Detroit Lake	Portland	165
Dorena Lake	Portland	167
Dworshak Reservoir	Walla Walla	49
Eastman Lake	Sacramento	22
El Dorado Lake	Tulsa	58
Elk City Lake	Tulsa	59
Englebright Lake	Sacramento	23
Eufaula Lake	Tulsa	118
Fall Creek Lake	Portland	168
Fall River Lake	Tulsa	61
Fern Ridge Lake	Portland	169
Fort Gibson Lake	Tulsa	120
Fort Peck Lake	Omaha	80
Fort Supply Lake	Tulsa	122
Foster & Green Peter Lakes	Portland	170
Francis Case, Lake	Omaha	184
Georgetown, Lake	Fort Worth	204
Glenn Cunningham Lake	Omaha	86
Granger Lake	Fort Worth	205
Grapevine Lake	Fort Worth	207
Great Salt Plains Lake	Tulsa	124
Harlan County Lake	Kansas City	85
Hensley Lake	Sacramento	25
Herbert G. West, Lake	Walla Walla	241
Heyburn Lake	Tulsa	125
Hills Creek Lake	Portland	172
Hillsdale Lake	Kansas City	62
Homme Lake	St. Paul	104
Hords Creek Lake	Fort Worth	209
Hugo Lake	Tulsa	126

Name	District	Page
Hulah Lake	Tulsa	127
J.W. Trimble Lock and Dam	Little Rock	129
Jim Chapman Lake	Fort Worth	210
Joe Pool Lake	Fort Worth	212
John Martin Reservoir	Albuquerque	44
John Redmond Reservoir	Tulsa	63
Kanopolis Lake	Kansas City	64
Kaw Lake	Tulsa	130
Kaweah, Lake	Sacramento	26
Keystone Lake	Tulsa	131
Koocanusa, Lake	Seattle	82
Lake Ashtabula	St. Paul	102
Lake Bonneville	Portland	159
Lake Bryan	Walla Walla	240
Lake Celilo	Portland	161
Lake Francis Case	Omaha	184
Lake Georgetown	Fort Worth	204
Lake Herbert G. West	Walla Walla	241
Lake Kaweah	Sacramento	26
Lake Koocanusa	Seattle	82
Lake Mendocino	Sacramento	28
Lake O' The Pines	Fort Worth	213
Lake Oahe	Omaha	189
Lake Sacajawea	Walla Walla	248
Lake Sakakawea	Omaha	106
Lake Sharpe	Omaha	193
Lake Sonoma	Sacramento	29
Lake Texoma	Tulsa	146
Lake Umatilla	Portland	176
Lake Wallula	Walla Walla	178
Lavon Lake	Fort Worth	215
Lewis and Clark Lake	Omaha	186
Lewisville Lake	Fort Worth	217
Lookout Point & Dexter Lakes	Portland	173
Lost Creek Lake	Portland	175
Lower Granite Lake	Walla Walla	243
Lucky Peak Lake	Walla Walla	51

Name	District	Page
Marion Reservoir	Tulsa	66
Martis Creek Lake	Sacramento	31
Melvern Lake	Kansas City	67
Mendocino, Lake	Sacramento	28
Milford Lake	Kansas City	69
Mill Creek & Bennington Lake	Walla Walla	245
Navarro Mills Lake	Fort Worth	219
New Hogan Lake	Sacramento	32
Newt Graham Lock and Dam	Tulsa	134
O.C. Fisher Lake	Fort Worth	220
Oahe, Lake	Omaha	189
Olive Creek SRA	Omaha	92
Oologah Lake	Tulsa	135
Optima Lake	Tulsa	137
Papio Creek Watershed Projects	Omaha	86
Pat Mayse Lake	Tulsa	222
Pawnee SRA	Omaha	92
Perry Lake	Kansas City	71
Pine Creek Lake	Tulsa	138
Pine Flat Lake	Sacramento	34
Pipestem Lake	Omaha	105
Pomona Lake	Kansas City	72
Proctor Lake	Fort Worth	223
Ray Roberts Lake	Fort Worth	224
Robert S. Kerr Reservoir	Tulsa	139
Rufus Woods Lake	Seattle	246
Sacajawea, Lake	Walla Walla	248
Sakakawea, Lake	Omaha	106
Salt Valley Lakes	Omaha	89
Sam Rayburn Reservoir	Fort Worth	226
Santa Margarita Lake	Los Angeles	35
Santa Rosa Lake	Albuquerque	99
Sardis Lake	Tulsa	141
Sharpe, Lake	Omaha	193
Skiatook Lake	Tulsa	142
Somerville Lake	Fort Worth	228
Sonoma, Lake	Sacramento	29

Name	District	Page
Stagecoach SRA	Omaha	93
Standing Bear Lake	Omaha	87
Stanislaus River Parks	Sacramento	36
Steinhagen Lake	Fort Worth	230
Stillhouse Hollow Lake	Fort Worth	231
Success Lake	Sacramento	38
Tenkiller Ferry Lake	Tulsa	144
Texoma, Lake	Tulsa	146
Toronto Lake	Tulsa	74
Trinidad Lake	Albuquerque	45
Tuttle Creek Lake	Kansas City	75
Twin Lakes WMA	Omaha	93
Umatilla, Lake	Portland	176
W.D. Mayo Lock and Dam	Tulsa	149
Waco Lake	Fort Worth	233
Wagon Train SRA	Omaha	93
Wallula, Lake	Walla Walla	178
Waurika Lake	Tulsa	150
Webbers Falls Lock and Dam	Tulsa	151
Wehrspann Lake	Omaha	88
Whitney Lake	Fort Worth	234
Wilson Lake	Kansas City	77
Wister Lake	Tulsa	153
Wright Patman Lake	Fort Worth	236
Wynoochee Lake	Seattle	249
Yankee Hill WMA	Omaha	94
Zorinsky Lake	Omaha	88

Appendix B

Districts of the Corps of Engineers

Alaska District
PO Box 898
Anchorage, AK 99506-0898
907-753-2520

Albuquerque District
4101 Jefferson Plaza NE
Albuquerque, NM 87109
505-342-3172

Baltimore District
PO Box 1715
Baltimore, MD 21203-1715
410-962-4616

Buffalo District
1776 Niagara St
Buffalo, NY 14207-3199
716-879-4200

Charleston District
PO Box 919
Charleston, SC 29402-0919
803-727-4201

Chicago District
111 N Canal St Suite 600
Chicago, IL 60606-7206
312-353-6400

Detroit District
PO Box 1027
Detroit, MI 48231-1027
313-226-4680

Fort Worth District
PO Box 17300
Fort Worth, TX 76102-0300
817-978-2196

Galveston District
PO Box 1229
Galveston, TX 77553-1229
409-766-3049

Honolulu District
Building 230
Fort Shafter, HI 96858-5440
808-438-9862

Huntington District
502 8th St
Huntington, WV 25701-2070
304-529-5453

Jacksonville District
PO Box 4970
Jacksonville, FL 32232-0019
904-232-2235

Kansas City District
601 E 12th St
Kansas City, MO 64106-2896
816-983-3542

Little Rock District
PO Box 867
Little Rock, AR 72203-0867
501-324-5551

Los Angeles District
PO Box 532711
Los Angeles, CA 90053-2325
213-452-3921

Louisville District
PO Box 59
Louisville, KY 40201-0059
502-582-5736

Memphis District
Clifford Davis Federal Bldg
167 N Main St, Rm B202
Memphis, TN 38103-1894
901-544-3348

Mobile District
PO Box 2288
Mobile, AL 36628-0001
334-690-2505

Nashville District
PO Box 1070
Nashville, TN 37202-1070
615-736-7161

New England District
696 Virginia Rd
Concord, MA 01742-2751
978-318-8238

New Orleans District
PO Box 60267
New Orleans, LA 70160-0267
504-862-2201

New York District
26 Federal Plaza, Rm 2108
New York, NY 10278-0090
212-264-9113

Norfolk District
803 Front St
Norfolk, VA 23510-1096
757-441-7264

Omaha District
215 N 17th St
Omaha, NE 68102-4978
402-221-3917

Philadelphia District
Wanamaker Building
100 Penn Square E
Philadelphia, PA 19107-3390
215-656-6515

Pittsburgh District
1000 Liberty Ave, Rm 1801
Pittsburgh, PA 15222-4186
412-395-7500

Portland District
PO Box 2946
Portland, OR 97208-2946
503-808-4510

Rock Island District
PO Box 2004
Rock Island, IL 61204-2004
309-794-5900

Sacramento District
1325 J St
Sacramento, CA 95814-2922
916-557-7461

San Francisco District
333 Market St, Rm 825
San Francisco, CA 94105
415-977-8658

Savannah District
PO Box 889
Savannah, GA 31402-0889
912-652-5279

Seattle District
PO Box 3755
Seattle, WA 98124-3755
206-764-3750

St. Louis District
1222 Spruce St
St. Louis, MO 63103-2833
314-331-8000

St. Paul District
190 5th St E
St. Paul, MN 55101-1638
612-290-5201

Tulsa District
1645 S 101st E Ave
Tulsa, OK 74128-4609
918-669-7366

Vicksburg District
4155 Clay St
Vicksburg, MS 39180-3435
601-631-5052

Walla Walla District
201 N 3rd Ave
Walla Walla, WA 99362-1876
509-527-7020

Wilmington District
PO Box 1890
Wilmington, NC 28402-1890
910-251-4626

APPENDIX C

Internet Resources

For information on recreational opportunities on federal land, point your web browser to www.Recreation.Gov. This web site is a multi-agency project that was developed to enhance access to information about recreation on federal lands. Agencies in addition to the Corps of Engineers include the Forest Service, Bureau of Land Management, Bureau of Reclamation, and Fish and Wildlife Service.

The Corps of Engineers also maintains an extensive system of web pages including division and district offices. Detailed information about projects nationwide is available from the following sources.

Corps of Engineers Headquarters Web Site

Headquarters .... www.hq.usace.army.mil

The headquarters web site is an excellent place to begin your search. All of the division and district web pages can be reached from this site.

Corps of Engineers Division Web Sites

Great Lakes & Ohio River Division .... www.usace.army.mil/lrd
Mississippi Valley Division .... www.mvd.usace.army.mil
North Atlantic Division .... www.nad.usace.army.mil
Northwestern Division .... www.nwd.usace.army.mil
Pacific Ocean Division .... www.pod.usace.army.mil
South Atlantic Division .... www.sad.usace.army.mil
South Pacific Division .... www.spd.usace.army.mil
Southwestern Division .... www.swt.usace.army.mil/swd

Corps of Engineers District Web Sites

Alaska District .... www.usace.army.mil/alaska
Albuquerque District .... www.spa.usace.army.mil

Baltimore District .... www.nab.usace.army.mil
Buffalo District .... www.ncb.usace.army.mil
Charleston District .... www.sac.usace.army.mil
Chicago District .... www.usace.army.mil/lrc
Detroit District .... www.lre.usace.army.mil
Fort Worth District .... www.swf.usace.army.mil
Galveston District .... www.swg.usace.army.mil
Honolulu District .... www.pod.usace.army.mil
Huntington District .... www.orh.usace.army.mil
Jacksonville District .... www.saj.usace.army.mil
Kansas City District .... www.nwk.usace.army.mil
Little Rock District .... www.swl.usace.army.mil
Los Angeles District .... www.spl.usace.army.mil
Louisville District .... www.orl.usace.army.mil
Memphis District .... www.lmm.usace.army.mil
Mobile District .... www.sam.usace.army.mil
Nashville District .... www.orn.usace.army.mil
New England District .... www.nae.usace.army.mil
New Orleans District .... www.lmn.usace.army.mil
New York District .... www.nan.usace.army.mil
Norfolk District http://155.78.30.111
Omaha District .... www.nwo.usace.army.mil
Philadelphia District .... www.nap.usace.army.mil
Pittsburgh District .... www.lrp.usace.army.mil
Portland District .... www.nwp.usace.army.mil
Rock Island District .... www.mvr.usace.army.mil
Sacramento District .... www.spk.usace.army.mil
San Francisco District .... www.spn.usace.army.mil
Savannah District .... www.sas.usace.army.mil
Seattle District .... www.nws.usace.army.mil
St. Louis District .... www.mvs.usace.army.mil
St. Paul District .... www.mvp.usace.army.mil
Tulsa District .... www.swt.usace.army.mil
Vicksburg District .... www.mvk.usace.army.mil
Walla Walla District .... www.nww.usace.army.mil
Wilmington District .... www.saw.usace.army.mil

Appendix D

Camping and Day Use Fees

Visitors to Corps of Engineers projects find well-maintained campgrounds with varying facilities. Camping fees vary from park to park depending on the facilities offered. Basically, campgrounds are divided into four categories. Listed below is a general description of each type and the fees associated with that type.

- ***Class A Campgrounds***

    Class A campgrounds are those having flush restrooms, showers, paved roads, sanitary disposal stations, designated tent or trailer spaces, refuse containers, and potable water. Campgrounds that have sites with hookups provide, at a minimum, electricity but many will also have water and sewer hookups. Class A campgrounds that have sites *without* hookups generally charge a fee from $8 to $15 or more. Fees for campgrounds *with* hookups will vary from $12 to $20 or more. Some campgrounds provide prime RV sites, double sites, 50-amp sites, screened shelters, and other amenities. Prices are slightly higher for these types of campsites.

    The operating season for Class A campgrounds will vary from state to state and park to park. Generally, campgrounds are open from spring through fall. Many campgrounds, especially in warmer climates, are open year-round. If a campground operates year-round, reduced fees may be available during winter months. In some campgrounds, facilities can also be limited during winter. Camping is limited to a 14-day stay during any 30-consecutive-day period.

- ***Class B Campgrounds***

    Class B campgrounds provide the same type of facilities as Class A but hot showers may not be provided nor flush restrooms. Class B campgrounds can have sites with or without hookups. Camping fees range from $6 to $12 or more.

The operating season for Class B campgrounds will also vary from state to state and park to park. Generally, campgrounds are open from spring through fall but many, especially in warmer climates, are open year-round. If a campground operates year-round, reduced fees may be available during winter months. Facilities may also be limited during winter. Camping is limited to a 14-day stay during any 30-consecutive-day period.

- *Class C Campgrounds*

Class C campgrounds are those having basic sanitary facilities, designated tent or trailer spaces, refuse containers, and potable water. Class C campgrounds can have sites with or without hookups. Fees range from a low of $5 to $10 or more.

The operating season for Class C campgrounds will also vary. Generally, campgrounds are open from spring through fall but many, especially in warmer climates, are open year-round. If a campground operates year-round, reduced fees may be available during winter months. Facilities may also be limited during winter. Camping is limited to a 14-day stay during any 30-consecutive-day period.

- *Class D Campgrounds*

Class D campgrounds are primitive areas that usually provide limited facilities, if any. Drinking water is usually not available in these campgrounds. There may be designated tent or trailer spaces or simply areas that are open to camping. Camping is permitted free of charge at many of these campgrounds but if a fee is charged, it is usually under $8. Class D campgrounds usually remain open year-round but this will vary from park to park. Camping is limited to a 14-day stay during any 30-consecutive-day period.

- *Other Campgrounds*

    In addition to Corps-operated campgrounds and parks, numerous other agencies such as state, county, and city agencies operate campgrounds at the lakes. Facilities, fees, and operating seasons vary from park to park. Many state parks charge an entrance fee in addition to camping fees. Generally, if the operating agency is other than the Corps of Engineers, this information is provided in the lake description.

Day Use Fees

Nominal day-use fees are charged in areas that are operated and maintained by the Corps of Engineers. Generally, a fee of $1 per person, up to $3 per vehicle, is charged at developed swimming beaches. A daily fee of $2 is charged for boat launching ramps that have restrooms, security lighting, courtesy docks, or other recreation facilities. Registered campers will not pay day use fees in addition to camping fees.

An annual non-transferable pass may be purchased for $25 that permits the holder and accompanying passengers in a private vehicle to use all boat ramps and swimming beaches at Corps-operated day-use areas nationwide without further charges. Annual passes can be purchased through the mail or in person at a Corps' lake office. They can also be purchased at park attendant stations.

Appendix E

National Recreation Reservation Service

A new campsite reservation system has been placed in operation for visitors to Corps lakes. Thousands of lakeside campsites are available through the system. Individual campsite reservations can be made up to 240 days in advance. The reservation service also offers the ability to reserve campsites throughout the national forest system. Information is available by calling toll-free 877-444-6777 (877-833-6777 TDD). Hours of operation are from 10:00 a.m. to 9:00 p.m. Eastern time. Reservations can also be made through the Internet by visiting the system's web site at www.ReserveUSA.com.

Information needed by the National Recreation Reservation Service to reserve your campsite:

- Specific campground you prefer
- Location by state and Corps lake
- Type of site you want
- Dates you want to camp
- Vehicles/trailers/tents you are bringing
- Credit card number

Appendix F

Golden Age and Golden Access Passport

Persons 62 years of age or older can obtain a Golden Age Passport from any Corps project office. The passport gives the holder and accompanying passengers in a private vehicle a 50 percent discount on recreation use fees charged at any recreation area administered by the Corps. The passport is available for a one-time fee of $10.

The Golden Access Passport is issued to persons who are blind or permanently disabled. The passport also provides a 50 percent discount on Corps of Engineers' use fees. There is no charge for the Golden Access Passport.

The Golden Age and Golden Access Passports are also honored at national parks, monuments, historic sites, recreation areas, and national wildlife refuges. Besides the Corps of Engineers, the passports can be obtained through the National Park Service, Forest Service, Bureau of Land Management, Fish and Wildlife Service, Tennessee Valley Authority, and the Bureau of Reclamation. The passports must be obtained in person and proof of age or permanent disability must be provided. Please note that the passports may not be honored at non-federal recreation areas.

Appendix G

Brief History of the U.S. Army Corps of Engineers

The U.S. Army Corps of Engineers traces its origins to the American Revolution. On June 16, 1775, when the Continental Congress established the Army, it provided for a Chief of Engineers. Colonel Richard Gridley, the first to hold that position, set to work immediately directing fortifications during the Battle of Bunker Hill.

Congress added companies of engineer troops, or sappers and miners, to the Army and, in 1779, formed them into a distinct Corps of Engineers. The Engineers' finest hour was at the Battle of Yorktown in October 1781, which forced a British surrender.

When war with Britain threatened again in 1794, Congress appointed temporary engineers to fortify key harbors. In 1802, the Corps of Engineers was made permanent and took charge of the military academy at West Point, N.Y.

Constructing seacoast fortifications continued as the engineers' primary responsibility. The Corps again saw combat in the War of 1812.

That war demonstrated the need to improve the nation's defense and transportation systems. In 1824, the General Survey Act authorized the President to use Army engineers to survey road and canal routes. A separate measure appropriated $75,000 to employ public engineers to improve navigation on the Ohio and Mississippi Rivers, beginning the Army's long involvement in civil works activities.

In May 1846, on the eve of the Mexican War, Congress authorized the first regular company of engineer troops. During the Civil War, their numbers increased, as engineer officers commanded combined troops, conducted surveys and reconnaissance, and directed siege operations.

In the following decade, the Corps' involvement in civil works mushroomed as appropriations jumped from $3.5 million for 49 projects and

26 surveys in 1866 to $19 million for 371 projects and 135 surveys in 1882. Key developments occurred on the Ohio River which the Corps had canalized to a depth of nine feet by 1929, and on the lower Mississippi, where growing pressures for navigation and flood control led Congress to establish the Mississippi River Commission in 1879. This permanent body included three Corps of Engineers officers.

As engineers debated effective flood protection measures, federal responsibility for flood control grew in response to recurring floods. With legislation in 1928, attention broadened from the Mississippi to include its tributaries. The Flood Control Act of 1936 recognized flood control in general as a proper activity of the federal government and gave responsibility for most federal projects to the Corps of Engineers.

After World War II, multi-purpose projects involving navigation, water storage, irrigation, power and recreation, in addition to flood control, predominated. In the process, the Corps became a leading producer of hydroelectric power.

The Corps role in protecting the natural environment also expanded. It was influential in the creation of Yellowstone as the first national park in 1874 and, in the 1870s, began to regulate construction of bridges to prevent obstruction to navigation. In 1899, Congress gave the Corps authority to regulate almost all kinds of obstructions to navigation.

The Corps of Engineers has had a special relationship with the District of Columbia since 1791, when former Army engineer Pierre L'Enfant designed the master plan for the new capital. In the mid-19th century, Lieutenant Montgomery C. Migs supervised construction of a permanent water supply system for the cities of Washington and Georgetown. In the post-Civil War period, Army engineers worked on reconstruction of the Capitol; completed the Washington Monument; helped design and supervise construction of the State, War and Navy Buildings (today's Executive Office Building next to the White House), and the Library of Congress; and oversaw dredge and fill operations, which created acres of public parkland.

After 1878, an Army engineer officer served on the District's three-man governing commission. The George Washington Memorial Parkway, the Pentagon and National Airport began as pre-World War II Corps projects.

Since the Civil War, engineer officers and troops have played key roles in six wars. During World War I, in combat and in such activities behind the lines as constructing ports, storage depots, hospitals, and barracks, the Corps performed a greater diversity of military services than ever before.

Its support of the Normandy landing and breakthrough of enemy lines, its bridge-building efforts, and support of amphibious landings during World War II stand out.

Throughout the Pacific Theater, the Corps built pipelines, dredged harbors, and built and repaired ports. Bases in Greenland and Iceland protected Atlantic shipping. The Corps also built the 1,671-mile Alcan Highway in Alaska and the Ledo Road from India to Burma.

At home, the Corps of Engineers took over responsibility for all Army construction in December 1941. This effort included military and industrial projects, a total mobilization that involved more than 27,000 projects at a cost of $15.3 billion. The Corps created a special district to oversee the Manhattan Project, a massive effort to construct production, and assembly facilities for atomic residential communities for workers.

After World War II, in less traditional roles, the Corps became the design and construction agent for NASA, supported the ICBM construction program, and worked on military civil projects overseas.

The above was prepared by the Corps of Engineers Public Affairs office.

INDEX

A

Abilene (TX) 209
Abiquiu Reservoir 96
Alamo Lake 19
Albeni Falls Dam 48
Albuquerque (NM) 97, 99
Alkali Creek 103
Angelina National Forest 226
Angelina River 226
Applegate Lake 157
Aquilla Creek 197
Aquilla Lake 197
Arcadia Lake 111
Arctic Circle 16
Arkansas River 44, 129, 130, 131, 139, 152, 154
Atlanta State Park 236
Aurora (CO) 43
Austin (TX) 204, 205

B

Baldhill Dam 102
Bardwell Lake 198, 199
Barling (AR) 129
Barnsdall (OK) 112
Bartlesville (OK) 112, 117, 127, 128
Bear Creek Lake 41
Beaver Creek 150
Beaver River 138
Belton (TX) 199, 231
Belton Lake 199
Benbrook (TX) 201
Benbrook Lake 201, 202
Bennington Lake 245, 246
Big Bend Dam 184, 193
Big Blue River 75
Big Bull Creek 62
Big Cypress Creek 213
Big Hill Creek 54
Big Hill Lake 54
Bill Williams River 19
Birch Creek 112
Birch Lake 112
Bird Creek 112
Bismarck (ND) 106, 189
Black Butte Lake 21
Black Hills 182, 183
Blue Mountains 245
Blue River (OR) 158, 159, 164
Blue River Lake 158, 159
Bluestem SRA 90
Boise (ID) 51, 52
Boise National Forest 52
Boise River 52
Bonneville Dam 159
Bosque River 233
Bowman (ND) 103
Bowman-Haley Lake 103
Branched Oak SRA 90
Brazos River 229, 235
Brazos River Valley 235
Bridge of the Gods 160
Bridgeport (WA) 246
Broken Bow (OK) 113
Broken Bow Lake 113, 114
Buchanan Dam 22
Buckskin Mountains 19
Burbank (WA) 248

Index

Bureau of Land Management 19
Burlington (KS) 63, 64

C

Calaveras River 32, 33
Canadian River 118
Caney River 127
Canton Lake 114, 115
Canyon Lake 202, 203
Cascade Locks (OR) 160
Cascade Mountains 158
Cedar Hill (TX) 212
Charles M. Russell National Wildlife Refuge 80
Chatfield Lake 42
Chautauqua Hills 61
Chehalis River 250
Chena River 16, 17
Chena River Lakes 16
Cherry Creek Lake 43
Cherryvale (KS) 54, 55, 60
Chief Joseph Dam 246, 247
Chouteau, Col. Auguste P. 116
Chouteau Lock and Dam 115
Chowchilla (CA) 22
Chowchilla River 22
Clear Fork of the Trinity River 202
Clearwater River 50
Clinton Lake 55, 56
Coast Fork of the Willamette River 163
Cochiti Lake 97
Coeur d'Alene (ID) 48
Cold Brook Lake 182
Coldwater Creek 138
Coleman (TX) 209

College Station (TX) 228
Colorado River Basin 209
Colton (WA) 243
Columbia River 48, 160, 161, 162, 176, 178, 240, 241, 246, 248
Columbia River Gorge 160
Columbia River Gorge National Scenic Area 159
Comanche (TX) 223
Conchas Dam 98
Conchas Lake 98
Conchas River 98, 99
Conestoga SRA 91
Cookson Hills 144
Cooper Lake 210
Cooper Wildlife Management Area 210
Copan Lake 117
Corsicana (TX) 219
Cottage Grove Lake 163
Cottonwood River 66
Cottonwood Springs Lake 183
Cougar Lake 159, 164, 165
Council Grove (KS) 56, 57
Council Grove Lake 56, 57
Crowder (OK) 118
Culebra Range 45

D

Dallas (TX) 197, 198, 207, 210, 212, 215, 217, 219, 224
Dalles Lock and Dam 161, 162
Deep Fork River 111
Delaware River 71
Denison (TX) 146
Denison Dam 146
Denton (NE) 91, 94

Denton (TX) 224
Denton Creek 207
Denver (CO) 41, 42, 43
Detroit (OR) 165
Detroit Lake 165, 166
Dexter Lake 173, 174
Dry Creek 29, 30
Duncan (OK) 150
Durant (OK) 146
Dworshak Reservoir 49

E

Eagle Creek 160
East Fork of the Trinity River 216
Eastman Lake 22, 23
Edmond (OK) 111
El Dorado (KS) 59
El Dorado Lake 58
Elk City (KS) 59
Elk City Lake 59
Elk River 59
Elm Fork of the Trinity River 225
Elm Fork Trinity River 217
Emerald (NE) 92
Emporia (KS) 74
Englebright Dam 24
Englebright Lake 23, 24
Enid (OK) 124
Ennis (TX) 198, 199
Espanola (NM) 96
Eufaula (OK) 118
Eufaula Lake 118, 119
Eugene (OR) 158, 163, 164, 168, 169, 172, 173
Eureka (KS) 61

F

Fairbanks (AK) 16
Fairview (OK) 114
Fall Creek 168
Fall Creek Lake 168, 169
Fall Creek National Recreation Trail 168
Fall River 61, 183
Fall River (KS) 61, 62, 75
Fall River Lake 61
Faris Caves 65
Fern Ridge Lake 169, 170
Flint Hills 56, 59, 61, 67, 68, 74, 76
Flint Hills (KS) 75
Flint Hills National Wildlife Refuge 64
Fort Cascades National Historic Site 160
Fort Gibson (OK) 120
Fort Gibson Lake 120, 121
Fort Gibson Stockade 121
Fort Manuel Trading Post 189
Fort Peck (MT) 80
Fort Peck Lake 80
Fort Randall Dam 184
Fort Smith (AR) 129, 149
Fort Supply Lake 122
Fort Thompson (SD) 184, 193
Fort Worth (TX) 201, 207, 223
Forth Worth (TX) 201, 212
Fresno (CA) 22, 25, 26, 34, 38
Fresno River 25, 26

G

Garland (TX) 215
Garrison Dam 106

Index

Gavins Point Dam 186
Georgetown (TX) 204
Glasgow (MT) 80
Glenn Cunningham Lake 86
Goodwin Dam 37
Gore (OK) 144
Grafton (ND) 104
Grand Coulee Dam 247
Grand Forks (ND) 104
Granger (TX) 205
Granger Lake 205, 206
Grapevine Lake 207
Great Salt Plains Lake 124, 125
Guadalupe River 203
Guymon (OK) 137

H

Hagerman National Wildlife Refuge 147
Hardesty (OK) 137
Harlan County Lake 85
Hasty (CO) 44
Healdsburg (CA) 29
Hensley Lake 25
Heyburn Lake 125
Hickman (NE) 93
Hills Creek Lake 172, 173
Hillsboro (KS) 66
Hillsdale (KS) 62
Hillsdale Lake 62
Hominy Creek 143
Homme Lake 104
Hords Creek 209
Hords Creek Lake 209
Horse Creek 27
Horsethief Canyon 65
Hot Springs (SD) 182, 183
Hugo (OK) 126

Hugo Lake 126
Hulah Lake 127, 128

I

Ice Harbor Dam 178
Ice Harbor Lock and Dam 248
Idabel (OK) 138
Illinois River 144, 145
Independence (KS) 59, 60

J

J.W. Trimble Lock and Dam 129
Jackfork Creek 141
Jackfork Mountains 141
Jamestown (ND) 102, 105, 106
Jasper (TX) 226, 230
Jean Pierre Chouteau National Recreation Trail 116, 134, 152
Jefferson (TX) 213
Jess, William L. Dam 175
Jet (OK) 124
Jim Chapman Lake 210
Joe Pool Lake 212
John Day Lock and Dam 162, 176
John Day River 176
John Martin Reservoir 44, 45
John Redmond Reservoir 63
Junction City (KS) 69, 70

K

Kahlotus (WA) 241
Kalispell (MT) 82
Kanopolis Lake 64, 65
Kansas City (KS) 62

Karl Mundt National Wildlife Refuge 185
Kaw Lake 130, 131
Kaweah River 26, 27
Kearney (NE) 85
Kellyville (OK) 125
Kennewick (WA) 178, 241
Kerr, Robert S. Lock and Dam 149
Kerr, Robert S. Reservoir 139, 140
Keystone Lake 131, 132, 133
Kiamichi Mountains 138
Kiamichi River 126, 141
Killeen (TX) 199, 231
Kings River 34
Knights Ferry (CA) 36
Kootenai National Forest 82, 83
Kootenai River 82, 83
Kramer (NE) 92

L

Lake Ashtabula 102
Lake Bonneville 159
Lake Bryan 240, 241
Lake Celilo 161, 162
Lake Francis 185
Lake Francis Case 184
Lake Georgetown 204, 205
Lake Hasty 44, 45
Lake Herbert G. West 241, 242
Lake Kaweah 26, 27
Lake Koocanusa 82, 83
Lake Mendocino 28
Lake O' The Pines 213
Lake Oahe 189, 190
Lake Pend Oreille 48, 49

Lake Sacajawea 248, 249
Lake Sakakawea 106, 107
Lake San Angelo 220
Lake Sharpe 193
Lake Somerville State Park 228
Lake Sonoma 29
Lake Tahoe 31
Lake Texoma 146, 148
Lake Umatilla 176, 177
Lake Wallula 178, 179
Lake Whitney 197
Lake Yankton 187
Lakewood (CO) 41
Lampasas River 232
Las Animas (CO) 44
Lavon Lake 215
Lawrence (KS) 55, 56
Leon River 223
Lewis and Clark Lake 186, 187
Lewiston (ID) 49, 243
Lewisville Lake 217
Libby (MT) 82
Libby Dam 82, 83
Lincoln (NE) 85, 89, 90, 91, 92, 93, 94
Little Caney River 117
Little Goose Lock and Dam 240, 242
Little Missouri River 107
Little River 114, 138
Long Tom River 169
Longview (TX) 213
Lookout Point Lake 173, 174
Los Angeles (CA) 35
Lost Creek Lake 175
Lowell (OR) 168, 173
Lower Granite Lake 243

Index

Lower Granite Lock and Dam 240, 243
Lower Monumental Lock and Dam 241, 248
Lucky Peak Dam 52
Lucky Peak Lake 51
Lufkin (TX) 230

M

Madera (CA) 25
Malcolm (NE) 90
Manhattan (KS) 75, 76
Marais des Cygnes River 68
Marion (KS) 66, 67
Marion Reservoir 66
Mariposa Indian War 26
Marquette (KS) 66
Martin Dies Jr. State Park 230
Martis Creek Lake 31
Marysville (CA) 23
McAlester (OK) 141, 153
McClellan-Kerr Arkansas River Navigation System 115, 129, 134, 139, 149, 152
McNary Lock and Dam 176, 178
Medford (OR) 157, 175
Melvern (KS) 69
Melvern Lake 67, 68
Middle Fork of the Willamette River 173, 174
Milford (KS) 70
Milford Lake 69, 70
Mill Creek 245, 246
Minnekahta Valley 183
Missouri River 106, 184, 186, 187, 189, 193
Mobridge (SD) 189

Modesto (CA) 36
Montesano (WA) 249
Moose Creek Dam 16
Mount Jefferson 165
Mountain Creek 212
Mountain Fork River 114
Mundt, Karl National Wildlife Refuge 185
Muskogee (OK) 115, 118, 139, 144, 149, 152

N

Nashua (MT) 80
Navarro Mills Lake 219, 220
Neosho River 57, 63, 64, 120
New Braunfels (TX) 202
New Hogan Lake 32, 33
Newt Graham Lock and Dam 134
Newt Grahm Lock and Dam 134
North Canadian River 115
North Concho Lake 220
North Concho River 221
North Fork of the Grand River 103
North Fork of the San Gabriel River 204
North Pole (AK) 16
North Santiam River 166

O

O.C. Fisher Lake 220, 221
Oakdale (CA) 36
Oakridge (OR) 172
Oklahoma City (OK) 111, 114
Olive Creek SRA 92
Olympic Mountains 250

Olympic National Forest 249, 250
Omaha (NE) 86, 87, 88
Oologah Lake 135
Optima Lake 137
Optima National Wildlife Refuge 137
Orange Blossom Bridge 37
Orland (CA) 21
Orofino (ID) 49
Osage City (KS) 69
Ottawa (KS) 72
Otter Creek 61
Ouachita Mountains 141
Ouachita National Forest 153
Ozawkie (KS) 72

P

Pacific Crest National Scenic Trail 160
Paola (KS) 62, 63
Papio Creek Watershed Projects 86
Paris (TX) 126, 222
Parsons (KS) 54
Pat Mayse Lake 222
Paterson (WA) 177
Pawnee SRA 92
Pecos River 99
Pend Oreille River 48
Perry (KS) 72
Perry Lake 71, 72
Phoenix (AZ) 19
Pickstown (SD) 184
Piedra (CA) 34
Pierre (SD) 189, 193
Pine Creek Lake 138, 139
Pine Flat Dam 34

Pine Flat Lake 34
Pipestem Creek 105
Pipestem Lake 105, 106
Pleasant Dale (NE) 93
Polecat Creek 125
Pomeroy (WA) 243
Pomona Lake 72, 73
Ponca City (OK) 130
Ponderosa Pine Scenic Byway 51
Porterville (CA) 38
Portland (OR) 159, 161, 176
Potato Hills 141
Poteau River 129, 154
Priest River (ID) 48
Proctor Lake 223
Pryor (OK) 121
Pueblo (CO) 45
Pueblo de Cochiti Indian Reservation 97
Purgatoire River 45

Q, R

Rawhide Mountain Wilderness 19
Rawhide Mountains 19
Ray Roberts Lake 224, 225
Red River 146, 150
Red River Basin 223
Republican City (NE) 85
Republican River 69, 85
Richland Creek 220
Rio Chama River 96
Rio Grande River 97
Ripon (CA) 36
Riverbank (CA) 36
Riverdale (ND) 106

Robert Aufderheide Memorial Drive 158, 164
Robert S. Kerr Lock and Dam 149
Robert S. Kerr Reservoir 139, 140
Rocktown Natural Area 77
Rogue River 175
Rogue River National Forest 157
Rogue River National Scenic Trail 175
Ruch (OR) 157
Rufus (OR) 176
Rufus Woods Lake 246, 247
Russell (KS) 77
Russell, Charles M. National Wildlife Refuge 80
Russian River 28

S

Salem (OR) 165
Salida (CA) 36
Salina (KS) 64, 77
Saline River 77
Sallisaw (OK) 139
Salt Fork of the Arkansas River 124
Salt Plains National Wildlife Refuge 124
Salt Valley Lakes 89, 90, 92
Sam Rayburn Reservoir 226
San Angelo (TX) 220, 221
San Angelo State Park 221
San Antonio (TX) 202
San Bois Mountains 153
San Gabriel River 206
San Joaquin River 37

San Luis Obispo (CA) 35
Sanders Creek 223
Sangre de Cristo Mountains 45
Santa Fe (NM) 96
Santa Margarita (CA) 35
Santa Margarita Lake 35
Santa Rosa (CA) 28, 29
Santa Rosa (NM) 98, 99
Santa Rosa Lake 99, 100
Sardis Lake 141
Savage, James D. 26
Sawtooth Mountains 52
Sawtooth Wilderness 52
Sequoia National Forest 34
Sequoia-Kings Canyon National Park 26
Sequoyah National Wildlife Refuge 140
Sheyenne River 102
Sierra National Forest 34
Sierra Nevada Mountains 22, 23, 25, 26, 31, 32, 38
Siskiyou Mountains 157
Sitting Bull 185
Sitting Bull Monument 189
Skiatook Lake 142, 143
Slough Creek 71
Smoky Hill River 64, 65, 66
Snake River 178, 240, 241, 242, 243, 244, 248, 249
Soda Lakes 41
Somerville (TX) 228
Somerville Lake 228, 229
South Branch of Park River 104
South Canadian River 98, 99
South Fork of the McKenzie River 165

South Platte River 42
South Sulphur River 210
Spiro (OK) 149
Spokane (WA) 48
Sprague (NE) 90
Spring Creek 103
Stage Coach SRA 93
Standing Bear Lake 86, 87
Stanislaus River 36
Stanislaus River Parks 36
Stanley (ID) 52
Starbuck (WA) 240
Steinhagen Lake 230
Stillhouse Hollow Lake 231, 232
Stockton (CA) 32
Stony Creek 21
Success Lake 38, 39
Sulphur River 237
Sulphur Springs (TX) 210
Sylvan Grove (KS) 78

T

Temple (TX) 199, 231
Tenkiller Ferry Lake 144
Texarkana (TX) 236
Tharp, Hale 27
The Dalles (OR) 161, 176
Tishomingo National Wildlife Refuge 147
Topeka (KS) 56, 63, 67, 69, 71, 72, 75
Toronto (KS) 62, 75
Toronto Lake 74
Town Bluff Reservoir 230
Trail (OR) 175
Trail of Tears 144
Trenton (ND) 106

Tri-Lakes Project 41, 42, 43
Trimble, James W. Lock and Dam 129
Trinidad (CO) 45
Trinidad Lake 45, 46
Trinity River 220
Truckee (CA) 31
Tucumcari (NM) 98
Tulsa (OK) 112, 115, 117, 125, 131, 134, 135, 142
Tuttle Creek Lake 75, 76
Twin Lakes WMA 93

U

Ukiah (CA) 28

V

Valley City (ND) 102
Valley Springs (CA) 32
Valliant (OK) 138
Vancouver (WA) 159
Vassar (KS) 73
Verdigris River 61, 74, 75, 135
Visalia (CA) 26

W

W.D. Mayo Lock and Dam 129, 149
Waco (TX) 197, 233, 234
Waco Lake 233
Wagon Train SRA 93
Wakarusa River 56
Walla Walla (WA) 240, 245
Walnut Creek 75
Walnut River 58, 59
Warm Springs Creek 29, 30
Warm Springs Dam 29

Index

Waurika (OK) 150
Waurika Lake 150
Waxahachie Creek 199
Webbers Falls Lock and Dam 151
Wehrspann Lake 86, 88
Wenden (AZ) 19
West, Herbert G. Lake 241
Westfir (OR) 159, 164
Whitney (TX) 234
Whitney Lake 234, 235
Wichita (KS) 58, 61, 66
Willamette National Forest 158, 164, 165, 168, 172, 173, 174
Willamette Valley 163, 165, 172
William L. Jess Dam 175
Wilson (KS) 77
Wilson Lake 77, 78
Winding Stair Mountains 141
Wister (OK) 153
Wister Lake 153, 154
Wolf Creek 122
Woodward (OK) 122
Wright Patman Lake 236, 237
Wynoochee Lake 249, 250
Wynoochee River 249, 250

X, Y, Z

Yankee Hill WMA 94
Yankton (SD) 186, 187
Yegua Creek 229
Yosemite Valley 26
Yuba River 24
Ziolkowski, Korczak 189
Zorinsky Lake 86, 88, 89